The Canadian Justice System: An Overview

Third Edition

Paul Atkinson

B.A., B.Ed., LL.B., LL.M.

 LexisNexis®

The Canadian Justice System: An Overview, Third Edition
© LexisNexis Canada Inc. 2013
August 2013

Library and Archives Canada Cataloguing in Publication

Atkinson, Paul, 1953-
    The Canadian justice system : an overview, Third edition / Paul Atkinson.

Includes index.
ISBN 978-0-433-47455-5

    1. Law—Canada. 2. Justice, Administration of—Canada.
I. Title.

| KE444.A85 2005 | 349.71 | C2005-906068-9 |
| KF385.ZA2A85 2005 | | |

Published by LexisNexis Canada, a member of the LexisNexis Group
LexisNexis Canada Inc.
123 Commerce Valley Dr. E., Suite 700, Markham, Ontario L3T 7W8

Customer Service
Telephone: (905) 479-2665 • Fax: (905) 479-2826
Toll-Free Phone: 1-800-668-6481 • Toll-Free Fax: 1-800-461-3275
Email: customerservice@lexisnexis.ca
Web Site: www.lexisnexis.ca

Printed and bound in Canada.

For Bev, Mike and Dan

SOMETHING TO KEEP IN MIND

"I have learned that a man has the right and obligation
to look down at another man, only when that man needs help
to get up from the ground."

Gabriel Garcia Marquez

"People working in the justice system have a great responsibility to
act with integrity and compassion. It should never be a role for the
power hungry or those with a bullying mentality."

Don Saunders

Foreword

All of us have opinions about the Justice System — and most of those opinions are derived from a combination of our individual experience, values and knowledge.

Some such opinions appear value-based: "I've never had a problem with drugs. I've had a problem with the police." — Keith Richards

Some are cynical: "There is no such thing as justice — in or out of court." — Clarence Darrow

Some are profound: "Injustice anywhere is a threat to justice everywhere. We are caught in an inescapable network of mutuality, tied by a single garment of destiny. Whatever affects one directly, affects all indirectly." — Rev. Dr. Martin Luther King

Where do laws come from? How are statutes made? Do judges make laws? How is our justice system organized? How do our civil, criminal and administrative justice systems interact? How are they different? How does our criminal justice system work? Why does it seem to change? What are future trends? What careers are there in the justice system?

Paul Atkinson has, in this book, succeeded in answering these questions and more. The book provides an accessible, entertaining and practical introduction to Canada's Justice System. It both informs and demystifies.

The book treats law and learning about law as ongoing, fluid, changeable, challenging and fun.

Its stated goal is to lay the foundation for ongoing learning. I am confident that it will do so for each and every reader.

Justice R. James Williams
Supreme Court of Nova Scotia
(Family Division)

Acknowledgment

Once again, Fran Cudlipp at LexisNexis has been kind enough to encourage me to produce a third edition of this text. I really appreciate Fran's support with this book and my evidence and business law texts and her positive approach to all our communications. The wonderful editors at LexisNexis consistently save me from inadvertent inaccuracies and my ongoing struggles with the wonders of modern technology.

My students and teaching colleagues have provided valuable feedback on the first two editions of the book. Wherever possible, I have followed their guidance in making improvements and pursuing up-to-date case and statutory references. As a result, I am confident that the book is improving with each edition. I trust you will find the contents stimulating and informative and an impetus for your own continued research into the intriguing intricacies of our ever-evolving system of justice.

Paul Atkinson
April 2013

About the Author

Paul Atkinson has taught law courses at Canadian colleges and universities for over 25 years. Paul studied law at the University of Alberta and Osgoode Hall Law School and education and economics at Brock University. Paul has worked as a lawyer in Halifax, Nova Scotia. Paul is also the author of *Proof: Canadian Rules of Evidence, Second Edition* and *Business Law in Ontario*.

Table of Contents

Chapter 1

Law-Related Careers and the Canadian Justice System

WHY YOU NEED AN OVERVIEW OF THE JUSTICE SYSTEM

If you are reading this text, chances are you are considering a law-related career. Good choice! Career opportunities in this field are diverse, challenging and stimulating. Your career path could lead you to the centres of human interaction where policies are formulated and important social programs are implemented through the law. Alternatively, your path may lead you to the very fringes of society where shadows tend to hide the dark deeds that are done until they impact on others and require legal controls. For over 25 years I have been teaching people like you, people who are planning careers in the Canadian justice system or who will be working with people impacted by various aspects of the system.

In these careers, you can never stop learning. The law is alive. It is constantly changing and evolving. In Canada, we have three levels of government that make new laws or amend existing laws each time they're in session. Each weekday, courts across the country are resolving disputes and interpreting and applying laws that governments have created. The courts are also making law. In our system of justice, court decisions are precedents that mold and shape the way the law will be applied in the future.

This text is designed to provide you with the foundational knowledge you will need to understand the way the various facets of the Canadian justice system work. Many of you will eventually require very specific knowledge of particular laws and the way they are applied to succeed in the fields you have chosen. Others will need a much broader understanding of legal issues and our justice system to cope with the diverse demands of the career paths you wish to pursue. Everyone beginning a practical study of our laws and the way they affect Canadians needs *context*; you need to grasp the big picture, where our laws come from, why they are implemented in a particular way, how they are used, by whom and when. This text will provide that background.

Over the next several pages, a variety of law-related careers will be discussed with an explanation of the importance of the material included in this book for someone who is considering each career path. I have had the good fortune to teach people who have been successful in most of these careers and have frequently drawn on their expertise to focus and refine the content of the Introduction to the Canadian Justice System course that I teach to hundreds of aspiring Canadian justice careerists each year. Since the first edition of this book was published in 2005, I have received useful suggestions from students and teachers who have used the book and have incorporated their ideas.

POLICE OFFICERS

There are approximately 50,000 Canadian police officers. Some work for municipal police services. These can range in size from a few officers to the thousands who work in our largest cities. Others work for provincial police services that operate exclusively in Ontario and Quebec. The largest single police employer is the Royal Canadian Mounted Police, which serves as our national police service, but also provides municipal and provincial policing on a contract basis in many parts of the country. British Columbia is home to the largest concentration of Mounties. The Department of National Defence maintains its own military police service. These officers can serve on Canadian Forces bases at home and abroad.

Initiatives around the world and financial pressures on the governments that fund police services are triggering a re-examination of the role of police. While the number of positions available for police officers as they have been traditionally trained and deployed in Canada may decline over the next several years, new opportunities may be opening for part-time or differently tasked and compensated officers.

Obviously, a detailed knowledge of criminal law and criminal procedure is of fundamental importance to all personnel filling these roles. Chapters 8 through 11 of the text focus on these aspects of the Canadian justice system.

Officers also need to know how to read statutes and how to distinguish between laws that are created by the federal, provincial, territorial or municipal levels of government. This information is introduced in Chapter 2. Policing personnel who don't understand that courts also create law by establishing precedents would be poorly equipped to perform their duties. Chapter 3 should assist individuals aspiring to these roles in acquiring this important contextual information.

Some people pursuing careers with police services may be so focused on the criminal justice aspects of the job that they fail to recognize at the outset how much more they need to know. Police officers are prominently positioned in the front lines of society. They are frequently called as a resource when people have legal problems that really fit into one of the civil or administrative categories of the justice system that are discussed in Chapters 5 through 7. Chapter 4 provides an introductory discussion of how legal matters are split among the three major categories in our system of justice and explains distinctions that police personnel need to have in mind when they respond to a call. There are times when the best thing an officer can do for a citizen in distress is to provide an appropriate referral to someone working in another area of the justice system.

The civil category of the law, where people sue one another, impacts on the daily functions of those engaged in policing for other reasons. Officers are in the middle of conflict situations on a regular basis. Police officers often become important witnesses in civil trials because they were called to the scene, or were there to investigate potential criminal aspects of an event that could also end up forming the basis of a lawsuit. Officers are also at risk of being sued themselves and need to know where those risks lie. An officer who doesn't recognize the limits of the powers he or she is expected to exercise will soon discover that many normal police activities can invite lawsuits. Whether the number of incidents that are recorded on video will create more or fewer lawsuits against police officers will become apparent in the next few years. Chapters 5 and 6 outline some of the key reasons that people sue others.

Administrative law is discussed in Chapter 7. This area of the law includes a wide range of legal decision-making that doesn't occur in court, but impacts on policing functions. The Parole Board is an administrative tribunal that decides if and when prisoners should be released from jail prior to the end of their sentences. Before a decision is made, police services are often asked to provide input on the effect the individual's release will have on the local community. Police are also informed of any restrictions that are placed on prisoners who are released so officers can monitor compliance. Police often refer victims of crime to provincial or territorial administrative boards that are empowered to provide financial compensation to people who have been injured by criminal behaviour. If a police officer is accused of inappropriate conduct, discipline hearings will be conducted by senior officers following administrative law principles.

Chapter 12 discusses trends in the Canadian justice system, all of which could impact upon the way a police officer performs his or her job in the future and especially on the availability of opportunities in policing.

In short, there should be something in each of the Chapters that could provide useful contextual information for someone considering a career in policing.

FORENSIC INVESTIGATORS AND ANALYSTS

The magical world of D.N.A., fingerprints, fibres, footprints, tire marks, blood splatters and human behaviour, forms a link between science and the law. Forensic investigators and analysts may become specialists in one or several scientific fields, but they need to a have a general knowledge of the entire justice system.

Since many forensic investigators and analysts will either work for police services or with police services on a regular basis, the list of need-to-know information about the law is very similar to that outlined above for police officers. Their specialized knowledge will involve them in investigations that may not be limited to the criminal courts, but may well extend to lawsuits and the decision-making processes of administrative tribunals. They will need to know the limits imposed by statutes and the common law on the investigative process and may be controlled in their activities by laws created by both the federal and provincial or territorial levels of government.

CORRECTIONAL WORKERS

Job opportunities on this career path are far more varied than most members of the public realize. People seldom think beyond the role of a correctional officer, or guard in a traditional jail setting. They fail to realize that the vast majority of offenders who are convicted of federal, provincial or territorial offences and require correctional supervision serve either their entire sentences, or a significant portion of their sentences, outside of correctional institutions.

Career opportunities exist in an array of community supervision capacities: half-way houses, group homes and parole and probation services. Even within the lock-up facilities, roles of correctional personnel vary a great deal. Some officers concentrate their efforts on security matters, while others are involved in training, counselling and vocational employment programs. Officers act as escorts when inmates leave correctional facilities for a variety of purposes. Many facilities employ medical staff, teachers, fitness coordinators, chefs and others with specialized training.

The corrections field is a shared responsibility in Canada, with both federal and provincial levels of government playing a significant role. Someone interested in a career in this field will benefit from an understanding of the division of law-making responsibilities, explained in Chapter 2. This Chapter also provides an initial look at the organization and analysis of *statutes*. As government employees and agents, correctional personnel are controlled in all of their actions by the limits of the government-created *statutes* that provide the initial power to provide correctional services and *regulations* which set parameters on how that power is exercised.

It would also be a mistake for someone planning to work in corrections to ignore Chapter 3, which discusses the role courts play in our justice system. Not only do courts set precedents, which create an integral component of the whole spectrum of legal controls, they also pronounce the sentences which correctional personnel have the responsibility of implementing.

Chapter 4 discusses the way our justice system is organized. Like police officers, people starting a career in corrections will understand that they will be central players in the criminal justice system, which gets detailed treatment in Chapters 8 through 11. They may not be quite as cognizant that decisions that are made by correctional officers affecting inmates or offenders in community supervision situations fall within the category of *administrative law*. Every note that is made in an offender's file could impact upon the outcome of an administrative decision reached by institutional supervisors or the Parole Board. Some key principles of administrative law are explained in Chapter 7 to provide this contextual guidance.

Correctional officers should not ignore the basic principles of our civil justice system. Again, like police officers, they are often at the centre of tense, conflict situations. They perform functions that require the careful application of security principles to avoid causing harm to others. Mistakes can lead to lawsuits. Chapter 5 will outline some of these risks.

Chapter 6 discusses civil law concepts that may have a bigger impact upon a correctional officer's personal life than on his or her professional responsibilities. Consider it a bonus. Chapter 12 discusses trends that directly implicate correctional personnel.

SECURITY AND RISK MANAGEMENT PERSONNEL

Private security and risk management is big business, with various experts suggesting that job opportunities may be two to three times those available to police officers and growing all the time. While there are many entry level jobs providing a security presence to deter and detect criminal and nuisance activities in airports, hospitals, retail settings, private businesses, remote job sites and at entertainment and athletic events, employers may also be looking for a whole lot more.

Security and risk managers should be involved in the initial planning and construction phases of all new facilities. Knowledge of security risks, combined with intelligent layout and use of appropriate technology can reduce long term security costs immeasurably. Even with existing facilities, cost efficient remedies can be added by experts who know what they are doing. The special knowledge required to implement security programs in relation to the widespread use of computers has created exciting job opportunities for security experts with that added know-how.

Most businesses consider the risks of being sued by customers and others who are present on facilities and the safety and personal security of employees at least as important as the risks associated with theft, trespass and other criminal concerns. They expect risk managers to be able to predict dangerous situations and to provide innovative solutions, operational policies and training packages to avoid the unpleasant legal ramifications of a lack of careful planning.

Someone entering this field had better be prepared to have a grasp of the entire spectrum of our justice system. Government and court created laws discussed in Chapters 2 and 3 will impact in terms of setting standards and evaluating potential risk situations. The risks of being sued are covered in Chapters 5 and 6 and people entering the security field will take a special interest in the property ownership issues that are discussed in Chapter 6. Employee rights and protections are greatly affected by administrative tribunals, which operate under the principles discussed in Chapter 7, while interaction with the criminal justice system, discussed in Chapters 8 through 11 is inevitable for the private security professional.

LAW CLERKS AND PARALEGALS

Law clerks and paralegals may work in a law office, government or private business setting under the supervision of a lawyer, or may provide legal services directly to clients. To pursue the full range of job opportunities in this field, the broader the knowledge of the Canadian justice system the better. Specialization cannot occur until the person working in the field understands how the entire system works. Actions performed on behalf of a client, whether performed under the supervision of a lawyer or not, can create ripples in several other legal aspects of the client's life.

Consider the simple example of a client involved in a car accident. The police investigate and lay a relatively minor charge in relation to the way your client was operating his or her vehicle, which collided with two other vehicles and knocked down a power pole. The client comes seeking advice in relation to the charge. Should the client simply admit guilt to the motor vehicle charge and pay the fine? What effect will this admission of guilt have if the client is subsequently sued by the other vehicle owners, one of whom was seriously injured in the accident? Could the hydro company also sue for the damage to the power pole? What effect will an admission of guilt have on your client's provincial driving record? Could he or she lose a driver's licence over this? How will the client's insurance rates be affected?

A law clerk, paralegal or court and tribunal agent cannot begin to answer these questions without having knowledge of government-created statutes and court-created common law, principles of criminal, civil and administrative law and how they all interact. If you are someone who would like to pursue a challenging career in one of these areas, Chapters 2 through 12 provide crucial contextual information that can start you on a course of study that will allow you to develop the legal skills to provide a useful service for clients who need guidance navigating the treacherous waters of the Canadian justice system.

CUSTOMS AND IMMIGRATION ADMINISTRATION

International trade will always be a crucial component of the Canadian economy and border security has never been more at the forefront of world-wide consciousness. This creates opportunities in both the private sector and with the Canada Border Services Agency.

The Canada Border Services Agency has approximately 15,000 employees working in over 1,000 locations in Canada and abroad. This federal government agency administers dozens of federal statutes, regulations and international trade agreements to ensure that people and goods entering the country are complying with the law and are being processed fairly and efficiently. The ability to recognize, analyze and implement government-created laws is crucial to performing these duties. The functions of the agency are governed by criminal investigation and administrative law principles, and mistakes could attract civil law consequences. Background knowledge of all the topics covered in this text is just a starting point for acquiring the expertise necessary to pursue this challenging career.

Being deeply immersed in the global economy, Canadian businesses have a huge need for employees who understand customs law and international trade agreements and the implications for cross-border trade. Private sector positions are far more numerous than most people realize and are often quite lucrative. The diverse understanding of Canada's justice system that is necessary for government employees working in this field is also a crucial component of the training background that private sector employers expect.

SOCIAL WORKERS

This book is intended to provide an introductory overview of the Canadian justice system. Social workers, victim support workers and mediators need this kind of background to explain the workings of the system to their clients.

Legal problems tend to come in bunches. The police investigate a complaint and charge me with a criminal offence. Newspapers report the incident and my employer decides to fire me before I can explain, or the criminal charge can be resolved in court. I believe the firing is unjustified, but my only recourse may be to start a lawsuit to get compensation from my trigger happy boss. Without my regular income, I'm forced to apply for social assistance. The local administrative officer in charge of the program tells me I'm going to have to wait several months, but I can appeal this decision. As the financial stresses mount, my spouse decides to get out of this mess. The evil "D" word is mentioned. Maybe child custody, support and property issues can be worked out, but I can see this ending up in court as well. I'm drowning in a legal mess and I don't know where to turn for help.

Social workers choose their career path because of a desire to help people with problems. Not only do problems come in bunches, they also tend to involve a mixed bag of federal, provincial, territorial and municipal laws and issues that fit into more than one legal category. Knowing how the justice system works and who the key players may be in each category is an invaluable asset for someone working as a social worker and for the social worker's clients.

LAWYERS AND JUDGES

If you want to work as a lawyer in Canada, representing clients and providing legal advice, you have to meet the licensing requirements of the provincial and territorial bar societies. These are professional organizations that have been given the power to control this profession by provincial and territorial government-created laws. Basic requirements include completing a law degree at an approved law school in a university, working under the supervision of a licensed lawyer for a designated period of time and the completion of qualifying examinations.

The law schools usually require that candidates for admission demonstrate an aptitude for rigorous study by successfully completing at least two years of another university program before applying. They more commonly admit candidates with at least one prior degree. Law schools also expect applicants to have excellent marks on the Law School Admission Test. This is a standardized aptitude test that is offered at a variety of locations across North America, several times a year. The law school course of studies itself is three years in length, covering all of the topics addressed in this book in much more detail, and expanding on a range of sub-topics and specialty areas of the law.

Minimum qualifications for judges, who are appointed to their positions by the Prime Minister or provincial premiers (as will be discussed in Chapter 3), are set by government-created laws. A candidate must have been licensed to practise as a lawyer in one of the provinces or territories for at least ten years before he or she can be considered for an appointment. Reading this text certainly won't be enough to secure one of these positions, but you have to start somewhere!

KEY TERMINOLOGY

administrative law	category of law that involves, boards, tribunals and government officers who make legal decisions (not courts)
regulations	government-created legal details added to statutes
statutes	government-created written laws

PRE-TEST

Try these questions as a pre-test of your knowledge of some of the legal issues that will be covered in the text. (References are made to the Chapters where each of the topics will be addressed.)

1. All Canadians charged with committing a criminal offence have the right to be tried by a jury of their peers.

   TRUE   FALSE
   (Chapter 10)

2. The most common justification used for suing someone is their lack of care, or negligence.

   TRUE   FALSE
   (Chapter 5)

3. The vast majority of people who are convicted of committing criminal offences are sentenced to spend time in jail.

   TRUE   FALSE
   (Chapter 11)

4. The person who starts a civil lawsuit is called:
   (a) the complainant;   (b) the whiner;
   (c) the prosecutor;   (d) the plaintiff.
   (Chapter 4)

5. These people have the power to arrest someone they see committing a criminal offence:
   (a) customs officers;   (b) private security guards;
   (c) police officers;   (d) teenagers;
   (e) all of the above.
   (Chapter 9)

6. You believe a landlord has refused to rent an apartment to a close friend because she is a single mother. In this situation, your friend's best legal solution would be to:
   (a) report the discrimination to the police;
   (b) sue the landlord in small claims court;
   (c) file a complaint with the human rights commission;
   (d) forget about it, she has no legal remedy.
   (Chapter 7)

CONSIDER THIS SCENARIO

You have been stopped by a police officer while driving on a local highway. The officer says she intends to charge you for speeding. The officer asks if you know you were going 40 km/hr over the speed limit. She also asks for your driver's licence, registration and proof of insurance.

You're sure there must be some mistake and think it might be wise to exercise your right to remain silent. You really don't think you should have to explain that you've left your wallet and I.D. on the kitchen counter, at home. Besides, this isn't your car. It belongs to your father and you're not really sure where he keeps the vehicle registration and insurance. You do know that he's a bit of a freaky old hippie and may stash a baggie of B.C. Bud in the glove compartment from time to time, so you've decided to avoid getting into that little complication.

7. In this situation:
   (a) there is no right to remain silent, that only exists in the United States;
   (b) if you exercise your right to remain silent, you may end up in jail;
   (c) the officer will be fully justified in going ballistic and tearing your whimpering carcass from the car;
   (d) your career goal of working in law enforcement may have just ended.
   (Chapters 5, 8, 9)

8. Which level of government created the speeding charge you are facing?
   (a) municipal   (b) federal
   (c) provincial or territorial
   (Chapter 2)

9. If you decide to fight the charge(s) arising out of this incident, in which level of court will your trial be held?
   (a) municipal court   (b) provincial court
   (c) superior court   (d) Supreme Court of Canada
   (Chapter 3, Appendix 4)

10. You realize that a section of this text provides a perfect answer for a question on a college or university assignment that you have been given. You don't really have time to re-word the information. In fact, you're not really sure you can say it any more clearly, so you simply copy the answer word for word from the book. If you were to follow this course of action, you would be:
(a) breaking the law;
(b) violating a school policy;
(c) breaching a contract;
(d) all of the above.
(Chapter 6)

Chapter 2

Sources of Law — Statutes

WHAT ARE STATUTES?

Statutes are laws that are created by one of the three levels of government — federal, provincial or municipal. Governments can only act, whether it involves taxing you, controlling your behaviour on the highways or spending your money on social programs like education and health, if they have gone through a full *parliamentary process* to create a statute authorizing that action.

At its simplest, the parliamentary process involves bringing a proposed law, or *bill*, to the House of Commons, provincial legislature, or municipal council. The bill will be given three *readings*, or forms of review, in this public forum and will be voted on by the elected members of Parliament or the provincial legislature, or by the city, town or county councillors. If the bill receives majority support in the federal House of Commons, it goes on to the Senate, where the process is repeated. If it also passes the vote at third reading in the Senate, it is sent to the Governor General for a final signature and becomes a law. At the provincial level, there is no Senate to conduct a review, but the Lieutenant Governor will have signing authority to finalize the statute and give it legal effect. For municipalities, the mayor or municipal clerk will add a signature to legally activate a *by-law* that has received a majority vote from the councillors.

In order to change, or *amend* a statute that has been created, government must go through the full parliamentary process again, even if the change involves only one section of a lengthy statute, or even a single word. Similarly, if government wants to *repeal*, or eliminate an entire statute, the full parliamentary procedure is required. Our governments cannot tinker with laws behind closed doors. It is a public process.

Statutes, in a collective way, are also called *legislation*. Individual statutes, created by the federal or provincial levels of government commonly carry the labels, *Act* or *Code*; for example, the federal *Divorce Act* or *Criminal Code* and Saskatchewan's *Age of Majority Act* or Newfoundland and Labrador's *Human Rights Code*. Laws passed by municipal levels of government are called *by-laws*.

THE CONSTITUTIONAL FRAMEWORK

Why is the *Criminal Code* a federal statute? Why do landlord and tenant laws differ from province to province? Does the city council in Charlottetown have the same law-making powers as Vancouver's city council? The answers to all of these questions start with an understanding of the written part of Canada's *constitution*. The constitution is the fundamental legal basis on which the government of Canada is organized. The constitution could be considered "super" law. It provides the framework on which all the rest of our legal structure is built.

Most readers will realize that prior to 1867, Nova Scotia, New Brunswick and Upper and Lower Canada (the areas we now know as Ontario and Quebec), were British colonies in North America. Political leaders in the colonies explored the benefits of joining together and their talks led to agreements on how power should be shared between a central, or *federal* government and the governments of each of the individual colonies, which would become *provinces* in a newly formed nation.

At the time, any agreement they reached required the approval of Britain's Parliament. A statute of that government, *The British North America Act* established Canada as a legal entity in 1867 and reproduced the division of lawmaking powers between federal and provincial levels of government that had been agreed upon by the component parts of the new nation. As other colonies were added to Canada, eventually leading to the configuration of 10 provinces and three territories that currently exist, they were subject to the same division of powers laid out in this statute. This statute is still the key document dividing power between the levels of government in our country, though in 1982 we made it our own statute and re-named it the *Constitution Act, 1867*.

Surprisingly little has been changed from the original list of powers that is found primarily in sections 91 and 92 of the *Constitution Act, 1867* and some additional sections that follow those. A big reason for this stability is the *amending formula* that is required to make a change to the constitution. Because it is such a fundamental part of the relationship between the different levels of government in our country, it is necessary for the federal level of government and *two-thirds* of the provincial governments to agree on any changes. Of course, two-thirds is a rather awkward fraction in a country with 10 provinces, but what it practically means is that the federal government and seven of the 10 provinces must agree before any change to the constitution can be made. As a little added requirement, those seven provinces also must contain at least 50 per cent of Canada's population.

Think about it! How often can you get politicians in seven out of the 10 provinces, plus the federal government to agree on anything? No wonder the division of powers is pretty much in the same state it was in when it first appeared in 1867. Let's face it, if a power were a potential money maker, like a new taxing power, both levels of government would want to claim it as their own. If a power was going to create a great deal of extra expense for whichever level of government landed it, neither the federal government, nor the provinces would want to have anything to do with it.

In fact, you can get a pretty good idea of how little has been changed since 1867 by taking a careful look at the excerpts from the *Constitution Act, 1867* that have been included as Appendix 2 at the back of this book, or the direct quotations from the statute used in the next several paragraphs. You may notice the rather exuberant use of capital letters at the start of every noun, without the capitalization being restricted to the start of a sentence or being attached to a proper noun. Not knowing much about the history of English grammar, I can only assume that this was a style that found favour in 1867, but had died by the time I reached elementary school. Since the *Constitution Act, 1867* has not been significantly altered over the years, this stylistic quirk has survived.

Of course, while dividing law-making power between levels of government based on a list from 1867 has led to an impressive level of legislative stability, there are also some practical problems. Who, for example, gets to exercise control over things that were simply never contemplated in 1867? Travel by airplane and nuclear energy are two examples that readily come to mind. Modern concerns for protecting the environment might be another useful example. We'll discuss the way these issues have been allocated, or seized, after we have a look at the basic division of powers.

FEDERAL POWERS

Section 91 of the *Constitution Act, 1867* contains the primary list of federal law-making powers. The section starts with a *preamble*, or introductory paragraph, that states that the federal government can "… make Laws for the Peace, Order and good Government of Canada, in relation to all Matters not coming within the Classes of Subjects by this Act assigned exclusively to the Legislatures of the Provinces". In other words, the federal government gets to deal with anything that could affect the whole country, as long as the subject matter doesn't show up on the list of powers that are specifically given to the provinces. Many of the provinces' spheres of power are listed in section 92. Sections 92A, 93 and 109 also assign law-making powers to the provinces, effectively excluding the federal government.

The federal government also gets exclusive law-making *jurisdiction* in relation to thirty different matters listed in section 91. Listed matters are called *enumerated powers*, because there is a number attached to each one. For example, the federal government's power over, "The Criminal Law … including the Procedure in Criminal Matters" is found in *enumerated power 27* in section 91.

Many of the powers listed in section 91 are simply practical matters for a central level of government to control. Enumerated power 5 is the "Postal Service", while power 14 is "Currency and Coinage". "Banking, Incorporation of Banks, and the Issue of Paper Money" are covered in power 15 and "Weights and Measures", allowing for the country-wide use of kilometers and kilograms, are properly allocated to the federal government in enumerated power 17.

Most people would expect the federal government to look after sea coasts, as they do because of power 12, but some may wonder why federal government employees look after the buoys and lighthouses on Lake Winnipeg, Lake Superior or Great Bear Lake. The federal government has been assigned "Beacons, Buoys and Lighthouses" in enumerated power 9 and are responsible for "Navigation and Shipping" due to power 10 in section 91.

To see the complete list of federal law-making powers included in section 91 of the *Constitution Act, 1867*, kindly turn to Appendix 2 at the end of this book.

PROVINCIAL POWERS

Provinces have their own list of 15 enumerated powers to make laws, contained in section 92 of the *Constitution Act, 1867*. Additional power over non-renewable resources in a province is granted by section 92A, while section 93 gives each province the very important power to make laws in relation to education.

Why do landlord and tenant laws differ among provinces? The reason is that enumerated power 13, in section 92 assigns law-making power over "Property and Civil Rights in the Province" to this level of government. Landlords own the *property*, tenants rent all, or a portion of the *property* for a designated period of time, and provinces make the laws that affect their interactions. Are hospitals in Alberta better equipped than those in Nova Scotia? It's a possibility because each province has jurisdiction over "The Establishment, Maintenance, and Management of Hospitals ..." due to enumerated power 7, section 92. Are bars and nightclubs in Montreal open later than those in St. John's? Enumerated power 9, makes "Shop, Saloon, Tavern ..." licensing issues a matter of provincial jurisdiction. This could account for differences in the way licensed premises operate in different parts of Canada.

How is it possible for someone to be fined $112.50 for driving 25km/hr over the speed limit if stopped by a police officer in Ontario, but to be facing a fine of $192.50 for the same speed if the person isn't caught until he or she has crossed the border into "Friendly" Manitoba? Surely it isn't just a matter of the Ontario Provincial Police officers being more lenient than the Royal Canadian Mounted Police (RCMP) officers who patrol Manitoba's highways, is it? No it isn't. Each province has law-making authority for "The Imposition of Punishment by Fine, Penalty, or Imprisonment for enforcing any Law of the Province ..." because of enumerated power 15 in section 92. Each province can control activities on their highways because highways are located on public lands and "The Management and Sale of Public Lands belonging to the Province ..." is a provincial area of responsibility because of enumerated power 5, in section 92, *Constitution Act, 1867*. As a result, although provinces commonly have a statute called, the *Highway Traffic Act*, the wording of the statutes is different and the penalties in each law are set at the level that the respective provinces feel is appropriate. You can never assume that provincial statutes sharing a name will contain identical provisions.

By the way, why are the highways of Ontario being patrolled by the Ontario Provincial Police, while RCMP officers are performing the same function in Manitoba? It is because "The Administration of Justice in the Province ..." has been assigned to provincial governments in enumerated power 14, section 92. Each province has the legal authority to choose the police service it desires to help enforce provincial and federal statutes within its boundaries. Ontario and Quebec have chosen to develop their own provincial police services. Manitoba, like the other provinces and territories, has chosen to contract with the RCMP, a federally-created service to perform the provincial policing function. Could these arrangements change in the future? That would be up to the individual provinces to decide.

While the federal government was given the general power in the preamble to section 91 to latch on to legal issues affecting the "... Peace, Order and good Government ..." of the whole country, the provinces received their own catch-all jurisdiction over "... all Matters of a merely local or private Nature in the Province" in enumerated power 16, section 92. They also have power over "Local Works and Undertakings ..." (enumerated power 10) and "Municipal Institutions in the Province" (enumerated power 8). As we shall see, this allows provinces to set up local, or municipal levels of government and pass delegated power along to these law-making bodies.

The complete list of provincial powers, as laid out in section 92, can be seen in Appendix 2.

MUNICIPAL POWERS

People who are aware that Canada has very active local levels of government in villages, towns, cities, counties or regions may be wondering where to find the municipal list of powers in the *Constitution Act, 1867*. There is no such list. Provinces, as we have just learned, have been assigned all the power over local matters. The province has also been given the power over "Municipal Institutions in the Province" (enumerated power 8, section 92). This gives provinces the power to create local governments. Any power municipal governments possess, must have been passed along to them by the provincial government in the province in which they are located. This is done in provincial statutes.

Most provinces have large, omnibus statutes that delegate a broad range of powers to municipal levels of government. Additional powers will be delegated in the context of a wide variety of other provincial statutes. For example, provinces frequently give municipalities the power to create special safety zones, requiring drivers to operate their vehicles at a reduced speed around designated school, or playground areas. This delegated power is likely to be found in just one section, or even a *subsection* of a much larger statute dealing with highway traffic issues.

While each province could, potentially, download significantly differing powers to the municipal level of government, there is a fairly high level of commonality across Canada with respect to matters that are assigned to municipalities. Local governments will be responsible for local land use and zoning decisions. Is a particular part of a community an appropriate locale for a factory or an apartment building? Must parking spaces be provided for customers of a corner variety store? Will a developer be required to set aside a portion of a new subdivision for parkland? How will services like sewage disposal, snow and garbage removal be provided? Municipal by-laws usually provide the answers.

It is important to note that the federal government cannot skip over the provinces and download any of their law-making responsibilities to municipal governments.

TERRITORIAL GOVERNMENT POWERS

Yukon, Northwest Territories and Nunavut have a different legal status than the provinces. Though the powers the territorial governments exercise are very similar to provincial powers, there are differences, even among the three territories. Rather than receiving constitutionally protected realms of power, all three territories are created by federal statutes, *Yukon Act*, *Northwest Territories Act* and *Nunavut Act* respectively. Section 18 of the *Yukon Act*, section 16 of the *Northwest Territories Act* and section 23 of the *Nunavut Act*, list powers that can be exercised by the territorial governments (called Legislative Assemblies in Yukon and Nunavut, and Council in Northwest Territories). These lists borrow their wording directly from the powers listed for provinces in sections 92 and 93 of the *Constitution Act, 1867*, but also add some unique features. Because they are bestowed by federal statute, powers could be taken away or added by the federal government without going through the complex amending formula process that would be required to change the constitutionally protected powers of provinces.

All three territories have some law-making powers that have not been specifically addressed in the constitutionally assigned powers granted to provinces. For example, each territory can legislate in relation to "intoxicants" (because of clause 18(1)(r) in the *Yukon Act*, clause 23(1)(p) in the *Nunavut Act* and section 49 in the *Northwest Territories Act*). The Northwest Territories and Yukon have both been granted a power to levy a tax on furs, through clause 16(1)(l) in the *Northwest Territories Act* and clause 18(1)(g) in the *Yukon Act*. This issue is not directly addressed in the *Nunavut Act*. The Northwest Territories are granted a unique law-making power in relation to the herding of reindeer in section 45 of their Act, while Nunavut's government has responsibility over the preservation of the Inuktitut language due to clause 23(1)(n) in their statute. Yukon has an enviable power, like that granted to the provinces in section 92A of the *Constitution Act, 1867*, to make laws in relation to the exploration for non-renewable resources (s. 19 of the *Yukon Act)*, while this has been a recent subject of negotiation between the other territories and the federal government.

THE CONCEPT OF *ULTRA VIRES*

Sometimes, a government will go through the whole parliamentary process and create a law even though that level of government has no *jurisdiction*, or law-making authority over the particular issue being addressed. This may be prompted by calls for help from concerned taxpayers, who may not recognize constitutional limits on the various politicians who can affect their lives. In their zeal to be helpful, the politicians don't always recognize the limits of their own law-making authority. It may not be until someone is charged with violating the law, and a judge is asked to determine the law's validity, that the error will come to light. In other instances, individuals who face negative financial ramifications or restrictions on their rights because of a particular law will launch court challenges to the law-maker's authority to create a law of this type.

If a judge is convinced that a level of government has created a law outside the parameters of their constitutional authority to make laws, a judge will label the government's behaviour as *ultra vires*. This is simply a fancy Latin label meaning the politicians have gone beyond their powers. The judge will then rule that the successfully challenged law is *of no force and effect*. In other words, the law is rendered unenforceable.

Recent court decisions provide useful examples. In a 2012 court case called, *Eng v. Toronto (City)*, three members of Toronto's Chinese community challenged the legitimacy of a City by-law that provided that, "no person shall possess, sell or consume shark fin or shark fin food products within the City of Toronto". The municipal councillors had passed the law in reaction to international media attention highlighting incidents of sharks being finned alive, then thrown back into the ocean to die. The fins are more valuable than the rest of the shark because they are used in shark fin soup, a traditional Chinese delicacy. Undoubtedly, Toronto citizens concerned with environmental issues had prompted their city councillors to act, and they were not alone. Justice Spence of Ontario's Superior Court of Justice noted that by the end of August 2012, "… at least six other Canadian municipalities had enacted by-laws substantially similar to Toronto's" (paragraph 11 of the court decision).

While the applicants who challenged the by-law were concerned that it had a discriminatory effect on the culture, commerce and lifestyle of Toronto's Chinese community, they also pointed out that the protection of sharks was not a proper legislative concern for the municipal level of government. Their argument was that if any level of government should be dealing with this issue, it should be the federal government. They logically opined "… that the By-law is constitutionally invalid because the province lacks the authority to delegate to a municipality the authority to pass by-laws to protect national resources that never come within provincial waters, such as sharks" (paragraph 4 of the decision). In other words, if the province doesn't have the legislative power to deal with such an issue, how can it delegate this type of control to a municipal government?

Lawyers representing the City tried to defend the by-law by suggesting that it was properly enacted to protect the health of the citizens of Toronto, which is a responsibility that the provinces legitimately download to municipalities in some contexts. Evidence presented to the court was that some experts had concern about the toxic effects of "excess" consumption of shark fin products, which could contain mercury. In rejecting this argument, Justice Spence pointed out that there was no evidence before the court of what level of consumption would be excessive and, "In any event, it does not appear that a single bowl of shark fin soup poses any health threat to the consumer" (paragraph 83 of the decision).

Yet the by-law would ban the sale of a single bowl of soup. As a result, Justice Spence found that the by-law was not a by-law for the valid municipal purpose of the health of Torontians and was "... *ultra vires* and without any force and effect" (paragraph 94 of the decision).

City councillors in St. Albert, Alberta (birthplace of my older son) found their law-making authority challenged in another 2012 case called *Smith v. St. Albert (City)*. These politicians had amended a business licensing by-law to prohibit local businesses from selling "restricted products". They defined these to include products displaying marijuana plants, water bongs and digital weigh scales. Justice Clackson of the Alberta Court of Queen's Bench pointed out that this amendment would have the practical effect "... to preclude the licensing or successful operation of what have become colloquially known as bong or head shops" (paragraph 24 of the decision).

The amendment to the by-law prompted the seizure of the business licence of Chad Smoke Shop 420, a St. Albert shop that had operated for about a year and had obviously caused some alarm among local politicians. Ronald Smith, the primary owner of that business went to court to challenge the by-law, with his lawyer arguing that the by-law was "... in pith and substance legislation in relation to criminal law" (paragraph 14 of the decision).

What's the problem with a municipal level of government creating a law that is, in effect criminal law? Well, as mentioned earlier in this chapter, the power to create criminal law is specifically assigned to the federal level of government in enumerated power 27 of section 91 of the *Constitution Act, 1867*. In fact, the federal government had used that power to formulate section 462.2 of the *Criminal Code*, which had already made it illegal to sell "instruments or literature for illicit drug use". In most circumstances, if the federal government has a particular law-making responsibility, the province will not have a similar power. A province can't download a power that it doesn't possess to municipal governments. Nor can the federal government skip the provinces and download one of their responsibilities to a municipal government.

Faced with this situation, Justice Clackson ruled, "... in legal effect and in practical effect, the impugned by-law is about criminal law, a power which is plainly beyond the competence of the municipality ... As such it is *ultra vires* the municipality and must be struck down" (paragraph 27 of the decision).

OVERLAPPING JURISDICTION

When you start working with the *Constitution Act, 1867*, you quickly notice that there are a few legal matters that seem to fall within the law-making authority of more than one level of government. For example, it will not come as a surprise to any Canadian that both the federal and provincial levels of government have the power to tax, though the wording of their respective powers is different. The federal government, in enumerated power 3, of section 91 is empowered to raise money, "… by any Mode or System of Taxation". In section 92, enumerated power 2, the provinces can raise money for provincial purposes through "Direct Taxation".

What practical difference does the wording make? People in most provinces who buy retail items are currently subject to both the federal Goods and Services Tax and a provincial Sales Tax, or a blended version of the two, the double whammy of the innocuous-sounding Harmonized Sales Tax. Both federal and provincial versions of these taxes are added on to the price at the point of sale. Customers see the tax being added. It may well be noted on the receipt. Both taxes are examples of *direct* taxation, the only tax a province can impose. What many taxpayers may not realize is that when the federal Goods and Services Tax was created years ago, it was not a totally new source of revenue. It was simply a direct tax replacing a "manufacturer's tax" that had been hidden. Because it was imposed at the point where the goods were manufactured, from a consumer's perspective the old tax was buried in the cost of the item. There is nothing to prevent the federal government from hiding taxes in this way, since they have the power to use "… any Mode or System of Taxation".

This came to light recently when the federal government announced, in an obvious attempt to pander to the large constituent of tax-paying hockey parents, that they were reducing the import duties on hockey equipment produced abroad. Prior to this announcement, most parents of young hockey players would undoubtedly have noticed that the equipment was expensive. It seems less likely that very many of them would have directed their minds to the fact that a great deal of the equipment for "Canada's game" is manufactured elsewhere. Nor would they have been tuned into the fact that a significant portion of the price they were paying was attributable to import duties added by the federal government before the equipment ever hit the shelves of their local retailer. The federal government is probably hoping that the grateful Canadian taxpayer won't notice that this narrow reduction in tariff revenue has been recouped (and then some) by introducing new taxes on a broad range of products that previously entered the country unscathed.

Some provisions in sections 91 and 92 of the *Constitution Act, 1867* appear to address the same issue, but don't necessarily create overlap in the day-to-day administration of government functions. For example, enumerated power 28 in section 91 gives the federal government the legal responsibility for "The Establishment, Maintenance, and Management of *Penitentiaries*". In section 92, enumerated power 6, provinces have been charged with "The Establishment, Maintenance, and Management of Public and Reformatory *Prisons* in and for the Province". What the heck is the difference? Well, the practical difference is in the length of sentence the convict will be serving, not in the nature of the accommodations. Both *prisons* and *penitentiaries* are jails. Back in 1867, it was agreed that the federal government would be responsible for housing prisoners sentenced to serve *two years or more*. Provinces imprison convicts serving sentences of *less than two years*. Consequently, for the purpose of the Canadian legal system, penitentiaries are simply jails that house prisoners serving sentences in excess of two years, while prisons are jails for people serving shorter sentences or for people who have been arrested and denied bail, but have not yet gone to trial.

The federal government is given legal authority over "Marriage and Divorce" in enumerated power 26, of section 91 in the *Constitution Act, 1867*. As a result, the *Divorce Act* is a federal statute that establishes a common set of rules for all Canadians who wish to terminate a legal marriage. There is also a federal *Marriage (Prohibited Degrees) Act*, but if someone was expecting to find the detailed process that must be followed to get married, or even to find out who is legally allowed to perform the service, he or she would not find that information in this federal law. Why? Enumerated power 12, in section 92 of the *Constitution Act, 1867* has given law-making responsibility over "The Solemnization of Marriage in the Province" to the provincial level of government. While the divorce process is consistent across Canada, the process related to getting married in the first place is not. The *Constitution Act, 1867* is the reason for this discrepancy.

It must be remembered that the division of law-making power in a constitutional document (particularly one that has been around for over 145 years) is never going to be perfect. There are bound to be new legal issues that arise and others that appear to create logical reasons for both the federal and provincial levels of government to claim responsibility. Oil and gas exploration in the area around Sable Island provides an interesting example.

Provincial politicians in Nova Scotia must have started to salivate when they learned that oil and gas exploration companies were turning their attention to the ocean waters, near this island, off the coast of Nova Scotia. At long last, they could profit from collecting the type of resource royalties that had made provincial sales tax unnecessary in oil-rich Alberta! After all, section 92A of the *Constitution Act, 1867* clearly gives provinces the power to regulate and tax non-renewable resources *in the province*. There, of course, was the rub. The federal government was able to say, "not so fast!" Through the strange wording of enumerated power 9, in section 91, the federal government could exercise law-making power over "Beacons, Buoys, Lighthouses, and *Sable Island*".

How the heck did that get on the federal list? Of course, back in 1867, giving this power to the federal government had nothing whatsoever to do with oil and gas exploration. In fact, from Nova Scotia's 1867 perspective, getting the feds to deal with Sable Island would be a matter of unloading a potentially expensive hassle. At that time, Sable Island was nothing more than a navigational hazard, stuck in the very busy ocean shipping lanes between Europe and North America. It would require manned lighthouses and the repetitive expense of rescue efforts directed at shipwrecked sailors and their cargo. What province would want responsibility for a nuisance like that?

When both a province and the federal level of government see the potential for profit, each level is quick to claim law-making authority. If an issue is likely to be an expense, arguments will be made that jurisdiction more logically rests with the other level of government. How are issues like this resolved? Ultimately, either level of government could ask our top court, the Supreme Court of Canada, to interpret the constitutional documents and decide in favour of one government or the other. The problem with this, as with any lawsuit, is that one level of government will win and the other will lose. The other alternative is for the province and the federal government to enter into a federal-provincial agreement, sharing in law-making responsibility and/or profits or expenses. Many jurisdictional disputes are resolved in this way.

FILLING IN THE GAPS

If a person were to look through an index of existing federal statutes (all of the statutes and an alphabetically arranged indexing system are available on Justice Canada's website, at <http://laws.justice.gc.ca>), it would be fairly easy to discover that with statutes like the *Aeronautics Act, Air Travellers Security Charge Act* and the *Airport Transfer Act*, air travel is a subject matter that is controlled by our government in Ottawa. Similarly, the federal *Nuclear Energy Act, Nuclear Fuel Waste Act* and the *Nuclear Safety and Control Act* provide pretty good clues that the federal government also regulates the nuclear energy industry. Why? Neither of these categories appear in the enumerated powers listed in section 91 of the *Constitution Act, 1867*. Perhaps, more importantly, they don't appear on the list of provincial powers enumerated in section 92 either. And, if you remember the wording from the preamble to section 91, the federal government has responsibility "… to make Laws for the Peace, Order and good Government of Canada, in relation to all Matters not coming within the Classes of Subjects by the Act assigned exclusively to the Legislatures of the Provinces …". In a sense, because these matters were never contemplated back in 1867 when the lists were compiled, the federal government gets them by default. They clearly don't seem to fit in the provincial catch-all category "Generally all Matters of a merely local or private nature …" found in enumerated power 16, section 92.

The environment is also a relatively new legal concern. Let's face it, back in 1867, hunters were decimating buffalo herds and doing their best to wipe out the passenger pigeon. Was anyone clamoring for laws to control the smog produced by coal-fuelled steam engines or to curb sewage being dumped into the new nation's waterways? It certainly wasn't enough of a pressing issue to have been placed on the list of law-making powers assigned to either the federal or provincial levels of government.

Of course, law-makers, like nature, abhor a vacuum. Both levels of government have found justifications for their respective forms of control over environmental matters. Ottawa can point to their "Peace, Order and good Government of Canada" fallback in the preamble to section 91. This is particularly useful for statutes like the *Canada Water Act*, which provides for agreements between the federal government and provinces with respect to the management of bodies of water that flow or sit across provincial boundaries. It also allows Canada to enter into management agreements across the international boundary with the U.S., where the boundary divides the Great Lakes and does nothing to stop the rivers and streams that flow merrily across it in a northerly or southerly direction.

Provinces have several *Constitution Act, 1867* justifications for environmental legislation. There's the responsibility for the "Management ... of the Public Lands" in enumerated power 5 of section 92 and the power to legislate with respect to "Property and Civil Rights" in enumerated power 13. Section 92A confers a right to make laws in relation to "development, conservation and management of non-renewable resources ... and ... sites and facilities in the province for the generation and production of electrical energy". (You will notice that section 92A, being a rare example of a post-1867 addition to the *Constitution Act, 1867* employs a more conservative approach to the use of capital letters.)

WORKING WITH STATUTES

It is a frightening principle of our Canadian justice system that we are all *presumed* to know what the law is! Think about it. A person could be charged with violating any of the thousands of laws that have been created by the federal, provincial, territorial or municipal levels of government having law-making power in the part of the country where the individual is located. It isn't going to help to respond by saying, "I didn't know there was such a law." As it's very concisely stated in section 19 of the *Criminal Code*, "Ignorance of the law by a person who commits an offence is not an excuse for committing that offence." Obviously, for people who are planning to work in the justice system, having a working knowledge of the laws that will affect their career path is crucial.

It only seems fair that governments should provide us all with reasonable access to the laws that can affect our lives. This was a pretty tricky proposition when the laws were only available in print form. A person needed access to a library that collected the statutes, or had to order copies of specific laws from the *Queen's Printer*, the official publisher of federal and provincial levels of government, or from the municipal clerk responsible for looking after local by-laws. Today, a person with internet access on a computer can look up any federal, provincial or territorial law on the appropriate government's website. Most of the popular search engines will locate the statutes with a simple prompt like, "Statutes of _____".

Many municipalities also make their by-laws accessible on-line. Locating the official website for the municipality is the first step; then, searching through the internal links should get you to the by-laws. If that doesn't work, communicating with the municipal *clerk*, the official keeper of the by-laws, would be most fruitful.

Prior to the use of computer sites for easy access to statutes, federal and provincial governments would publish *sessional volumes* of the new laws they had created in the annual law-making sessions of that level of government. Legal *citations* for the statutes direct someone who is looking for a particular statute to the correct book. For example, if someone wanted to locate the *Nuclear Fuel Waste Act*, the *citation* for that statute is: S.C. 2002, c. 23. The "S.C." portion tells you that this is a Statute of Canada, a federal law. "2002" is, of course, the year the statute was created, and tells you which sessional volume of statute books contains this particular law. The reference to "c. 23" means that the law can be found at "Chapter 23" in the book. It probably also means that the *Nuclear Fuel Waste Act* was the 23rd law the federal government created that year.

It used to be a regular practice of both the federal and provincial governments to gather all of the existing statutes of their respective levels together in a multi-volume, alphabetically arranged set of *Revised Statutes*, every 10 or 15 years. The revised statutes contain laws with all of the *amendments*, or changes that have been made to the laws edited in, with a straight-forward, sequential numbering of all the *sections*, or sub-divisions of the individual statutes. The last time the federal government put together a set of revised statutes was in 1985. Some of the provinces have compiled sets of revised statutes more recently.

An example of a citation for a statute that could be found in one of these revised compilations would be the citation for Newfoundland and Labrador's *Fatal Accidents Act*. The citation for that statute is: "R.S.N.L. 1990, c. F-6, as am." The "R.S.N.L. 1990" portion is indicating that this law can be found in the Revised Statutes of Newfoundland and Labrador that were compiled in 1990. The reference to "c. F-6" is telling someone who is looking for the statute to look in Chapter 6 of the volume of laws that start with the letter "F". Remember, in the revised volumes of the laws they have been organized alphabetically. The final part of the citation, "as am.", is warning a person who is looking up the statute that changes or *amendments* have been made to the law since the compilation was done in 1990, and means, "as amended". In this case, the provincial government made changes to the law in 1995, 2008, 2009 and 2010.

If you are using the print form of statutes for your research, the amendments would have to be found in the sessional volumes of the session of the provincial legislature in which the changes were made. On the computer versions of federal and provincial statutes, amendments will be incorporated into the body of the statutes that are available on-line, shortly after the amendment has gone through the parliamentary process. This is another practical reason to use a computer to do legal research involving government-created laws.

Some of the government websites warn that the computer versions are not the official versions of the statutes. For example the website containing Prince Edward Island's statutes includes this warning attached to each law: "This document is *not* the official version of the Act. The Act and amendments as printed under the authority of the Queen's Printer for the province should be consulted to determine the authoritative statement of the law." How archaic! Many of the other Canadian governments have realized the advantages of public accessibility to updated, computer versions of their laws and have legitimated their website versions. The most advanced example may be Manitoba, where electronic versions of their statutes are the official version. This has led to citations for Manitoba laws to look like, *The Good Samaritan Protection Act*, C.C.S.M. c. G65. In Manitoba's citation, the "C.C.S.M." stands for the "Continuing Consolidation of the Statutes of Manitoba".

This is a solid recognition of both the dynamic nature of our laws and that the technological advances of the 21st century are here to stay. It is also helpful for legal research purposes.

WHAT A STATUTE LOOKS LIKE

Statutes can be very long and intricately worded, or quite brief. The following statute from British Columbia isn't overly lengthy, but it does include many of the elements commonly found in federal and provincial statutes.

GUIDE ANIMAL ACT
R.S.B.C. 1996, c. 177

Definitions
1.   In this Act:
     "guide animal" means a guide animal
        (a) prescribed under section 8, or
        (b) for which a certificate has been issued under section 7
     if that animal is used by a person with a disability to avoid hazards or to otherwise compensate for a disability;
     "minister" includes a person designated by the minister for the purposes of this Act;
     "person with a disability" means a person who is apparently blind or otherwise disabled and is dependent on a guide animal or white cane;
     "white cane" means a cane or walking stick at least the upper 2/3 of which is white.

Rights with a guide animal
2.   (1) A person with a disability accompanied by a guide animal has the same rights, privileges and obligations as a person not accompanied by an animal.
     (2) In particular, a person with a disability accompanied by a guide animal may, in the same manner as would a person not accompanied by an animal, enter and use an accommodation, conveyance, eating place, lodging place or any other place to which the public is invited or has access so long as the guide animal is
        (a) prevented from occupying a seat in a public conveyance or eating place, and
        (b) held by a leash or harness.
     (3) This section applies despite any enactment enacted before or after the enactment of this Act.

Rights under section 2 not to be interfered with

    3.   A person must not interfere with the exercise of a right or privilege under section 2 or charge a fee for a guide animal accompanying a person with a disability.

Tenancy rights

    4.   (1) In this section:

      "manufactured home site" has the same meaning as in the *Manufactured Home Park Tenancy Act*;

      "rental unit" has the same meaning as in the *Residential Tenancy Act.*

      (2) A person must not

        (a) deny to a person with a disability a rental unit or manufactured home site advertised or otherwise represented as available for occupancy by a tenant, or

        (b) impose a term or condition on a person with a disability for the tenancy of a rental unit or manufactured home site if that term or condition discriminates

      because of the disability or because the person with the disability intends to keep a guide animal in the rental unit or manufactured home site.

      (3) Subsection (2) does not apply if the advertisement or representation specifies occupancy of the rental unit may entail sharing sleeping, bathroom or cooking facilities in the space with a person from another family.

White cane

    5.   A person who is not a blind person according to accepted medical standards must not carry or use a white cane.

Onus on defendant

    6.   In a prosecution for contravention of section 5, the onus is on the defendant to prove that he or she is blind according to accepted medical standards.

Certificate

    7.   (1) A person with a disability may apply to the minister for a certificate to use as evidence that section 2 applies.

      (2) The minister must issue a certificate under section (1) if the minister is satisfied that the animal is to be used as a guide animal.

      (3) A person to whom a certificate under this section is issued must surrender the certificate to the minister and the certificate is void if the minister is satisfied that the guide animal for which the certificate was issued has died, become permanently disabled, ceased to render the services to which the certificate relates or is not qualified as a guide animal.

Power to make regulations

   8.   (1) The Lieutenant Governor in Council may make regulations referred to in section 41 of the *Interpretation Act.*

   (2) Without limiting subsection (1), the Lieutenant Governor in
Council may make regulations as follows:

      (a) specifying those animals or classes of animal that are guide
      animals;

      (b) specifying the conditions that must be met for an animal to
      become or continue to be a guide animal.

Offence and penalty

   9.   (1) A person who contravenes this Act commits an offence.

   (2) A person who commits an offence under subsection (1) is liable
on conviction to a fine of not more than $200.

From an organizational perspective, you will see that this statute is broken
down into *sections.* Each section is designated by a whole number in bold nu-
merals. This is a law drafting technique used by federal, provincial and territorial governments and also by many municipalities.

Each section performs a different function in the law. For example, section
"**1**" helpfully provides definitions for terms that will be used in the rest of the
law and may be open to more than one meaning if not clarified. Let's face it,
despite the title of the statute itself; the less imaginative among us are likely to
think only of dogs when we contemplate guiding companions for the blind or
other disabled people. By its careful use and definition of the much broader term
"guide animal", British Columbia's legislators have opened the possibility of
any number of other trainable creatures. I have heard, for instance that pigs are
very smart (and clean, when not being forced to wallow in some mud-based sty).
Perhaps they would make wonderful guide animals. The B.C. government has
provided an opportunity for alternative helpful beasts.

By the same token, through the insertion of their own definition of a "person
with a disability", B.C. law-makers have provided for the possibility that disabled persons other than the blind may have a need to be accompanied by a guide
animal or to use a white cane. If you were to compare this statute to Ontario's
Blind Persons' Rights Act, you would find that law-makers in Ontario haven't
been nearly as comprehensive in the disabled persons for whom they provide
rights, nor have they looked beyond the possibility of canine guides.

It is quite common, though by no means universal, for government-created
laws to include their own "definition" or "interpretation" sections like the one in
this statute. In fact, you may have already noticed that there are additional definitions provided in section **4** of this statute. Those terms appear to have a narrower function in relation to the contents of that section alone. Definitions in the
body of a statute are a useful tool for anyone seeking a precise understanding of
the law or needing to apply the legislation to real-life situations. When included,

such definitions supersede any broader meanings that may be attached to the terms in standard dictionaries.

It is also pretty common for headings to be inserted prior to the start of each section, stating in a general way the subject matter of that particular section. The heading, "Rights with a guide animal" announcing section **2** of this statute is an example. From a strict legal interpretation perspective, these headings have no effect at all on the meaning of what is to follow, but do provide quick guideposts for someone who is skimming through the law in search of the most immediately relevant provisions.

If you take a careful look at section **2**, you will notice that it is subdivided with whole numbers contained in parentheses: (1), (2) and (3). These are called *subsections* and are the standard method of breaking up related information in a section to help make the law more easily understandable. While subsection (1) of section **2** provides a broad protection for the rights and privileges of a disabled person accompanied by a guide animal, subsection (2) clarifies where these rights apply. Subsection (3) seems to suggest that these rights apply no matter what any other statute might say. For example, if a Kamloops' by-law were to state that animals are not allowed on city buses, subsection **2**(3) of the *Guide Animal Act* means that the Kamloops by-law would not bar a guide animal accompanying a disabled rider.

Subsection **2**(2) is broken down a little further, with lower case letters in parentheses: (a) and (b). These are both grammatically and legally known as *clauses*. The clauses in subsection (2) are used to clarify that a disabled person can get into restaurants and trains and buses with their animal companion, as long as the guide animal is kept on a leash and stays off the seats.

As a keen grammar hound, you may have already noticed that each *subsection* is a sentence. You won't find a "period" until you reach the end of the subsection, no matter how many clauses (or *subclauses*, a phenomenon we thankfully don't encounter in this statute) it might contain.

This statute, like many government-created laws also makes certain types of unacceptable behaviour illegal. For example, section **3** makes it illegal to interfere with a disabled person's rights or to charge a fee for allowing a guide animal to accompany the person. Section **4** makes it illegal to deny a disabled person rental accommodations because he or she lives with a guide animal. It seems sad that the provincial government had to anticipate the possibility of this level of sleaze. Section 5 makes it illegal for someone who is sighted to use a white cane. Apparently, the government of B.C. doesn't want you attracting extra sympathy during your fraudulent panhandling schemes, nor do they want you sneaking into restaurants with Fido, who provides no help at all in guiding you to the buffet table.

It is necessary to skip to subsection **9**(2) to discover the penalty that could be imposed on someone who violates the provisions of this statute. Like many punishments you will find in federal and provincial or territorial laws, this one provides a maximum penalty that a judge could impose on someone found guilty, "… a fine of not more than $200". This means that the judge has the discretion to impose any punishment he or she deems appropriate up to this maximum limit.

You may find it interesting to compare the maximum punishments that the Ontario government has chosen for similar behaviour in their *Blind Persons' Rights Act*. Section 6 of their law imposes a much harsher maximum fine of $5000 on people who interfere with the rights of the blind, with a maximum fine of $500 for someone posing as a blind person in order to attain a benefit.

Section 8 of the *Guide Animal Act*, which is labelled as the "Power to make regulations" is an example of a type of provision that you will find in a large number of federal and provincial statutes. It is designed to provide a legal authority to change secondary details related to the law, without having to go through the full parliamentary process. In this case, the power is given to "the Lieutenant Governor in Council" (code words for the provincial cabinet) to specify which animals can be considered "guide animals".

REGULATIONS

Going through the full parliamentary procedure to change details of the law that may require frequent alteration is burdensome and impractical. In order to streamline this process, statutes will frequently give a specific power to the *government cabinet minister* responsible for administering that law, or the *cabinet* (as was done in section **8** of the *Guide Animal Act*), to alter the details by way of *regulation*. Of course, if such a power is given to the cabinet, or a cabinet minister, all the input for change is coming from the party in power. The opposition parties don't get an opportunity to challenge the changes before they are made and once the regulations are "published" in the official government gazette they have the same legal power or *force of law*, as a statute.

As a result, none of the regulations deal with large policy issues and they must be consistent with the general legal framework that is provided in the statute that allows for their creation. Details like the fee for a hunting or fishing licence, or the style and size of package labelling that needs to be provided on hazardous goods, are examples of the type of legal detail that will be found in regulations.

Obviously, it is important for people who will be working with laws to be able to access these details. On-line legal research through the government websites provides handy links to the relevant regulations when you search the statute that sets the legal policy. When I availed myself of this process in researching the *Guide Animal Act*, I was able to discover this:

GUIDE ANIMAL REGULATION
B.C. Reg. 664/74

Certificate issuance

1.   The minister may issue a certificate pursuant to section 7 of the Act if the guide dog has been trained in any of the following facilities:

(a) The Seeing Eye, Inc., Morristown, New Jersey;
(b) Guide Dogs for the Blind, Inc., San Rafael, California;
or any other facility which, in the minister's opinion, provides an acceptable standard of training.

This regulation provides an interesting example for a couple of reasons. While the general rationale behind using regulations is to allow for frequent changes of detail, this particular regulation hasn't been altered in a very long time. In fact, the regulation's citation, B.C. Reg. 664/<u>74</u> is actually telling us that the regulation was made way back in 1974 and must have originally been created under a much earlier version of the *Guide Animal Act*. Judging by the fact that the regulation addresses the issuing of certificates in relation to guide "dogs", rather than the more expansive "animals", it may be that the earlier version of the statute was also more limited in scope.

One would also hope that by now a disabled person could access a guide animal trained somewhere closer to B.C. than either New Jersey or California. In fairness, the wording of the regulation does allow the responsible government minister to find a dog trained at any facility providing "an acceptable standard of training" appropriate for certification purposes.

WHEN AMENDMENTS TO STATUTES ADD NEW CONTENT

When governments make amendments that add new provisions to an existing law, they are careful not to disrupt the logical organization of the material already included. As a result, if a whole new section or subsection is added to a statute, decimals are utilized to minimize any disruption. For example, the following section was inserted in the *Criminal Code* in 2004.

> **27.1** (1) Every person on an aircraft in flight is justified in using as much force as is reasonably necessary to prevent the commission of an offence against this Act or any other Act of Parliament that the person believes on reasonable grounds, if it were committed, would be likely to cause immediate and serious injury to the aircraft or to any person or property therein.

The *Criminal Code* had already contained section **27**, which generally allows a person to use force to prevent the commission of an offence. When the federal government decided that further clarification was necessary to show that a person could also intervene on an aircraft in flight, the logical place to put this addition was between the existing sections **27** and **28**. By labelling the addition section **27.1**, this could be accomplished smoothly.

Of course, when a statute is altered as frequently and as extensively as the *Criminal Code* this can lead to some pretty complex numbering. One area where the federal government has really been ambitious is in adding to the types of court orders that judges can issue to authorize peace officers to gather evidence that may be useful in a criminal investigation and to require suspects to provide samples for DNA analysis and other comparison purposes. This has resulted in sections being labeled like section **487.0551,** which is strategically located between sections **487.055** and **487.0552.**

Section **487.055** itself has experienced some interesting internal meddling as evidenced by both a subsection labeled as **487.055**(3.11) and a clause labelled as **487.055**(1)(c.1).

KEY TERMINOLOGY

amend	to change a law
amending formula	the requirement that the federal government and two-thirds of the provinces have to agree on any change to Canada's constitution
amendments	changes made to existing laws
bill	a proposal for a government-created law
by-law	a written law made by a municipal government
cabinet	the key members of the party in power in the federal or provincial government who act as special advisors to the Prime Minister or the premiers and guide government policy decisions
cabinet minister	a member of the party in power who has been given special responsibilities for overseeing a government department and attends cabinet meetings
citation	reference information for locating a statute or case report
clause	a portion of a subsection of a statute, labelled with a small case letter in parentheses
constitution	the fundamental legal basis on which the government of Canada is organized
direct taxation	the taxing power given to provinces — the person being taxed has to be made aware of the tax
enumerated powers	listed law-making powers given to a particular level of government
federal	the central government with power to create laws that apply across the country
force of law	having the same impact as a valid government-created law
intra vires	within the law-making power of a particular level of government

jurisdiction	the power to create laws in that geographic area or in relation to that legal issue
legislation	statutes, or written laws
maximum penalty	the largest penalty stipulated for breaking a law
municipal clerk	local government administrator with special responsibility for organizing, filing and making municipal by-laws available to members of the public
parliamentary process	process followed by government to enact laws
penalty	punishment for breaking a law
penitentiaries	federally operated jails, house prisoners with sentences longer than two years
preamble	an introductory portion of a statute, often outlines the purpose of the law
presumed	a judge will assume a particular state of affairs unless he or she receives contrary evidence
property	a collection of rights that includes ownership in relation to land, goods, business concepts, inventions of artistic creations
provinces	ten distinct geographic portions of Canada that have designated law-making power
Queen's Printer	government agency responsible for making laws available to the public
readings	stages in the parliamentary process for creating laws, may involve a literal reading, referral to committees for further review and a vote
reformatory prisons	provincial jails
Sable Island	island off the east coast of Nova Scotia
section	the primary division in a statute
sessional volume	a book containing the statutes created by the federal government or a provincial or territorial government during a particular year

subsection

a portion of a section of a statute, grammatically it will be a sentence and will be labelled by a number in parentheses

ultra vires

beyond the law-making power of a level of government

STATUTES MENTIONED

Aeronautics Act, R.S.C. 1985, c. A-2, as am.

Age of Majority Act, R.S.S. 1978, c. A-6, as am.

Airport Transfer (Miscellaneous Matters) Act, S.C. 1992, c. 5, as am.

Air Travellers Security Charge Act, S.C. 2002, c. 9, Part 2

Blind Persons' Rights Act, R.S.O. 1990, c. B.7

British North America Act, see *Constitution Act, 1867*

Canada Water Act, R.S.C. 1985, c. C-11

Clothesline Act, S.N.S. 2010, c. 34

Constitution Act, 1867 (U.K.), 30 & 31 Vict., c. 3 reprinted in R.S.C. 1985, App. II, No. 45

Criminal Code, R.S.C. 1985, c. C-46, as am.

Divorce Act, R.S.C. 1985, c. 3 (2nd Supp.), as am.

Fatal Accidents Act, R.S.N.L. 1990, c. F-6, as am.

The Good Samaritan Protection Act, C.C.S.M., c. G65

Guide Animal Act, R.S.B.C. 1996, c. 177

Guide Animal Regulation, B.C. Reg. 664/74

Highway Traffic Act, R.S.O. 1990, c. H.8, as am.

Marriage (Prohibited Degrees) Act, S.C. 1990, c. 46, as am.

Northwest Territories Act, R.S.C. 1985, c. N-27, as am.

Nuclear Energy Act, R.S.C. 1985, c. A-16, as am.

Nuclear Fuel Waste Act, S.C. 2002, c. 23, as am.

Nuclear Safety and Control Act, S.C. 1997, c. 9, as am.

Nunavut Act, S.C. 1993, c. 28, as am.

Yukon Act, S.C. 2002, c. 7, as am.

CASES MENTIONED

Eng v. Toronto (City), [2012] O.J. No. 5661, 2012 ONSC 6818 (S.C.J.)

Smith v. St. Albert (City), [2012] A.J. No. 1333, 2012 ABQB 780 (Q.B.)

TEST YOURSELF

Which level of government has the power to make laws in relation to each of these subject matters? For an extra challenge, provide the source of the law making jurisdiction (section number and enumerated power) for each answer. Watch for overlapping powers!

1. Landlord and Tenant Rights

2. Sexual Assault

3. Sales Tax

4. Marriage Licences

5. Bankruptcy

6. Speeding Tickets

7. Nuclear Energy

8. Native Education

9. Prisons

10. Wills

Chapter 3

Sources of Law — Common Law

COMMON LAW

As we have already discussed, governments make law in the form of statutes and by-laws. Judges also make law by establishing *legal precedents* when they resolve the disputes that come to court. This is our second primary source of law.

From the first few years that Henry II sent his representatives on a circuit around Merry Old England to resolve disputes among the king's subjects, these early circuit "judges" recognized the importance of being consistent. In a sense of fairness, judges tried to resolve common disputes in a common way. Not surprisingly, this approach to justice was labelled *common law.*

The idea caught on, spreading to British colonies throughout the world, including the colonies in Canada, and also those in what became the United States, the Caribbean, India, Australia, New Zealand, South Africa, Hong Kong and elsewhere. A significant portion of the world continues to value common law principles in their justice systems and to create precedents that judges in other similarly inclined nations will consider before deciding cases that have common features.

From the outset, a practical way of helping to ensure consistency was for each judge to make some sort of written record of the cases that were dealt with and the way the judge had resolved the dispute. This logically included a short description of the *facts*, or what had happened to the parties to get them into court in the first place. It also included the judge's view of the *legal issues*, or questions that would have to be answered to resolve the dispute in a fair, or just manner. Lastly, the judge would provide his or her answer to the legal questions. This answer is also called the *decision*, and is really the core of the legal *precedent* that is being established for this judge, or for another judge who may encounter a similar circumstance in the future. The whole summary, written by the judge who dealt with the case, came to be known as a *case report.*

When the early circuit judges got together, they would share these records of their cases, so there could be a pattern of consistency and predictability among the judges. Eventually, private publishing firms were wise enough to start collecting these decisions and published them as books of precedents. Not only would they be of interest to other judges, but when professional lawyers started acting as advocates for people whose disputes were likely to end up in court, these books of precedents became valuable tools for predicting the likely outcome of a client's case. This was the start of the private *case reporting* services that are available today and can be found in any good law library. Some of these sets of precedents are organized according to subject matter, or the type of legal issue being decided, like *Canadian Criminal Cases*, or *Reports of Family Law*. Others are collected according to the geographic jurisdiction of the courts. Examples of this type would be *Alberta Reports,* or *Dominion Law Reports*, a service that collects cases from across Canada.

THE PRINCIPLE OF *STARE DECISIS*

Stare decisis is a Latin expression that, at its simplest, just means to stand by, or follow the decided cases. It is the expression that is attached to the common law concept of relying on the precedents set by prior court decisions. In practice, it is a little more complicated.

In the Canadian justice system, not all courts are considered equal. There is a *hierarchy* of courts, with some levels of court, and the decisions they make, being treated as being more important than decisions made by "lower" levels of court. A bare bones chart of courts in any of our provinces or territories would look like this:

Supreme Court of Canada
↑
Provincial or Territorial
Court of Appeal
↑
Trial Courts

The *trial courts* are, of course, the busiest level of court. It is where every dispute enters the formal justice system that is available for resolving disputes. Judges at this level deal with large numbers of cases and may have the least time to consider the big picture issues like where each case the judge decides fits within broader concepts of justice, or the full array of conflicting legal principles that could potentially apply to an individual case. Judges at this entry, or *lowest* level are also aware that if one of the parties to the dispute is unhappy with the outcome of the case, he or she would normally be entitled to *appeal* the trial judge's decision to the next *higher* level of court, the provincial or territorial court of appeal.

A *provincial or territorial court of appeal* does not have to spend long, confusing hours listening to witnesses relate their individual views of what happened or assessments of the evidence related to the case. Nor do they have to decide which of the witnesses they hear from are most believable. They review the decisions that were made by the trial judges, who probably did have to sort through a cacophony of conflicting stories. The only people the appeal judges have to listen to are lawyers with significant legal education. The lawyers actually assist the judges by directing their attention to the relevant statutes and common law precedents that apply to the situation being reviewed. Appeal judges seldom make their own decisions quickly, often taking months to sort through the legal principles and to scrutinize the recorded actions of the trial judges under review. Nor do they work alone, as most appeals that are dealt with by this level of court involve panels of at least three judges. They can discuss the issues among themselves before coming to a conclusion. In addition, appeal level judges often have graduate lawyers working for them as legal researchers or "clerks". As a result, the decisions of appeal court judges are considered to have a higher value as legal precedents within the province or territory where they do their work than do the decisions of trial judges.

Parties to court cases who are unhappy with decisions that have been made by a provincial or territorial court of appeal may wish to appeal these decisions to the *Supreme Court of Canada*. This is the last level of review that is available for most court judgments and this court will deal with cases from any provincial or territorial court of appeal, but they won't automatically do the review just because someone is dissatisfied. To get the Supreme Court of Canada to review your case, it is usually necessary to apply for *leave*, or permission first. They will only grant the permission if the case presents a unique legal issue (one that hasn't been dealt with at that level), or if it involves an issue that has some national importance. The Supreme Court of Canada is the highest level of court in the justice system and its decisions have the greatest precedent value.

How does this hierarchy of courts affect the concept of *stare decisis?* The decisions that are made by our highest court, the Supreme Court of Canada, are *binding* on all the judges deciding similar cases in any of the lower levels of court. A trial judge dealing with the same issue has to follow the precedent set by the Supreme Court of Canada, as do the judges in the provincial or territorial courts of appeal.

Judgments that are made by provincial or territorial courts of appeal are *binding within their provincial or territorial jurisdiction.* In other words, trial judges in that province or territory dealing with the same issue would be legally bound to follow the court of appeal precedent.

Judgments that are made by trial court judges are *influential*. Other trial judges will try to follow them for the sake of consistency, but are not legally bound to do so. If a judge feels that the reasoning of the earlier decision is faulty, based on fundamental legal principles, the judge could choose to establish a different precedent for dealing with this kind of case.

Similarly, court decisions that are made in other provinces or territories, even if they were made at the court of appeal level in that other jurisdiction, are *influential*, not binding, outside the jurisdiction where they were made. In fact, a common law decision from any country in the world could be *influential* on a judge in a Canadian court, but Canadian judges are not legally bound to follow these precedents. They will do so if they feel that the foreign judge's reasoning is sound and worth applying to the similar case that must be resolved in Canada.

HOW DOES SOMEONE BECOME A JUDGE?

In Canada, judges are appointed by the federal or provincial government. In order to qualify for an appointment, a person would have to have been trained as a lawyer, with the appropriate university degree and would have been fully qualified to work as a lawyer in the relevant province or territory for a considerable period of time (generally, at least ten years) prior to becoming a judge.

Today, most judges indicate an interest in becoming a judge by submitting an application. These applications will be reviewed by a panel made up of representatives of the bar association (the lawyers' professional organization), judges who are already sitting and citizens. The panel will provide a list of appropriate candidates from among the applicants to the federal Minister of Justice or the provincial or territorial Attorney General. These government cabinet ministers will, in turn, make recommendations on suitable candidates to the Prime Minister, or the provincial Premier, or Territorial Commissioner. These top elected officials then make the final choices based on the recommendations they have received. The actual appointment of the judges is done by the Queen's representative in Canada, the Governor General, or Lieutenant Governor.

In Canada, the judges in the Supreme Court of Canada, the provincial or territorial courts of appeal and the *superior* trial courts in each province or territory are all appointed by the federal government. This is because the power to make these appointments was given to the federal level of government in section 96 of the *Constitution Act, 1867.*

Each province or territory, with the exception of Nunavut, also has a provincial or territorial trial court. The power to create these courts comes from enumerated power 14 in section 92 of the *Constitution Act, 1867.* The provincial or territorial government appoints the judges to these trial courts. Nunavut is the only province or territory in Canada that has a fully unified trial court, combining the powers of the superior and provincial or territorial trial courts. In some of the provinces, specialized courts are unified to deal with family law matters that have some elements that could only be dealt with in a superior level of court, like divorce and other elements that could be dealt with by a provincial court or territorial court, like child welfare and child custody.

The *Youth Criminal Justice Act* sets out special procedures for people between the ages of 12 and 17 who are facing criminal charges. While many provinces designate their provincial and territorial court judges as *Youth Court* judges under this law, it is also necessary for some *superior* trial court judges to be designated as *Youth Court* judges. This is because the *Youth Criminal Justice Act* establishes a special category of the most serious criminal offences, like murder, where even someone between the ages of 14 and 17 could face an adult sentence. Because adult sentences for these serious offences would entail maximum potential punishments much longer than 5 years in custody, these youth would have a constitutional right to elect a trial by judge and jury. Only the *superior* trial court judges supervise jury trials.

In general, provincial or territorial trial courts are where most people facing criminal charges make their first court appearance. If the criminal charge is not too serious, or if the accused chooses to stay in that court, the entire trial could be held there. These courts also handle all provincial charges and municipal by-law offences. They are by far the busiest criminal courts in the Canadian system of justice.

On the "civil", or lawsuit side of things, the types of matters the provincial or territorial trial courts deal with vary among provinces and territories. Some provincial and territorial trial courts handle child protection issues and family custody and support matters. In other provinces or territories, these issues are handled by unified family courts. Many provincial or territorial trial courts are also designated as small claims courts, handling lawsuits under a specified dollar value. In Ontario, even those types of cases are handled under the superior level of trial court.

Superior trial courts only handle the more serious criminal charges, when the accused person chooses to go to that level of court. If the accused person wants a *jury* trial for his or her serious criminal charge, it would have to be held in the superior trial court. As noted above, provincial or territorial trial courts don't hold jury trials. The superior trial courts also deal with the majority of lawsuits. Some specific legal issues, like divorce have to be dealt with in superior court. Of course, in provinces and territories with unified family courts, those courts have the powers of both provincial/territorial and superior courts.

Once appointed, judges are not easily removed. This is so judges can act independently, without having to worry about being fired by the government for making unpopular decisions. It is also very important for judges to be seen to be independent of the government because they deal with so many cases in which the government plays a role. In criminal cases, "society" is represented by Crown Prosecutors, lawyers who are employed by the government. It is also possible for the government to be in court because the government is being sued, or needs to sue someone else. If a person accused of committing a crime, or someone involved in a lawsuit with the government thought the judge had to follow the government's wishes, a courtroom would not seem to be a very fair or impartial tribunal for resolving disputes.

To protect the independence of our judges, an appointment as a judge lasts until the age of 75. A judge could retire earlier, but cannot be forced out of his or her position by the government before then. Any complaints about the behaviour or competence of judges are dealt with, initially, by a committee of other judges, not by any government official. A judge could only be removed from his or her position after a thorough review by this committee and if the committee recommends removal as the appropriate course of action to the government. Even then, the removal could only occur after a full debate and vote in the public forum of the federal House of Commons and Senate, or the provincial or territorial legislature. Across Canada, removal recommendations have been extremely rare, though some judges have decided to resign when subjected to review by their peers.

FINDING CASE REPORTS

As mentioned earlier, case reports started to be "published", and available to a broad range of people conducting legal research when private publishing companies realized there was a market for this branch of the law-making process. For most of Canada's legal history, it was these private publishing companies and not the courts themselves, or the government that made case reports available.

As a result, not every judge's decision on a court case has found its way into one of the privately published reporting services. Until the recent advent of computer accessibility, many court judgments just ended up in the court filing systems, with copies being sent to the lawyers for the parties that were involved in the case. For every level of court, except the Supreme Court of Canada, case reports were only published if someone on the private publishers' editorial boards, or one of the lawyers involved in the case, alerted the editors to the value of particular cases as precedents. One of the private publishers recognized the importance of publishing all the decisions of our highest appeal court, the Supreme Court of Canada, some time ago, so all of this court's judgments are published in a series called, *Supreme Court Reports*.

The private publishing companies have organized their case reporting services both geographically and by legal subject matter or topic. Examples of the former include series like *Ontario Reports*, *Atlantic Provinces Reports* or the *Western Weekly Reports*. Topical reporting services would include series like *Canadian Environmental Law Reports* or *Canadian Criminal Cases*.

It is quite expensive to buy these services, as they are updated with new volumes of case reports on a regular basis. As a result, for most people, access to the print versions of these case reports may only be feasible through a well equipped law library, like those in university law schools or in some courthouses. Larger lawyers' offices may have their own libraries, complete with the case reporting services most applicable to the issues they deal with on behalf of clients. In addition, it is possible to pay for computer access to a very broad spectrum of privately published case reports, through legal search services like one provided by *LexisNexis*, the publisher of this text. College and university libraries often have a limited number of the case reporting services and may also pay for access to the computer-based search services to broaden search opportunities for finding relevant cases when necessary.

A very significant advantage to using these commercial services is that all the cases are thoroughly indexed. You can find cases using case names, jurisdiction or, more practically, using key words of the legal issue that needs to be researched. For example, if a researcher were looking for cases in which *drunkenness* was successfully used as a *defence* to a *criminal charge*, the ability to use a key word indexing system to locate relevant precedent-setting cases can be a valuable time-saving tool.

With the advent of wide-spread use of computer technology, courts across Canada have increasingly made the majority of their judgments available to anyone with computer access to the internet. As a result, many more cases are now available to a broader segment of the public. However, these cases have not been subject to an editorial selection process. Consequently, cases with little new to add to the body of law as precedents are included along with the ones that really set the law in a new direction. Indexing is not done with the same consistency and may not be as user friendly as that available in the commercial reporting services. In addition, since this is a relatively new phenomenon, it may not be possible to get access to older court decisions in this way. Nevertheless, this has provided a wonderful new opportunity to access recent court decisions. If, for example, you were to read or view a media report of a precedent-setting court decision, it would be relatively easy to find the actual judgment if you knew the name of the people involved, or even if you had a rough idea of the date of the decision and accessed the website of the court that resolved the case. To try the process yourself, why not try to find an electronic version of the case report reproduced below? As you can see from the heading, the case is called *R. v. Chin Le* and the case report was released by the Court of Appeal for Saskatchewan on January 31, 2013.

READING CASE REPORTS

Let's look at substantial excerpts from a recent case report.

R. v. Chin Le
Court of Appeal for Saskatchewan
January 31, 2013

Cameron, Lane and Herauf JJ.A.

Herauf J.A.:

[1] This is a sentence appeal by the Crown that seeks to overturn a conditional sentence order imposed upon Tan Chin Le ("Mr. Le") following a guilty plea to possession of cannabis marihuana for the purpose of trafficking, contrary to s. 5(2) of the *Controlled Drugs and Substances Act*, S.C. 1996, c. 19.

[2] In an oral decision this Court … set aside the conditional sentence order and imposed an incarceral sentence of 14 months with 4 months credit for the time served on the conditional sentence order. The Court undertook to provide written reasons for the decision. These are those reasons.

[3] The facts are relatively straightforward. On August 6, 2011 the RCMP conducted a traffic stop on Highway 1 near Swift Current, Saskatchewan. The RCMP stopped a vehicle driven by Mr. Le. The co-accused, Thi Phuong Thao Dinh ("Ms. Dinh"), was located in the passenger seat. Ms. Dinh was the registered owner of the vehicle and she is also the common-law spouse of Mr. Le.

[4] A hockey bag was found in the vehicle. The hockey bag contained 34 pounds of marihuana in heat sealed bags. The street value of the marihuana ranged from $37,400 to $88,400. Mr. Le had no criminal record at the time of the sentencing. In a pre-sentence report, and before the sentencing judge, Mr. Le accepted <u>full</u> responsibility for his involvement in the offence. ...

[5] The sentencing judge described the respondent as a "simple courier" but noted he was "transporting a significant amount of cannabis".

[6] Mr. Le was sentenced by the sentencing judge to a conditional sentence order of two years less a day. The conditions included house arrest for one year followed by a curfew for the remainder of the sentence. There were a number of additional conditions such as residency requirements, random search clause, surrender of passport, etc.

[7] This Court has consistently treated offences where large quantities of marihuana have been transported as very serious. For example, in *R. v. Neufield* (1999), 180 Sask. R. 96, Cameron, J.A. speaking for the Court stated:

> Possession of comparatively large amounts of marijuana for the purpose of trafficking commercially ... has long been regarded as an offence of considerable gravity ...

[8] *R. v. Bolla*, 2005 SKCA 111, 269 Sask. R. 295, is a more recent decision of this Court. *Bolla* involved a Crown sentence appeal from a conditional sentence order following a trial where the respondent was convicted of possession of marihuana for the purpose of trafficking. The respondent was the owner-driver of a semi trailer. His truck slid off the road near Moose Jaw ... loaded with boxes of noodles. Two large boxes of marihuana were concealed within them. ... The boxes contained 51.17 pounds of marihuana with a value ranging from $153,000 to $464,000 depending on how it was sold.

[9] Richards J.A., writing for the Court in *Bolla*, concluded that a conditional sentence was demonstrably unfit. The Court substituted a sentence of 18 months imprisonment with credit for the time served on the conditional sentence. The Court noted:

> Mr. Bolla has no criminal record ... However he did not offer a guilty plea and testified untruthfully at trial ... the interprovincial transportation of marihuana is and continues to be a significant problem. Thus, in view of the amount and value of marihuana involved here, a term of imprisonment is the punishment dictated by recent precedents.

[10] While the amount and the street value of the marihuana involved in *Bolla* was greater than in this case, it does not detract from this Court's longstanding practice of treating seriously offences that involve commercial trafficking of large amounts of marihuana. The gravity of the offence is considerable ... In addition, the sentencing judge's description of Mr. Le as a simple courier does nothing to diminish his culpability in the crime involved. In *R. v. Nishikawa*, 2011 ABCA 39, 505 A.R. 63, the Alberta

Court of Appeal spoke about how couriers are a necessary and integral part of a larger drug operation. The court stated:

> But most important, the theory that someone who serves as a courier of large quantities of drugs is "not vital to the scheme" and only serves a "peripheral" role must be rejected. The reality of the drug trade is that the supply chain depends on a wide variety of individuals, all of whom are indeed vital to the criminal enterprise as a whole. That certainly includes the couriers of the drugs ... It must be remembered that trafficking in a prohibited drug includes transport and delivery of that drug. By including these activities in trafficking, Parliament signalled the high level of culpability that must attach to those carrying out these roles ... .

[11] For the above reasons alone we could have found the sentence to be demonstrably unfit and substituted an incarceral sentence in its place. There is an additional ground that must be addressed. Ms. Dinh, the co-accused, had previously pled guilty before the same sentencing judge and received a conditional sentence. When it came to sentencing Mr. Le, the sentencing judge felt obligated to treat both accused in a similar fashion and therefore sentenced Mr. Le to the identical sentence imposed upon Ms. Dinh. We find that this was an error in principle to sentence both accused to identical sentences and also resulted in Mr. Le's sentence being demonstrably unfit. During the sentencing proceedings for both Mr. Le and Ms. Dinh (which took place on separate dates) a substantial amount of time was devoted to the comparative degree of culpability of Mr. Le and Ms. Dinh in this transaction. Mr. Le's acceptance of <u>full</u> responsibility to the circumstances of the offence ... was raised by Crown counsel with the sentencing judge during Mr. Le's sentencing hearing. This was raised to clarify that Mr. Le was taking responsibility. Nevertheless, the trial judge felt in the interests of parity, identical sentences had to be imposed.

[12] The acceptance of full responsibility by Mr. Le contrasts with the more limited involvement of Ms. Dinh. In an earlier appeal by the Crown of Ms. Dinh's sentence, this Court did not interfere with the sentence on the premise that her involvement in the offence was different from that of Mr. Le. Mr. Le's acceptance of full responsibility, in our view, means just that: he was primarily responsible for picking up and arranging for the transportation of marihuana from Calgary to Saskatoon, via Swift Current and Rosetown for some unexplained reason. In other words, their roles were different and the sentencing judge erred in treating them the same.

. . . . .

In Concurrence: The Honourable Justices Cameron and Lane

The title of this case, *R. v. Chin Le* would alert an experienced legal researcher to the fact it is a report of a *criminal* case, not a civil lawsuit. The "R." is a symbolic reference to *Regina*, a Latin expression for "The Queen". The Queen is used to represent Canadian society. When someone is charged with committing a crime, it is considered a crime against society, not an individual victim. Society's representatives, in the form of police officers and *Crown prosecutors*, investigate the allegation and represent society's interests in seeking a just outcome of the case and punishment of a wrongdoer if the accused person is convicted in court. A civil lawsuit case report would have a title formed using the names of the person suing and the person being sued, like *Ediger v. Johnston*, a negligence lawsuit alleging medical malpractice that was dealt with by the Supreme Court of Canada in April of 2013. Another example would be *Everything Kosher Inc. v. Joseph and Wolf Lebovic Jewish Community Centre*, a contract dispute resolved by the Ontario Superior Court of Justice the same month. As you can see from the latter case name, businesses and community organizations can be considered "persons" for the purposes of suing or being sued.

If the title of the case was *R. v. J.F.*, this could alert a researcher to the fact that the person accused of committing the crime in question would probably be someone who fits the age range of a "youth" under the *Youth Criminal Justice Act*. Part of the special procedural protections provided for people between 12 and 17 years of age in our criminal justice system is a ban from having their names published. The intent is to protect a young person from being publicly labelled as a criminal at too early a stage in their development, perhaps hindering efforts at rehabilitation. As a result, the name of an accused in the title of a youth court case is expressed only with initials. This way, the case can still be distinguished from others, but the accused being dealt with in court is unidentifiable by someone reading the case report. Initials are rarely used in cases involving adult accused. When it is used in that circumstance, it is to protect the identity of a victim. For example, if a parent has been accused of assaulting his son or daughter, the parent's name would be expressed in initials so no societal attention would be directed at the child victim.

We are told that this case report comes from the Saskatchewan Court of Appeal. Because it is a precedent set by an appeal level of court, the principle of *stare decisis* would tell us that this decision would be a *binding* precedent on any trial judge in Saskatchewan that would have to deal with a similar situation in the future. Would the case be binding on judges dealing with similar cases outside the province of Saskatchewan? Would it even be binding on another panel of judges in Saskatchewan's Court of Appeal? No, it would be *influential* as a precedent in those circumstances, but not binding.

We are also told the names of the three judges sitting as the panel on the Court of Appeal to deal with this case: Justices Cameron, Lane and Herauf. Why three judges? They sit in an odd number for appeal cases so that if there are conflicting opinions among the judges about the way the case should be handled, the majority (in this case, 2 of the 3) would resolve the case and set the precedent that would bind or influence future judges. As it turns out, a peek at the end of this judgment shows that all three Saskatchewan Court of Appeal judges were in agreement about the correct way to resolve this appeal. Justice Herauf may have actually written the Court's decision (someone has to), but the ruling is unanimous. The words, "In concurrence" before the names of Justices Cameron and Lane mean they agree with the written reasons provided by Justice Herauf.

If one of the judges were to disagree with the way the case should be handled, he or she would explain the rationale for the disagreement. In case reports, the reasoning of any judge that did not form part of the majority of appeal judges dealing with the case would be labelled "dissenting" in some way, often right before that judge's name at the start of his or her judgment.

It is important to recognize that a case report is not like a *transcript* of a court case, which would be a written record of everything that had been said during a trial or sentencing hearing. A transcript would include every question asked by the lawyers and every answer provided by the witnesses. It would also record every comment made by the lawyers and the judge during the trial or sentencing hearing. The transcript of the trial or sentencing hearing would be part of the documentary material that appeal court judges would consider in assessing the validity of an appeal. In this case report, the appeal court judges quote from the sentencing hearing transcript (at paragraph 5), because he believes that comments that the trial judge made during the original sentencing hearing illustrate legal errors that the trial judge made in arriving at the appropriate sentence for Mr. Le.

A case report, like this one, is a judge's summary of the key facts that got the matter into court, the judge's view of the legal issues that have to be resolved and the judge's decision on the appropriate way to resolve those legal issues. It is the case reports, not transcripts, that are studied by legal researchers to determine the law-making precedent that has been established by a particular court case.

The appeal judges' names at the start of this case are followed by the initials "JJ.A." This simply tells us that these judges are "Justices of Appeal", or appeal court judges. If just one appeal judge is mentioned, the letters, "J.A." would be used. A trial judge's name would be followed by the single letter, "J."

Sometimes, case reports will indicate that a judgment has been made "orally". This alerts us to the fact that this judgment was delivered, out loud, in court and recorded by the official court reporter, rather than being written out by at least one of the judges and delivered to the lawyers for the parties that were involved in the court process. In this case, Mr. Justice Herauf mentions in paragraph [2] that an oral judgment was originally provided, but that what we are reading are the promised written reasons supporting the decision by the appeal court to change the sentence the trial judge had imposed on Mr. Le. The written form, while perhaps lacking drama, is often the way that judgments are communicated, particularly judgments made by appeal courts. Appeal judges often "reserve" their judgment following the legal arguments made by the lawyers. This allows the judges to discuss and further research the legal issues before providing a written decision on the appropriate outcome for the case.

Recently, in addition to judgments being sent to the parties directly involved in the case, electronic copies of the judgments will also be uploaded to a website that publishes the decisions of that particular court. Alert researchers can read the legal precedent almost immediately after the parties to the case have been made aware of the outcome.

You will have noticed that each paragraph in the case report is numbered for easy reference. Since this is an appeal court case, Justice Herauf, in paragraph [1] of the report, starts by telling us what happened to the accused person at his trial in the Saskatchewan Provincial Court. Mr. Le entered a guilty plea to a charge of possession of marijuana for the purpose of trafficking and was given a "conditional sentence" by the trial judge. Paragraphs [3] and [4] describe the circumstances of Mr. Le's arrest and the fact that a significant quantity of marijuana was found in a hockey bag (Only in Canada, you say?) in a car that he was driving. The car was actually owned by Mr. Le's common-law spouse, who was "riding shotgun", as my students express it, in the passenger seat. Though the spouse was also charged with the possession for the purpose of trafficking offence, Justice Herauf emphasizes that Mr. Le took <u>full</u> responsibility for the narcotics by underlining the word "full" in paragraph [4], then again in paragraph [11]. This will become an important factor in the appeal court's conclusion that Mr. Le should receive a harsher punishment than his spouse. As we will learn in paragraph [11], the trial judge had sentenced them both identically and the Court of Appeal had already dismissed the Crown prosecutor's appeal of the spouse's sentence before dealing with this Crown appeal of Mr. Le's sentence.

If you were to look up the criminal law statute relevant to the charge the accused was facing, the key provisions would be found in the federal *Controlled Drugs and Substances Act*:

> **s. 5 (2)** No person shall, for the purpose of trafficking, possess a substance included in Schedule I, II, III or IV.
>
> **(3)** Every person who contravenes subsection (1) or (2)
>
> > (a)   ... [where] the subject-matter of the offence is a substance included in Schedule I or II, is guilty of an indictable offence and liable to imprisonment for life.
>
> . . . . .
>
> **Schedule II**
>
> 1. Cannabis, its preparations, derivatives and similar synthetic preparations, including: ...
>
> (2) Cannabis (marihuana)

Like the penalties the government-created statutes impose for many criminal charges, this section tells a sentencing judge what the *maximum* punishment is for someone caught possessing marijuana for the purpose of trafficking. In this case, the maximum possible punishment is LIFE! While you may find this shocking, you will discover as you work with criminal statutes that Canada has a significant number of offences that entail a potential maximum punishment of life. In reality, this gives a judge a broad discretion, controlled as we shall see by common law precedents, to impose what he or she feels is an appropriate penalty under this upper limit. There are many sentencing options other than jail, including fines, probation and the "conditional sentence" the trial judge chose to employ in this case. These alternatives, and some restrictions on their use, are laid out in the *Criminal Code*. Section 742.1 deals with conditional sentences. A portion of that section (as worded at the time Mr. Le was originally sentenced) stipulated the following:

> **s. 742.1** If a person is convicted of an offence, other than a serious personal injury offence ..., a terrorism offence or a criminal organization offence and the court imposes a sentence of less than two years and is satisfied that the service of the sentence in the community would not endanger the safety of the community and would be consistent with the principles of sentencing set out in sections 718 to 718.2, the court may ... order that the offender serve the sentence in the community, subject to the offender's compliance with the conditions imposed ... .

It would appear from this wording that a conditional sentence, (which some people describe as house arrest because it involves the convict staying out of jail with a large number of restrictions on his or her actions and movements) was a legitimate sentencing option for a judge dealing with someone like Mr. Le. But Justice Herauf tells us in paragraph [1] that the Crown prosecutors are appealing this sentence. If a statute seems to allow for this type of sentencing, on what legal basis could the prosecutors be challenging the trial judge's decision? Well, as we have been discussing, there are two primary sources of law: statutes and the common law. The prosecutors must believe precedents set by the courts add some extra qualifiers to the use of conditional sentences for someone in Mr. Le's situation.

Justice Herauf and his colleagues agree with the prosecutors who have launched the appeal. In paragraphs [7], [8] and [9], they point out that two precedents from the Court of Appeal for Saskatchewan, *R. v. Neufield* (1999), 180 Sask. R. 96 and *R. v. Bolla*, 2005 SKCA 111 make it clear that the Court of Appeal have "consistently treated offences where large quantities of marijuana have been transported as very serious" and in a similar situation, "concluded that a conditional sentence was demonstrably unfit".

You probably noticed that there is some sort of code of numbers and letters following the case names of the Court of Appeal precedents that Justice Herauf mentioned. Once you learn how to read this gobbledygook that follows the case names, properly called the *citation* information, you will be able to look up the cases yourself in a case reporting service. This will allow you to check out the full text of any precedent you are interested in investigating further. For example, the "(1999)" that follows the name of the *R. v. Neufield* case tells you that this precedent was set in 1999. The segment of the *Neufield* citation, "180 Sask. R." tells you that this case report can be found in "Volume 180" of the geographic-case reporting service called the *Saskatchewan Reports* (Sask. R.). Important case reports decided in Saskatchewan are collected by the publishers of this service until they have enough to fill a book. Each individual book compilation of court decisions is called a "volume" and these volumes or books are numbered sequentially as more and more cases are added to the collection. You would look for this case in the book labelled 180.

The "96", at the end of the *R. v. Neufield* citation, tells you to check on page 96 of Volume 180 of the Saskatchewan Reports. This part of the citation gives you the page number of the book, or volume where the case report you are looking for begins. In other words, the full citation is a complete tracking device, allowing you to locate case reports. You should now be able to apply this knowledge of the way citations work to figure out what year the *R. v. Bolla* case was decided.

The citation for the *R. v. Bolla* case, "2005 SKCA 111" is an example of an on-line reference. The "SKCA" portion of the citation is a short form method of telling you that the case is a decision of the Saskatchewan Court of Appeal. Cases like this one can be found on the website of the Canadian Legal Information Institute (CanLII). The Institute is a non-profit organization run by the Federation of Law Societies of Canada and the website includes court decisions from each Canadian province and territory as well as statutes and regulations. It is a handy research tool.

The appeal court judges in *R. v. Chin Le* felt that the trial judge should have paid more attention to these precedents. As you will be aware from our discussion of the principles of *stare decisis*, since both the *R. v. Neufield* and *R. v. Bolla* cases were decided by the Court of Appeal for Saskatchewan, a trial court judge in Saskatchewan is legally bound to follow these precedents. Both should have warned the trial judge that the use of conditional sentences would be inappropriate in a case like this one.

The trial judge also made it clear (as quoted at paragraphs [5] and [10]) that he thought the fact that Mr. Le was a "simple courier" was an important factor in imposing a lighter sentence. At paragraph [10], Justice Herauf quotes a decision from the Alberta Court of Appeal that he obviously found influential:

> ... the theory that someone who serves only a "peripheral" role must be rejected. The reality of the drug trade is that the supply chain depends on a wide variety of individuals, all of whom are indeed vital to the criminal enterprise as a whole. That certainly includes the couriers of the drugs ... .

There was really no suspense in the way this judgment was written. In paragraph [2], Justice Herauf made it clear that the Court of Appeal would be substituting a much harsher sentence of 14 months in jail for the conditional sentence that the trial judge had imposed. This was consistent with the substitution of an 18-month sentence for a conditional sentence in the *R. v. Bolla* precedent, set by the Saskatchewan Court of Appeal eight years earlier. While a new panel of the Saskatchewan Court of Appeal was not legally bound to follow its own earlier precedent, it chose to do so and pointed out to a trial judge that he or she was not in a position to deviate from the Court of Appeal's legal guidance on sentencing in this type of case.

In an interesting aside, if you were to look up **s. 742.1** of the *Criminal Code* today, you would find that the federal government has altered the wording of this section since Mr. Le was sentenced. The changes narrow a judge's ability to use a conditional sentence in a number of ways. One of the new restrictions states that a conditional sentence is not an option if the offence with which the person has been charged involves a maximum penalty of 14 years *or life*. In other words, a trial judge's freedom to choose a conditional sentence for possession of marijuana for the purpose of trafficking is not only restricted by court decisions like *R. v. Chin Le*, it is no longer a sentencing option according to the relevant statute either.

GETTING THE WHOLE PICTURE (THE INTERACTION BETWEEN STATUTES AND COMMON LAW PRECEDENTS)

When the judges in the Court of Appeal for Saskatchewan were asked to decide whether the trial judge should have sent Mr. Le to jail for transporting a large quantity of marijuana, they were being asked to analyze the application of the wording of statutes (sections of the *Criminal Code* and the *Controlled Drugs and Substances Act*) and prior court precedents to an incident that occurred in real life. When their analysis was complete, the judges had created a precedent that could, in the future, affect other people charged with the same offence. In deciding what, exactly, amounted to appropriate sentencing principles, they have set a standard that other judges may, or may not, be bound to use, in assessing similar incidents. The judges have added detail to the law.

Another simple example will help to illustrate how complex the law can be and to emphasize the importance of developing legal research skills that cover both statutes and common law if you plan a law-related career. Imagine that the local municipal government has created a by-law that says: *No person shall deposit litter on the streets of Ourtown*. Certainly nothing complex on the face of the statute, but consider a few of these issues as by-law enforcement officers seek to enforce it.

A 10-year-old child leaves a corner store and drops a candy bar wrapper on the sidewalk. Can the child be charged with violating the by-law? Are there age limits on laying charges? Even if the child could be charged, is it possible to get a conviction in court based on these facts? Does a candy bar wrapper fit a definition of *litter*? Does tossing a wrapper on the sidewalk fit the restriction on depositing litter on the *street*? What if the wrapper was blown from the child's hand by a gust of wind? Should we still pin the punishment on this pint-sized perpetrator? What the heck is the punishment for breaking this law anyway? None of the answers are clear from looking at this simple little statute alone, but all could affect the way the law is to be applied. Perhaps, we should consider the questions one at a time.

Canadian 10-year-olds do not go to court to face charges. Even though this little by-law is silent on the issue, other statutes are not. For example, section 13 of the *Criminal Code* states: "No person shall be convicted of an offence in respect of an act or omission on his part while that person was under the age of twelve years." The *Youth Criminal Justice Act* provides special procedures for criminal charges that involve youth from the ages of 12 to 17, but provide nothing for dealing with younger criminals. Of course, both of these are federal statutes and affect charges under federal laws, but not charges under a municipal by-law, like this one. Nevertheless, each of the provinces and territories have procedural statutes that set similar age limits that would apply to charges under provincial statutes *and municipal by-laws* enacted within those jurisdictions. In other words, this statute is affected by another statute. To get the full picture on the law, you must be aware of the interaction between municipal by-laws and provincial or territorial statutes.

Even if the accused had been 14, the other issues remain. How would a court deal with the appropriate way to define words like *litter* or *street* when the peculiar context relating to a specific charging incident becomes relevant? A judge would follow a legally logical process, which may well differ from the process you or I would follow if we were seeking a definition. Let's face it, we'd probably proceed directly to a dictionary. A judge, on the other hand, would check first to see if the word had been defined in the statute itself. Often, statutes contain definition, or *interpretation* sections to define potentially contentious words. The judge is bound by these definitions, when available. The next place to look is in *related statutes*. In other words, if the municipal government that created this by-law had defined the words in other municipal by-laws, those definitions would be applied. Failing locating a related municipal definition, judges would look for a statutory definition in provincial or territorial statutes in the jurisdiction where this municipality is located. It is not too difficult to imagine that an environmental statute might contain a definition for *litter* and any number of municipal, provincial or territorial statutes related to planning, development or traffic control could provide a definition of *street*. Would it end at the curb, or would it extend across the boulevard and onto the sidewalk? You would have to analyze the related statutes to know.

If the statutes did not prove fruitful, a judge would seek common law direction. In other words, they would be looking for previous court decisions that set precedents on the way these words should be interpreted. There are, of course, published *legal dictionaries*. These specialized dictionaries provide references to court decisions where judges have interpreted the words.

It would only be when this thorough search of legal authorities failed to yield a definition that a judge would resort to the standard type of dictionary that you or I might pull off the shelf, or access on-line, seconds after being stumped by a new word. To get the whole picture of the law as it is applied to defining terminology used, you may have to know not only about related statutes, but also about the common law precedents that have previously looked at the words.

Could the accused be convicted under the littering by-law if the wind had torn the litter from his hand? Expressed another way, can a person be convicted of an offence if he or she lacked any *intention* to violate the law? As we'll discuss in Chapter 8, if an accused person is charged with committing a serious criminal offence, like murder, the Crown prosecutor would have to present evidence that would prove, not only the action of causing a wrongful death, but also that the accused intended to harm the victim. Sometimes, expressed using Latin terminology, the Crown has to prove both the *actus reus* (action) and *mens rea* (intent). Often though, this requirement becomes obvious simply from looking at the wording of the statutory section that defines the wrongful activity. For example, section 229 of the *Criminal Code* says:

s. 229 Culpable homicide is murder

(*a*) where a person who causes the death of a human being

    (i) means to cause his death, or

    (ii) means to cause him bodily harm that he knows is likely to cause his death, and is reckless whether death ensues or not.

There is no such wording in our littering by-law. It doesn't look as though a prosecutor would have to demonstrate that an accused intended to litter for the person to be convicted. If you knew some of the relevant common law, you would know that the Supreme Court of Canada has dealt with this issue in a case that involved an allegation that the City of Sault Ste. Marie had been responsible for discharging potentially harmful materials into a body of water, under a provincial environmental protection statute. In *R. v. Sault Ste. Marie (City)* (1978), 40 C.C.C. (2d) 353, the Supreme Court of Canada stated that charges could fall into three categories; straight *criminal* charges, which would require proof of *actus reus* and *mens rea*, and two categories of regulatory offences, *strict liability* and *absolute liability* charges. Since the latter two categories seldom carry as high a risk of jail time and are aimed at public welfare issues, like protecting the environment, or controlling traffic flow on our streets, people could be convicted of the wrongful action, without the need for a prosecutor to prove that the act was intentional.

Even without the need for the prosecutor to prove intent, could there be any defence for a person who is able to say, "I was being careful, but the wind was just too strong?" Would a judge be prepared to take an excuse like that into consideration? Again, the answer comes from the common law established in the *Sault St. Marie (City)* case. The Supreme Court judges said that most regulatory charges would fit into their strict liability category. For these charges, an accused would be entitled to use a due diligence defence. In other words, if the accused could legitimately prove that he or she was being careful, but had committed the prohibited action despite the care exercised, the act might be excusable. If the wording of the statute itself made it clear that the action would be enough and that excuses should not be considered, an offence would be categorized as absolute liability. Again, you have to understand common law to apply this very simple statute to a particular accused in the circumstances in which he or she is alleged to have committed the offence.

KEY TERMINOLOGY

absolute liability	proof of the *actus reus* component of this type of criminal or quasi-criminal charge is enough to get a conviction
actus reus	an illegal action or omission
appeal courts	courts that deal with challenges to the decisions made by other courts
appellant	the person who starts an appeal of a court decision
binding	a court decision that a judge has a legal obligation to follow in dealing with another case
case report	the written judgment or decision of a court case that includes the judges' view of the facts of the case, the legal issues that must be resolved and the judges' decision on the correct legal resolution
case reporting service	a service that collects, organizes and publishes case reports
common law	a system of resolving common legal disputes in a common way by relying on precedents
criminal charge	the allegation that a person has violated a particular section of a criminal statute
decision	a judge's answer to the legal issues that have to be resolved in a court case
defence	a legal response to a criminal charge that could entitle an accused person to be acquitted or convicted of a reduced charge
drunkenness	intoxication, can be used as a partial defence to some criminal charges
due diligence	exercising care to avoid doing something illegal
hierarchy of courts	ranking some courts as more influential than others; for example, appeal courts are more influential than trial courts and the Supreme Court of Canada is the most influential of all

influential	convincing, likely to affect another judge's approach to dealing with a legal issue
intention	the mental element of criminal behaviour; meaning to bring on a particular result, or being reckless as to consequences
interpretation section	a portion of a statute that provides definitions for terminology used in that law
jury	a group chosen from the community to decide on the guilt or innocence of an accused person in a criminal case, or on liability of someone who is being sued
leave	seeking the permission of a court of appeal to proceed with an appeal
legal dictionaries	special dictionaries dealing with legal terminology
legal issues	the questions that have to be answered by a judge or jury in resolving a legal dispute
mens rea	the mental element that may have to be proven to secure the conviction of someone accused of committing a crime
precedents	previous court decisions that may be influential or binding on a judge dealing with a similar legal issue
Provincial trial courts	courts with provincially appointed judges, where trials are held before a judge alone with no possibility of jury trials — busiest criminal courts, handling all summary charges, first appearances on most other charges and indictable charges when the accused person chooses
related statutes	written laws from the same level of government that deal with some of the same issues, or use the same terminology
small claims court	a civil court, using simplified procedures to deal with claims involving dollar amounts under a limit set by statute

stare decisis	the common law system of relying on precedents that considers court decisions from a higher level of court binding and decisions from the same level, or from another jurisdiction, influential
strict liability	criminal or quasi-criminal charges that don't require proof of *mens rea*, but will enable an accused to raise a due diligence defence
superior trial courts	trial courts with judges appointed by the federal government, where jury trials are an option
Supreme Court of Canada	highest level of appeal court in the country, its decisions are binding on all other judges
transcript	a written record of the questions asked, answers given and statements made when someone is speaking in court or during another type of legal proceeding
trial courts	courts where evidence is provided by witnesses to assist a judge or jury in arriving at a decision involving a criminal charge or civil lawsuit

STATUTES MENTIONED

Constitution Act, 1867 (U.K.), 30 & 31 Vict., c. 3, reprinted in R.S.C. 1985, App. II, No. 5

Controlled Drugs and Substances Act, S.C. 1996, c. 19, as am.

Criminal Code, R.S.C. 1985, c. C-46, as am.

Youth Criminal Justice Act, S.C. 2002, c. 1, as am.

CASES MENTIONED

Ediger v. Johnston, [2013] S.C.J. No. 18, 2013 SCC 18 (S.C.C.)

Everything Kosher Inc. v. Joseph and Wolf Lebovic Jewish Community Campus, [2013] O.J. No. 1588, 2013 ONSC 2057 (S.C.J.)

R. v. Bolla, [2005] S.J. No. 533, 2005 SKCA 111, 269 Sask. R. 295 (C.A.)

R. v. J.F., [2013] S.C.J. No. 12, 2013 SCC 12 (S.C.C.)

R. v. Le, [2013] S.J. No. 33, 2013 SKCA 9 (C.A.)

R. v. Neufield, [1999] S.J. No. 461, 180 Sask. R. 96 (C.A.)

R. v. Nishikawa, [2011] A.J. No. 818, 2011 ABCA 39 (C.A.)

R. v. Sault Ste. Marie (City), [1978] S.C.J. No. 59, 40 C.C.C. (2d) 353 (S.C.C.)

TEST YOURSELF

Read the following case report and be prepared to answer some questions about the court case and its relevance. The case involved a young woman in Alberta who was charged with assault causing bodily harm. At trial, she was found guilty and the judge imposed a sentence. There was an appeal and this case report is from the appeal court.

R. v. Bach
Alberta Court of Appeal
February 24, 1986

Before: The Honourable Justices McClung, Cavanagh and Forsythe

McClung, J.A. (orally, for the court)

[1] In this case the Crown appeals the granting of a conditional discharge to Ms. Bach who found her boyfriend with another *in flagrante delicto*. The attack took place with a meat cleaver. The boyfriend was badly cut on the hand while warding off Ms. Bach's displeasure. Despite the serious potential of the incident it quickly diffused. She is normally a responsible girl, employed, and it is conceded by all that it is unlikely she will be back in a courtroom. She has no record and enjoys the obvious support of her family. Mr. Smyth (defence lawyer) tells us that since the trial she has changed and it may be that a record of conviction is not so onerous to her in her present job.

[2] But it is difficult to envisage any circumstance where a weapon assault, resulting in bodily harm, could attract a discharge, be it conditional or absolute. A conviction for this type of offence is information to which the public and law enforcement is entitled. Nor does this class of offence meet the standards of *R. v. Macfarlane* [(1985), 55 A.R. 222 (Alta. C.A.)] which guidelines the granting of discharges in this province. We think that weapons offences are far too fashionable to maintain the discharge in this type of case.

[3] Leave to appeal must be granted and the appeal will be allowed.

[4] In lieu of the discharge we substitute a suspended sentence and probation for a period of 6 months on the conditions prescribed by the learned sentencing judge.

1. Who was responsible for this case getting to the Court of Appeal?

2. Why would the trial judge's decision have been appealed?

3. How did the Court of Appeal judges deal with the main appeal issue?

4. What was the rationale for the Appeal Court decision?

5. For whom might this particular court decision have precedent value? Why?

6. Would this decision be *influential* or *binding* in a trial court in your province or territory? Briefly explain.

7. Check the year of this court decision. Is that an important factor to consider when assessing the precedent value of this case? Why or why not?

8. Did this court rely on previous court precedents in arriving at a decision? Briefly explain.

9. Could this court decision have been appealed? If so, to which court would the appeal go? If not, why not?

EXTRA CHALLENGE: Locate a *Criminal Code* and check on the *maximum penalty* Ms. Bach was facing for a charge of assault causing bodily harm.

Chapter 4

General Categories in the Justice System

THREE DISTINCT CATEGORIES OF JUSTICE

The *criminal justice* system, used when society alleges that a person has done something wrong and should be punished, and the *civil justice* system, applying when one person sues another to get financial compensation for harm that has been caused, both use our courts as the ultimate decision-making forum. The processes, documents and *standards of proof* used in the criminal justice system differ from those used when civil justice matters are being settled. This is true even though crimes and lawsuits might be dealt with in the same court building and often may be decided by the same judges. This Chapter examines the similarities and the differences.

Administrative justice covers issues that are handled by specialty boards and other government-appointed decision-makers, like the Parole Board, the Human Rights Commission and the people working for the Ministry of Transport who decide whether or not you have the qualifications to get a driver's licence. These boards and government agents have their own distinct processes for arriving at fair decisions. Sometimes, the process used looks an awful lot like a trial held in court. Other times, decisions are based entirely on written documents that are submitted, or on tests that are performed successfully. This Chapter will discuss distinguishing features of the administrative justice system and general fairness principles that apply.

AN ADVERSARIAL APPROACH TO JUSTICE

Canadian civil and criminal trials and even some administrative tribunal hearings are run as contests, where the participants are generally expected to know the rules. The rules can be quite complex, creating a real disadvantage if one of the contestants, or *parties* is not being assisted by a procedural expert, like a lawyer or paralegal in ensuring that the contest is fair.

In the *adversarial* system of justice employed in Canada, the role of the judge or administrative hearing officer is very passive in relation to the gathering and presentation of the *evidence*, the information on which the outcome of the case will be decided. The judge or hearing officer allows the *parties* to select the witnesses they feel will be most useful. Each party's *counsel* (lawyer or paralegal, if they are fortunate to have one) will decide on the order the witnesses will be called and will then ask questions of these witnesses to draw out the relevant information. It is expected that the bias of one party, in gathering evidence slanted to that party's perspective of the appropriate outcome of the case, will be balanced by the evidence gathered and presented by the other party. An opposing party, or his or her legal representative will also be allowed to *cross-examine* opponent's witnesses, asking challenging questions to test the accuracy of the information that has been presented.

The judge or hearing officer, as an independent arbiter and expert in the law and legal procedure, will make decisions about whether or not a particular witness or an element of their evidence is appropriate to use in the case, but usually only if the opposing party makes an *objection*. In most circumstances, it is only in responding to objections that judges apply rules of evidence laid out in government-created statutes or court-created precedents.

Justice Charron of the Supreme Court of Canada made the role of a judge in an adversarial system of justice quite clear in a case called *R. v. S.G.T.*: "... judges are expected to be impartial arbiters of the dispute before them; the more a trial judge second-guesses or overrides the decisions of counsel, the greater is the risk that the trial judge will, in either appearance or reality, cease being a neutral arbiter and instead become an advocate for one party".

Justice Doherty of the Ontario Court of Appeal recently added some revealing comments when he criticized a judge for asking witnesses too many questions during a recent trial: "Trial judges are, at bottom, listeners ... It is counsel's job, not the trial judge's, to explore inconsistencies in a witness' testimony" (paragraph 33 of *R. v. Huang*).

CRIMINAL JUSTICE SYSTEM

The criminal justice system is used to deal with people facing the true criminal charges, found in federal statutes like the *Criminal Code of Canada* and the *Controlled Drugs and Substances Act*. This system is also used for people facing *quasi-criminal* charges under provincial statutes, like Ontario's *Highway Traffic Act*, Alberta's *Fisheries Act* or Nova Scotia's *Liquor Control Act*. Individuals who violate municipal by-laws and want to fight their parking tickets, or charges for failing to secure the proper permits to operate a local business, would find themselves in a court using criminal justice procedure.

If governments, as society's representatives, decide to label certain behaviours as unacceptable and deserving of punishment, this will be done in a *statute*. We do not have *common law*, or judge-created crimes.

The police, as agents of society, usually investigate allegations of criminal behaviour and exercise their discretion in laying charges if this behaviour appears to violate one statute or another.

When the accused person is brought to court to face the charges, a prosecutor, employed by the government, will represent society as an advocate, calling witnesses who may have evidence of the accused person's guilt. The prosecutor will also ask the judge to impose an appropriate sentence, as society's punishment, if the person is judged to have committed the offence.

Neither the police, nor prosecutors are in a position to decide on the guilt or innocence of an accused person. That can only be done by an *impartial* decision-maker. In our criminal justice system, this is a role for a judge, or a jury. As was mentioned in Chapter 3, once a judge has been appointed to his or her position, he or she cannot be easily removed. This gives the judge the independence to make impartial decisions, whether or not these decisions are popular, or would fit the political climate at the time the decision is made.

Not everyone who faces a trial in our criminal justice system has a right to a jury trial. Section 11(*f*) of the *Canadian Charter of Rights and Freedoms*, ensures an accused person the right to choose to have a jury IF he or she is facing a charge with a maximum punishment of five years or more in jail. In practical terms, that means that juries are only available for serious federal offences. No charges under provincial or territorial statutes or municipal by-law offences qualify for jury trials. When there is a jury in a criminal trial, it will be made up of *twelve* people from the community where the accused person is alleged to have committed the crime. The jury is given the task of deciding the guilt or innocence of the accused. All 12 jurors must reach a unanimous decision to convict. The jurors do not decide on the appropriate sentence for someone who has been convicted. That is the judge's role.

The statutes that define the behaviours that are considered to be crimes, usually specify a *maximum* punishment that a judge can impose on a person who has been judged to be guilty. Often, this includes a maximum jail sentence that could be used as punishment. Depending on the circumstances of the crime and the criminal, the judge has the discretion to impose an appropriate type of sentence that falls under this maximum and may include elements other than jail. Fines, periods of community supervision, probation and restrictions on the use of motor vehicles or weapons are among the array of sentencing tools available.

It is a very serious matter to accuse someone of committing a crime. A conviction may not only result in a loss of freedom, it could also damage the convict's reputation in the community, future job prospects and the ability to travel to foreign countries. As a result, the criminal justice system requires a very vigorous *standard of proof* in order to convict someone of a crime. If the prosecutor cannot present witnesses who have sufficient evidence to convince a judge or jury of the accused person's guilt *beyond a reasonable doubt*, the accused person will be *acquitted* (judged "not guilty").

The *onus*, or legal responsibility, for proving that a crime has been committed by this person is always on the prosecutor. The accused does not have to prove anything, though his lawyer may want to present any evidence that could raise a reasonable doubt in the mind of a judge or jurors.

Since society is accusing a person of behaviour that is unacceptable, the prosecutor, representing society, has a legal duty to *disclose* all the evidence that has been gathered in relation to the alleged offence to the accused, or his or her lawyer, BEFORE trial. This allows the accused an opportunity to prepare a defence against the allegations. Because criminal defendants have no onus to prove anything, the defendant or his or her legal representative is generally not required to disclose the evidence that they may use to the prosecutor in advance of the trial.

Often, following disclosure, an accused person may decide that he or she is prepared to admit to committing the crime, or a related crime, and will come to court and enter a "guilty" plea. This streamlines the trial considerably and the judge could move into the sentencing stage of the process right away.

CIVIL JUSTICE SYSTEM

The civil justice system allows people who have been harmed by the behaviour of others to *sue* the individuals or corporations they allege have caused the harm for financial compensation. There are other types of *remedies* a court might be prepared to order, some of which will be discussed in Chapters 5 and 6, but financial compensation is, by far, the most common.

The person who starts a lawsuit must have a legitimate legal reason to sue, called a *cause of action*. Most causes of action come from *common law*. They have been created by judges resolving disputes between individuals, rather than by government-created statutes. *Breach of contract*, or failing to do what you've agreed to do, is a very popular reason for someone to be sued. *Negligence*, which could generally be considered harming someone by not being careful enough, is an even more frequently used justification for a lawsuit. The parameters for each of these causes of action are examples of judge-made law. You have to understand the precedent-setting cases to understand what is required.

There are some types of disputes that are dealt with in the civil justice system that do involve causes of action that are set out in government-created statutes. For example, if someone who has been legally married wants to get a divorce, whether or not he or she qualifies to sue for a divorce is laid out in the federal *Divorce Act*.

Another example of a civil justice issue that is controlled by statute is the area of child welfare. Each province in Canada has a statute that describes family circumstances that may be harmful to a child and will justify the intervention by children's aid societies to protect the child from harm. Before removing a child from the care of his or her parents on any long term basis, a children's aid society would have to apply to a judge in the civil justice system for a court order. A parent or other guardian would be entitled to attend and dispute the need for intervention.

Some of the causes of action that judges created first, in resolving disputes between individuals, are the civil equivalents of criminal charges. For example, for someone to be charged criminally with assault, society would have to allege that his or her behaviour fit within the definition found in section 265 of the *Criminal Code* of Canada. For the victim to sue in the civil justice system for financial compensation for injuries suffered in the same assault, he or she would have to show that the person being sued applied force, or threatened to apply force, without the victim's consent. The same perpetrator of the harm could end up facing two separate court cases, one to decide if he or she has done something criminal, and therefore should be punished by society, the other to decide if he or she must pay financial compensation to the victim.

Before starting a lawsuit, most people would have to go to a lawyer in private practice to discuss the harm they have suffered and to ask if they have a legitimate, legal reason to sue. If so, the lawyer would then expect to be paid to prepare the appropriate documents to start the lawsuit. Although the procedural rules in the civil justice system are set by provincial governments, and the required documents have provincial idiosyncrasies, they are all variations of a *statement of claim*.

The statement of claim will describe the person who is starting the lawsuit, or *plaintiff*, and the person or persons being sued, the *defendant(s)*. It will also describe what is alleged to have happened to cause the harm to the plaintiff and will request financial compensation of a certain amount, also known as *damages*.

The statement of claim must be filed in the civil court system before time limits for starting a lawsuit (set by individual provinces) have lapsed and must be *served* on the potential defendants. The defendants will then have a time limit to respond with their own written document, called a *statement of defence*, disputing the claim. Usually, defendants have to hire their own lawyers to prepare these documents and assist them through the court processes.

The civil justice system in each province has a number of procedural steps to encourage plaintiffs and defendants to settle their disputes before they get to court, the ultimate decision-making body. One of these is the concept of *discovery*. Through this process, both the plaintiff and the defendant will exchange any important documents they plan to rely on if the dispute goes to trial, well in advance of the trial date.

In addition, the lawyer for the plaintiff will be able to ask questions of the defendant and the defendant's lawyer will be able to question the plaintiff at an "oral discovery" meeting, where all statements are made under oath and the questions and answers are recorded by a qualified court reporter.

If those procedural steps aren't enough to lead to a settlement, most provinces require a pre-trial conference where a judge will try to narrow the issues in the dispute and encourage an agreed resolution. Some provinces also require a mediation session for certain types of disputes.

A trial becomes a forum of last resort. In Canada, most trials are held by a judge, without a jury, even though the plaintiff and defendant have the right to choose a jury for a broad range of civil justice issues. Civil juries are commonly made up of six jurors (as compared to the 12 in criminal court). A majority of jurors can make a decision in civil court, it does not have to be unanimous.

When a civil case goes to trial, the *onus* of proving the valid cause of action and the appropriate financial compensation for the harm caused is on the plaintiff. The *standard of proof* required in not as rigorous as that in the criminal justice system. A plaintiff will be successful in the lawsuit if he or she can prove the case *on a balance of probabilities*. This simply means showing that the plaintiff's side of the story is more likely to be true than the defendant's version of what happened. If we were looking at a comparison of the civil and criminal standards of proof, using the scales of justice, simply tipping the scale in your favour represents a win in civil court. In criminal court, the prosecutor, who always has the onus, would have to weigh the balance of evidence on the prosecution side right to the ground to prove the case *beyond a reasonable doubt*.

One interesting aspect of the civil justice system is that a judge or jury can apportion responsibility, or *liability*, among a number of different parties. For example, if a person caused a car accident while driving impaired, but also had to contend with brakes that failed because of faulty work done by a mechanic in trying to avoid the accident, a court could decide that the drunk was 80 per cent responsible for the accident and the mechanic 20 per cent (or 70 per cent - 30 per cent if that is more appropriate). If the plaintiff, who was injured, was carelessly walking along a dark road, on the wrong side, dressed in black, the jury could deduct a percentage of any damages awarded because of the contributory liability of the person who is suing.

Criminal Justice — Civil Justice Comparison

	Criminal Justice System	Civil Justice System
WHO	Society v. an individual	Individual v. Individual
	R. v. Defendant	Plaintiff v. Defendant
PROCESS	Charge	Sue
OBJECTIVE	Punish, deter	Compensation
GROUNDS	Statute Violation	Cause of Action
ONUS	Prosecutor	Plaintiff
PROOF	Beyond a reasonable doubt	Balance of probabilities
FINDING	Guilty or Acquitted	Liability or none (can be shared)
RESULT	Jail, fine, probation	Financial compensation (DAMAGES)

ADMINISTRATIVE JUSTICE SYSTEM

The courts cannot handle every sphere of government-controlled decision-making that effects people in a society as complex as Canada in the 21st century. As a result, a great deal of the decision-making is assigned to specialty boards and tribunals and other government agencies and administrators. Some deal directly with individual rights and protections. Examples would include, provincial workers' compensation boards, human rights tribunals, social assistance and welfare agencies and agents authorized to issue fishing and hunting licences. Others deal with sectors of the economy. The Canadian Radio-Television and Telecommunications Commission, the Atomic Energy Control Board and local public utilities would fit this niche. A few of the administrative decision-making bodies have clear links to our criminal justice system. The Parole Board of Canada, provincial criminal victim compensation boards and the officials in transportation ministries who suspend the drivers' licences of people who have been convicted of impaired driving would be examples.

Governments create and give specific powers to these decision-makers through statutes. Unlike judges, who have a broad range of discretionary powers that have developed through common law principles, administrative decision-makers must follow the legislative guidelines they have been given. If they stray, their actions are considered *ultra vires*, or beyond their power and people adversely affected could challenge the decisions in court.

In reviewing challenged decisions of administrators, Canadian courts have developed some basic principles of justice, or *fairness* that all administrative decision-makers should follow. The key is that the person who is likely to be affected by a decision is given a reasonable opportunity to participate in the decision-making process. This can involve a range of rights, depending, in part, on the potential impact of the decision. As a starting point, fairness will require an advance notice that a decision is going to be made and a chance for the affected person to make submissions before that occurs. Courts have also said that affected persons should be able to expect that the individual or panel making the decision will be impartial. In other words, the decision-maker should not be biased.

Many administrative bodies hold hearings that include processes very much like those followed in court. The affected parties may be entitled to advance disclosure of evidence they will encounter and have the right to be represented by a lawyer or other agent. They might also have an opportunity to cross-examine anyone who presents evidence that is harmful to their position. Provincial governments in Alberta and Ontario have addressed many of these common law concerns by creating statutes that set out procedures that designated administrative tribunals must follow.

The process for appointing administrative decision-makers is not consistent. For years, members of the public have complained that some of these decision-makers get their jobs, not because of any knowledge of the legal system, or even the subject area that they are being chosen to administer, but because of close ties, or political affiliations with the politicians who supervise the appointments. These jobs, many of which involve attractive pay scales, have been used as rewards for assisting the political party in power in some way. It is true that many of the appointments are made "at the pleasure of the government". This means that the decision-makers could all be replaced if an election in that jurisdiction changes the party in power. This is a far cry from the lengthy legal experience expected of people who are appointed as judges. Judges also have firmly entrenched independence and protection from dismissal at the whim of government.

PRACTICAL OVERLAP

It is important to realize that one incident could fit into more than one category of our justice system. For example, a person who is involved in a car accident might face criminal charges related to driving while impaired. If the accident has injured someone, this same wrong-doer could find himself being sued in the civil justice system by the victim.

Following his conviction for impaired driving, a government administrator, working for the provincial transportation ministry, will undoubtedly send this same person a notice stating that his driver's licence has been suspended. The criminal, civil and administrative systems of justice have all had an impact on this one individual and one incident.

KEY TERMINOLOGY

Acquitted	being judged "not guilty" after a criminal trial
adversarial	operating like a contest
balance of probabilities	the standard of proof in the civil justice system
beyond a reasonable doubt	standard of proof in the criminal justice system
breach of contract	not doing what was agreed to be done
cause of action	legal reason you can sue someone
counsel	legal representative — lawyer or paralegal
cross-examine	ask challenging questions of an opponent's witness
damages	financial compensation given to someone who has won a lawsuit
defendant	the accused person in a criminal trial, or the person who is being sued in a civil trial
disclose	provide evidence to the other party in advance of a trial
discovery	exchange important documents, question key opposition witnesses prior to a civil trial
evidence	information presented to a court or tribunal to be used in arriving at a decision
liability	legal responsibility for harm caused
objection	a challenge to the use of evidence or a style of question by an opposing party
onus	the responsibility for proving something
parties	the individuals directly involved in a criminal trial, lawsuit or administrative hearing
plaintiff	the person who starts a lawsuit
remedies	solutions that a court can order following a civil trial

standard of proof   the degree to which something must be proven

statement of claim   the document used to start a lawsuit

statement of defence   the document used to respond to a statement of
                                claim in a lawsuit

STATUTES MENTIONED

Controlled Drugs and Substances Act, S.C. 1996, c. 19, as am.

Canadian Charter of Rights and Freedoms, Part 1 of *Constitution Act*, 1982, being Schedule B to the *Canada Act, 1982* (U.K.), 1982, c. 11.

Criminal Code, R.S.C. 1985, c. C-46, as am.

Fisheries (Alberta) Act, R.S.A. 2000, c. F-16

Highway Traffic Act, R.S.O. 1990, c. H.8, as am.

Liquor Control Act, R.S.N.S. 1989, c. 260, as am.

CASES MENTIONED

R. v. Huang, [2013] O.J. No. 1695, 2013 ONCA 240 (C.A.)

R. v. S.G.T., [2010] S.J. No. 20, [2010] 1 S.C.R. 688 (S.C.C.)

TEST YOURSELF

Into which LEGAL CATEGORY (civil, criminal or administrative) does each of these situations fit?

NOTE: Some situations may fit into more than one of these categories.

1. Driving to university this morning, Beatrice was charged with "failing to yield" at a stop sign.

2. Ronoldo has been living in Canada for the past four years, but his student visa expires next month. He is thinking of marrying a Canadian student he met and wonders if this will allow him to stay in the country after his visa expires.

3. Lila is being beaten by her drunken bum of a husband and has had enough!

4. Desiree is trying to get social assistance, but her case worker says she doesn't qualify.

5. Your car was rear-ended this morning by an impaired professor's vehicle.

6. You have tried to get the city to re-zone your property so you can turn the café you operate into a bar offering "adult entertainment". City council keeps refusing your request.

7. Marie decided to sell her living room furniture and put an ad in the paper. A prospective purchaser has given her a $100 down payment and is coming back to pick up the furniture. Marie's spouse says she has to call off the deal. The couch is apparently "lucky" (where he sits to watch every game played by his beloved Edmonton Oilers).

8. 15-year-old Zach was caught stealing candy bars from the corner variety store.

9. Willie and the Poor Boys have been practising their hard rock tunes in a garage Willie claims to have sound-proofed. Neighbours have complained several times about the racket and are threatening to do something.

10. A union has been trying to organize workers at a local fast food eatery. The manager of the business is refusing to let union reps on the business property to speak to the workers.

Chapter 5

Civil Justice System — Torts

WHAT ARE TORTS?

Torts are legal justifications for suing someone. Most of them have been created by judges through common law precedents, though in some provinces and territories statutes cover certain elements of tort law. Since most tort law is a creation of the courts, some torts have been recognized throughout Canada's legal history, with antecedents in English common law. *Trespass* and *assault* would be ready examples. These older torts are the civil equivalents of criminal or quasi-criminal charges, stemming historically from a time when the distinctions between civil and criminal wrongs did not exist. Other torts are relatively new and evolving, the principles relating to *strict liability* fit this category. While breach of contract is a very common reason for a lawsuit, it is not considered a tort. As a result, some people like to think of torts as the non-contractual justifications for suing someone.

VICARIOUS LIABILITY

Many years ago, courts developed a legal principle to hold employers legally and financially responsible for the actions of their employees that result in successful lawsuits. It is important to realize that the concept does *not* remove the employee from the lawsuit, nor does it protect an employee from having to contribute to financial compensation of the party who has been harmed if the employee has income or assets that make a contribution possible. However, a motivating factor in developing the principle known as *vicarious liability* was undoubtedly that employers are likely to have more assets (property or insurance coverage) to pay for the harm caused to an innocent party. Besides, it hardly seems unreasonable to expect employers to provide their employees with proper training and supervision so the workers will avoid harming others.

The concept of *vicarious liability* only applies if employees have done something "in the normal course of their employment" triggering a lawsuit. In other words, employers will not be held responsible for lawsuits that employees cause on their own time, or through their leisure activities.

NEGLIGENCE

At its simplest, the tort of *negligence* arises when someone is injured because someone else has been careless. Not surprisingly, it is the number one reason that people are sued. Injured in a car accident? It could be because someone wasn't careful enough. Might have been another driver, the mechanic who failed to repair your brakes properly or the municipal maintenance crew that over-looked the pothole; in fact, it may have occurred due to contributions from all these people and your own lack of care because you were distracted by a ringing cell phone in your vehicle. A family member has been attacked by a violent con-vict who has been mistakenly released from jail too early? Wow, seems likely someone screwed up there. A surgeon forgot to remove a sponge before you were sewn up following your latest operation? *Malpractice* is just a subdivision in the very large negligence community.

A judge will rule that someone is *liable*, or legally and financially responsible for being negligent if three key elements of the tort can be established:

(1)   the person being sued *owed a duty of care* to the person he or she harmed;

(2)   the harmful behaviour of the person being sued fell below the *standard of care of a reasonably careful person*; and

(3)   the harm was *caused* by the lack of care.

Let's expand upon each of these elements. How does a judge decide whether or not the person being sued, the defendant, owed a *duty of care* to the person who was harmed, the plaintiff? The judge will ask this question: should the de-fendant have *reasonably foreseen* that the plaintiff could be harmed by the de-fendant's actions at the time the defendant started the activity that ultimately resulted in the harm? In using this concept of *reasonable foreseeability*, courts are making it clear that not every single person who might be harmed by your actions is going to be able to sue you.

To put this in a practical context, consider your personal duty of care to oth-ers when you drive a car. Think about the reasonable foreseeability of whom you might harm if you were careless. Do you owe a duty of care to your passengers? I think it is obvious. How about drivers of other vehicles on the roads that you'll use? That seems reasonable. Should we include pedestrians crossing the road, or using adjacent sidewalks, cyclists sharing your route? As a frequent cyclist and pedestrian myself, I would hope so. How about the errant parachutist who sud-denly drops onto the roadway, directly into the path of your car? I suspect if this individual were to sue, your lawyer might successfully convince a judge or jury that the parachutist's appearance was NOT reasonably foreseeable and that you should not be held liable for any injuries your car may cause. In fact, maybe you should be suing the careless parachutist for failing to properly plan the descent, causing serious damage to your vehicle and your nerves. A court case involving the application of the concept of duty of care has been included in Appendix 5 at the end of this text. The case is called, *Boudreau v. Bank of Montreal*.

The second element to consider is whether a defendant's behaviour that is alleged to be negligent falls below the standard of a reasonably careful person undertaking the same task. To look at it another way, if the defendant has done everything a reasonably careful person would do to avoid harming others, he or she should be able to establish a successful defence to the lawsuit and won't be held to be financially responsible, even if harm was done.

Imagine that you work as a correctional officer. Your employer has established a list of procedures that you and the other guards are expected to follow any time you transport a prisoner from the lock-up to a court appearance. Sadly, one of the prisoners that you are escorting manages to escape. A vehicle is stolen and a high-speed chase ensues. The stolen vehicle crashes into several parked cars before the prisoner is recaptured. Owners of damaged property are quick to sue, alleging your negligence.

In this scenario, assessing whether you have done everything a reasonable correctional officer would do to prevent the event occurring may be as simple as checking to see if you have followed the procedures established by your employer. If you have missed a step, you may be found to be negligent. Even if you have complied fully, a judge or jury may find that your employer was careless in designing the procedures. Other correctional facilities may have developed more sophisticated processes or be using more effective technological aids to prevent escapes like this one. If you fail to keep up with advancements in industry standards, you heighten the risk of being successfully sued if anyone suffers harm.

The third requirement for a successful negligence claim is that there is a direct connection between the lack of care and the harm that is caused. If there is such a link, a defendant will be legally responsible for the full extent of the damage. The concept of foreseeability that applied with respect to the first element of negligence has no application at this stage. The common law principle that will be applied is often called the *thin skull rule*. It means that the defendant must accept the idiosyncrasies of the person who has been harmed.

Consider the simple example of a traffic officer, gesturing dramatically as he or she directs traffic at an intersection. Perhaps, the officer fails to notice a cyclist who is passing from the side. Focusing fully on a car that is approaching the intersection directly ahead, the officer swings an arm holding a flashlight to point it at this vehicle. In doing so, the officer knocks the cyclist from her bike. She is unable to break her fall and the cyclist's helmeted head strikes the ground. Quite possibly, the fall didn't seem too violent and one would only expect bruising and a minor headache. Nevertheless, this particular cyclist suffers from a rare condition that triggers massive swelling of the brain if it is jolted in any significant way. She is severely injured, needs to be hospitalized for a lengthy period and has to undergo years of intensive therapy to regain even minimal movement. She is unable to return to her high paying job and will require in-home care for herself and her young children for several years. If the officer is found to have been careless in causing these injuries, the officer and the officer's employer will be financially liable for the full extent of the harm.

New, intervening actions might create new liability and break the chain of responsibility with the first person who acted negligently. Think about a private security officer who notices some liquid spilled in the front lobby of head office. Realizing the potential danger, the officer starts to call maintenance but is interrupted by a colleague asking for immediate assistance. By the time the diversionary crisis is sorted out, the security officer has forgotten the spill. Shortly thereafter, an important customer fails to notice the danger, slips and suffers a minor knee injury. Now, acting to minimize the problem, the security officer calls for an ambulance. The ambulance service responds promptly, but sadly, the driver of the ambulance carelessly runs a red light en route to the hospital and the customer suffers horrible head and spinal injuries in the crash.

Who should be held responsible for the various injuries the customer has suffered? Arguably, none of this would have happened if the security officer had arranged for the spill to be cleaned up in a timely manner. On the other hand, that just caused a minor knee injury. Surely, the ambulance drivers should also be expected to exercise care in performing their own services. In civil lawsuits, a judge or jury can apportion financial responsibility among a number of different parties who have caused harm.

In fact, the judge or jury can even reduce the financial compensation that will be paid to a plaintiff by an appropriate percentage based on the plaintiff's own carelessness in contributing to what has occurred. This common law concept is called, *contributory liability*, or in this case, *contributory negligence*. In our scenario, the fact that the customer was attempting to text a message or read a newspaper while rushing through the lobby, may have contributed to a failure to notice the spill. If the customer had also refused to be strapped to the stretcher by ambulance personnel, there's an argument to be made that this exacerbated the injuries suffered in the crash. Both factors could result in a reduction in the financial compensation that must be paid by the defendants.

ASSAULT AND BATTERY

Historically, judges created two torts, *battery*, involving an uninvited application of force to a person and *assault*, which only required a *threat* of force, with a reasonable fear that the threat might be acted upon. Not surprisingly, the incidents that resulted in lawsuits often involved behaviour that incorporated both torts. It seems that with the passage of time, judges more commonly refer to the combined range of behaviour as *assault*.

This, of course, seems even more logical when it is recognized that these torts are civil equivalents of the alternative behaviours that constitute *assault* under section 265(1) of the *Criminal Code*. Clause (*a*) of that subsection deals with the application of force (the *battery* equivalent), while clause (*b*) only requires an attempt or threat to apply force. Either behaviour could result in a criminal *assault* conviction. Of course, judges dealing with civil lawsuits do not assess behaviour using the *Criminal Code* wording, but the terminology used in the common law decisions that have shaped these torts is quite similar.

Since *battery* is an *uninvited* application of force, evidence that there has been some *consent* by the plaintiff to having the force applied would create a *defence* to a lawsuit relying on this cause of action. While on the surface, it would seem rather strange that someone who has been injured would have consented to the injury, this defence is commonly used. It is not too hard to imagine that someone who initially agreed to engage in a consensual fight might sue if the fight went badly for this willing participant and injuries resulted.

Even if there is proof of consent, judges may be required to draw the line on how much violence was likely to be expected when the plaintiff initially indicated consent. Consider, for example, a hockey player. He or she may take to the ice, fully aware that a certain level of physical contact is to be expected in this game. As a result, a judge may be prepared to imply that there was consent to being struck within the rules of the game, and even beyond, with the common realization that penalties are regularly assessed for excessive application of force. However, is it reasonable for a judge to conclude that an injured hockey player could never sue an opponent who has assaulted him or her, even if the assaultive behaviour went well beyond the norm? Judges have not carried the defence that far and will limit the parameters of a consent to what would be reasonable in the circumstances. Excessive levels of force will not be successfully excused through the use of a consent defence.

Police officers, correctional personnel and individuals working in private security regularly find themselves in situations where it may be necessary to apply some force to protect themselves, others or property. These have all been recognized as legitimate common law defences to assault and battery claims. Judges allow themselves a sliding scale for the assessment of a defendant's responsive behaviour by considering what is reasonable in the circumstances. Professionals in these fields must be cool enough to make a measured response, because any excessive levels of force can result in civil liability and the need to pay financial compensation to someone who has been harmed. No one should be surprised in this day and age if their excessive use of force is captured on some camera/phone or security video. It may be impossible to explain away your over-the-top reaction to a perceived threat when it is broken down frame-by-frame in all its ugly detail.

TRESPASS

What we call *ownership* of property is really just a bundle of rights in relation to the item or piece of real estate. We can also be in *possession* of property that we don't own and there is a smaller bundle of rights that attaches to the concept of possession. A tenant's possession of his or her apartment would be an example. One of the rights that judges have long recognized in relation to both ownership and possession is a *right to exclude others*.

If guests have stayed too long, we can ask them to leave. If you arrive at the dock to discover a stranger sitting in your boat, you could ask the stranger to disembark. When my younger son discovers his older brother wearing his hat, he could kindly (in my dreams) ask him to return it. If any of these people were to take unreasonably long in complying with the request, they would be *trespassing* and a *reasonable* amount of force could be used to encourage compliance. Trespass is a common law cause of action with a long legal history.

Most provinces and territories have statutes that deal with trespass in relation to real estate. You could examine Ontario's statute, which has been included in Appendix 4 at the end of this book. These statutes commonly make trespassing on real estate *quasi-criminal* and fines could be imposed. Some of the statutes also include civil remedies up to a certain dollar amount to compensate the injured party for any damage that has been done to his or her property by the trespasser. If the statutory limit on compensation seems too low, or if the trespass has occurred in relation to property that isn't covered by the statute, the injured party could still sue using common law principles.

In most of the statutes, it is not necessary to have "no trespassing" signs posted, nor would you have to ask a trespasser without any legitimate reason to be on your property to leave before calling the police. Simply entering your private property without permission would usually be enough, particularly if the land is fenced or "cultivated", making it apparent to an intruder that someone might own the land.

Under common law, "breaking the bounds" of private property is enough to amount to a trespass, though unless there is some damage done it probably wouldn't warrant a lawsuit. Occasionally, if there is repetitive trespassing, the property owner may go to court and ask for an *injunction*, a court order requiring the trespasser to stay off the property in future. If the order was ignored and the trespass repeated, further punishment could be imposed by a judge for *contempt*, wilfully failing to comply with an order from the court.

CONVERSION

Conversion is the civil lawsuit equivalent of theft. If someone were to steal something of yours and use it for their own purposes, you could sue for any money you lost or had to expend as a result, or for an accounting for any profits that the person made using what is rightfully yours. This tort seems to be used most often by businesses who will sue competitors who have stolen trade secrets like a valuable recipe or confidential marketing information.

Occasionally retailers have sued thieves in an attempt to recover some of the expense of store security that otherwise would have to be passed on to customers. Unfortunately, thieves are infrequently in possession of assets or income that would make them a fruitful source of significant financial compensation awards in a civil lawsuit.

FALSE ARREST AND IMPRISONMENT

Stopping someone from going where he or she wants, without a legitimate legal reason, may amount to a *false arrest*. Retail security personnel and police officers are particularly vulnerable to being sued under this cause of action, though even a lowly law teacher might run afoul of the law in this regard.

Suppose I have a student who has a pressing need to use the washroom facilities during one of my highly fascinating lectures. Unlike in elementary school, post-secondary students seldom raise a hand to seek permission to flee in these circumstances. Exercising excessive concern that someone may miss a gem from my lecture, I loudly confront the exiting individual and intimidate the student into returning, without ever cluing in to the reason for the hasty, but otherwise unobtrusive sprint for the door. A serious bladder problem and the stress of my over-reaction unfortunately result in a humiliating accident for the student.

Could this student sue for *false arrest* to try to secure compensation for the damaged clothing and the trauma and embarrassment caused by my actions? If the student did sue, I'd respond by saying that as the person in charge of ensuring that there is an atmosphere conducive to learning in my classes, I have an obligation to control student behaviour that may be disruptive to others. Does this give me a legitimate, legal reason for stopping the student from going where he or she wanted? If you were a juror, how would you decide?

Before you answer, let's change the context a little. A retail security officer notices a shifty looking teen with baggy clothing sorting through a display of expensive cell phones. The officer doesn't actually see the teen slip anything into his clothes but doesn't have a great angle and is highly suspicious. Suddenly, the teen runs past the checkout counter without stopping to pay for anything and sprints into the mall. Should the officer pursue the teen and make an arrest to check for stolen goods? Does *suspicion* provide a legitimate, legal reason for an arrest?

The security officer would be making an arrest because he or she has reason to suspect that a crime has been committed. What power does a private security officer have to arrest anyone? The answer requires some knowledge of the arrest powers laid out in the *Criminal Code*. Section 494 of that statute says that *anyone* may arrest, "… a person whom he finds committing an *indictable offence*". We'll discuss the categories of offences in Chapter 8, but for now you have my assurance that theft, which is technically a *hybrid* offence, could fit the general categorization of an indictable offence for these purposes. The problem, of course, is that the section requires finding the person committing the offence. A recent amendment to section 494 extends the power of arrest to situations where someone like a security officer has knowledge that an indictable offence was recently committed in relation to property for which he or she has responsibility. However, the section still says nothing about suspicion being enough to justify an arrest.

A *peace officer*, who is defined in section 2 of the *Criminal Code* to include police officers, but not private security personnel, has a broader power to arrest, granted by section 495 of the *Criminal Code*. He or she, in addition to being able to arrest someone found committing an offence, can also arrest based on *reasonable grounds for believing* the person has committed an offence. This reasonable belief could come from reliable information supplied by others. But the officer still needs reasonable and probable grounds to make an arrest. Common law cases analyzing this power have made it clear that suspicion is not enough to justify an arrest.

Obviously, the law treats the restriction of someone else's freedom through arrest as a very serious matter that should only occur when legally justified within fairly narrow parameters. Would a security officer, or a police officer run the risk of being successfully sued if he or she were to act on suspicion rather than more substantial evidence that someone has committed a crime? Yes. Should a law teacher exercise care before he or she prevents a student from leaving a class? This one will.

Adding to the restrictions on someone's free movement through a form of confinement, again without a legal justification, could constitute the related tort of *false imprisonment*.

If the security officer were to escort a theft suspect back to the store premises, he or she might place the suspect in the manager's office while awaiting the arrival of police. Someone would probably have to stand guard in the doorway to prevent the suspect from bolting, or hiding the booty somewhere in the office before the police arrive. From a legal perspective, the suspect could be said to be imprisoned, since he or she has been confined and is clearly being prevented from leaving. If, after a search, it turns out that nothing has actually been stolen, there was no legitimate legal reason for any of the restraint. A second cause of action would have been added to the former suspect/potential plaintiff's arsenal.

DEFAMATION

Publishing a comment that could damage someone else's reputation may justify a lawsuit for *defamation*. Once a plaintiff can establish that the potentially harmful comment has been published, the onus shifts to the defendant to justify the statement. Being able to prove that the comment was the truth provides a potential defendant with a solid defence to any claim. It is not illegal to publicly call someone a bloodthirsty murderer if the statement is accurate, or, perhaps more importantly in defending lawsuits, if it can be substantiated.

In order to sue, the comment must have been "published", but this wouldn't have to be as widespread as a television broadcast, or a newspaper report. You can come to my office, shut the door and call me the most vile, repulsive, toadeating scumbag on the face of the earth, a disgrace to the teaching profession. Alternatively, you could address these comments to me in a personal letter. This would not be defamation. And it is not just because I happen to find toads tasty. If no one else hears or reads the comments, how could they damage my reputation?

On the other hand, if one of my teaching colleagues happens to come into the office and overhear while you vent your displeasure, this would be all the publication a court would require. If my reputation with this colleague is high enough to be lowered by your comments, this limited audience supplies a technical basis for suing, though the financial compensation I'd be able to claim may be pretty limited. My potential claim might increase if the comments were overheard by my boss and they affected promotions, or, God forbid, resulted in me being fired.

There are still a couple of locations where you can speak freely, without fear of being sued for defamation. People who will be working in law-related careers will be relieved to know that what you say in court, or in a procedure before an administrative tribunal is protected by a common law *privilege* that prevents anyone from using statements made in this setting as a justification for a lawsuit. This is to ensure that judges, lawyers, paralegals and witnesses will be candid in contributing to a search for the truth and not intimidated by concerns with being sued. The privilege extends to the documents that are used in the court or tribunal process, including *informations* or *indictments*, used to initiate criminal proceedings, written records of witness statements that would be disclosed to an accused person in a criminal case, *statements of claim*, *statements of defence* and other documents used in civil cases, and reports prepared in advance by expert witnesses who may be testifying during the court or tribunal hearing.

Anyone who has heard the insults fly around a session of the federal House of Commons, or a provincial or territorial legislature, may have realized that comments made in those settings are also covered by a common law privilege from use as a basis for a lawsuit. You may even have heard the target of an insult invite his or her tormenter to repeat their jibes outside. That, of course, would allow for a lawsuit based on insults that could be damaging to the target's reputation, with the privilege related to the context of parliamentary proceedings being stripped away.

Newspapers and other media across Canada have been granted a *privilege* to provide fair and accurate reports of both court and legislative proceedings in provincial and territorial statutes. The statutes prevent the media sources from adding commentary, without running the risk of being sued and usually require them to publish a contradiction or explanation by a potential plaintiff if the publication has broadcast something that could harm the person's reputation.

Two Supreme Court of Canada cases, *Quan v. Cusson* and *Grant v. Torstar Corp.*, recognized a common law defence for newspapers and reporters, which the judges of the Supreme Court called, "responsible communication on matters of public interest". If reporters can prove they were diligent in trying to verify allegations about a matter that would be of interest to the public, they may be able to successfully defend themselves in defamation lawsuits, even if some of the factual information they have published turns out to be inaccurate. The judges warn that this should not be considered a licence to ruin the reputations of people who are involved in matters of public interest. Nevertheless, the cases recognize the importance of a free discussion in a search for the truth on matters of public significance and the value Canadians place on freedom of expression.

INVASION OF PRIVACY

There are federal and provincial statutes that aim to prevent government agencies and some corporations from disclosing confidential information that they control. In addition, five Canadian provinces, British Columbia, Manitoba, Saskatchewan, Quebec and Newfoundland and Labrador have statutes that create a right to sue other members of the public who invade your privacy. As an example, subsection 1(1) of British Columbia's *Privacy Act* provides: "It is a tort, actionable without proof of damage, for a person, wilfully and without a claim of right, to violate the privacy of another."

Canadian courts in the provinces and territories without specific privacy statutes have lagged behind many other common law jurisdictions in providing court-created protections for privacy rights. Cases like the recent Ontario Court of Appeal decision in *Jones v. Tsige* may be signalling a greater willingness on the part of our judges to provide some protection. In that case, the appeal court judges ruled that it was an *intrusion upon seclusion* for a bank employee with a romantic interest in the plaintiff's ex-husband to access the plaintiff's banking records to satisfy some personal curiosity. The judges were influenced by American case law that had recognized a common law right to sue in situations like this.

NUISANCE

Like *trespass*, nuisance is a tort that was developed by judges to protect property interests. However, in nuisance the interference with property is more indirect. *Nuisance* is a tort that allows an owner of real estate, or a tenant in possession of real estate, to sue a neighbour if the neighbour is doing something on his or her own property that unreasonably disrupts the enjoyment and use of the land of the plaintiff. Creating excessive noise or odours, indiscriminate spraying of insecticides, releasing toxic fumes or dumping pollution in a river or stream that crosses neighbouring properties, could all attract claims using this cause of action. The list of potentially annoying activities has not been closed by the courts and continues to grow as new hindrances trigger lawsuits. Judges focus more on the impact on the reasonable enjoyment of neighbouring lands than on the specific type of conduct generating the complaint.

People who think, "I can do anything I want on my own land" will soon find that this is not true. Neighbours can sue for financial compensation for the harm that is caused and could also request that a judge impose an *injunction*, a court order preventing the continuation of the annoying activity.

There are practical limits on when nuisance claims will be successful. Pre-existing uses of neighbouring lands and municipal zoning can be limiting factors. For example, if you move into an area that is zoned as commercial or industrial and the factory across the street was engaging in noisy manufacturing processes for years before you moved in, a judge may be reluctant to use this tort to curtail their activities. Similarly, if you have been a city dweller your whole life, then move to the country and complain about the odours from the pig farm upwind, sympathy for your sensitivity may be limited. However, if the farm boasting three little piggies suddenly blossoms into Hog Heaven, home to hundreds of ham on the hoof, a judge may be more willing to order restrictions on the odorous impact. It should be noted that some provinces have placed statutory limits on the right to sue for nuisance in relation to "normal" farm activities. Nova Scotia's *Farm Practices Act* is an example.

STRICT LIABILITY

Some activities or "things" are so inherently dangerous that a judge will rule that you are *strictly liable* if someone is harmed because you have undertaken this activity or chosen to keep the thing on your property. This means that the judge will not be interested in any negligence-type explanations about how careful you were about avoiding the harm. If the harm was caused because of your actions, or your handling or storage of the dangerous thing, you will be held financially responsible.

Once again, the category of dangerous things or activities is not closed and courts will assess claims made using this tort on a case-by-case basis. Precedents have already been set with respect to property owners who choose to keep *wild* animals, toxic chemicals, explosives and weapons. In fact, this area of the law got its start in an English case called, *Rylands v. Fletcher*. The "dangerous thing" in that case was a large reservoir of water. When the water escaped, it flooded underground mines on a neighbouring property. The principle derived from the case is that if you choose to keep inherently dangerous things and they escape and cause harm, you should be financially responsible.

In some provinces and territories, statutes also impose strict liability. For example, dog owners, or owners of particularly dangerous breeds of dogs have been made statutorily liable for any harm their animals cause to humans, other animals or property. Statutory liability is also imposed on taverns and restaurants with liquor licences. Allowing a customer to leave in an impaired condition can make the business financially responsible for any harm caused as a result.

KEY TERMINOLOGY

assault	an uninvited threat of force, with a reasonable fear it will be acted upon, or an uninvited application of force
battery	an uninvited application of force
cause of action	legal justification for suing someone
contempt	a wilful failure to follow a court order
contributory liability	when the plaintiff's actions are a contributing factor in the harm done
contributory negligence	the plaintiff has contributed to his or her own injuries through lack of care
defamation	published statements that damage someone's reputation
defence	a rationale for the defendant's actions that eliminates or reduces liability
duty of care	the duty to be careful toward others
false arrest	stopping someone from going where he or she wants to go without a legitimate legal reason
false imprisonment	confining someone without a legitimate legal reason
hybrid offence	a criminal offence that can be treated as a summary or indictable offence
indictable offence	serious criminal offence
indictment	document used in processing indictable offences
information	document used to start the court process in relation to most criminal or quasi-criminal charges
injunction	court order preventing someone from doing something
intrusion upon seclusion	a common law right to sue for an intrusion on a person's private affairs
liable	legally and/or financially responsible

malpractice	negligence by a doctor or other medical expert
negligence	a lack of care that entitles someone to sue
nuisance	doing something on your own property that damages the value of someone else's property
ownership	the largest bundle of property rights
possession	the control of property
privilege	a special legal right
quasi-criminal	having many of the same characteristics as a criminal offence
reasonably foreseeable	predictable
right to exclude others	a right to deny access to your property
standard of care	the degree of care that must be exercised
statement of claim	the document used to start a lawsuit
statement of defence	the document used to respond to a statement of claim
strict liability	being civilly liable without the ability to use being careful or any other excuse as a defence
suspicion	an inkling that someone may be responsible without much proof to support the belief
thin skull rule	being responsible for all damage caused even if the victim was particularly sensitive
threat	causing someone to fear harm
torts	non-contractual justifications for suing someone
trespass	encroaching on someone else's property without permission or any other legal reason
uninvited	without any prompting or invitation
vicarious liability	holding employers legally and financially responsible for the actions of their employees

CASES MENTIONED

Boudreau v. Bank of Montreal, [2013] O.J. No. 1551, 2013 ONCA 211 (C.A.)

Grant v. Torstar Corp., [2009] S.C.J. No. 61, 2009 SCC 61 (S.C.C.)

Jones v. Tsige, [2012] O.J. No. 148, 2012 ONCA 32 (C.A.)

Quan v. Cusson, [2009] S.C.J. No. 62, 2009 SCC 62 (S.C.C.)

Rylands v. Fletcher (1868), L.R. 3 (H.L.)

STATUTES MENTIONED

Farm Practices Act, S.N.S. 2000, c. 3

Privacy Act, R.S.B.C. 1996, c. 373

TEST YOURSELF

1. You work part-time as a security officer at the university/college you attend. Yesterday, your supervisor asked you and a co-worker to remove a number of rowdy students, who were staging a sit-in on the front steps to protest tuition increases. They had the entrance clogged, preventing anyone from entering or leaving without stumbling over them. You politely asked them to move away from the doors. One young woman responded by getting right in your face, screaming, spitting and calling you a "gutless weasel, scum sucking lap-dog for the Man!" You were pretty embarrassed since a number of your classmates were close by and two of your professors. When you tried to place a hand on the young woman's shoulder to calm her down, she swung her protest sign, which was taped to a pipe and screamed, "Rapist, get your hands off me!" The pipe opened a large gash on your forehead and knocked you unconscious. You awoke in the hospital with dreams of lawsuits dancing in your head.

    (a) In this situation, could you successfully sue the protester? If so, what would the *causes of action* (legal justifications for suing) be? If not, why not?

    (b) Would the protester have a legal basis for a counter-suit against you and/or your employer? Briefly explain.

2. You celebrate the completion of your mid-term exams with some alcoholic beverages in the university/college pub, which is operated by the student council. The server is a friend of yours and turns a blind eye on your increasingly drunken state. Not only does he continue to serve you, but he ignores the fact that you have car keys in your hand as you stagger out the door, singing at the top of your lungs. Sadly, you start the car and head across the parking lot. You fail to notice that one of your professors is walking across the lot, with her head down, reading a textbook. Your car strikes her and knocks her to the ground, causing life threatening injuries.

   (a) In this situation, if the professor decides to sue, what *causes of action* could her lawyers use? Briefly explain.

   (b) How is a court likely to apportion liability for the harm caused? Why?

3. Consider your future career goal. Which torts will be the biggest concerns for you in this line of work? Why?

Chapter 6

More Civil Justice System Concepts

CONTRACTS

Contracts are agreements that courts will help enforce if one of the parties fails to do what he or she has promised. The individuals are generally free to reach an agreement on the terms and only seek a legal solution if something goes wrong after the agreement is in place. Contracts are a more common part of day-to-day life than most people think and the courts are asked to resolve a very tiny percentage of contracts that are formed. When you take a loaf of bread from the shelf in your corner store and proceed to the checkout counter to pay for it, you are initiating a contractual relationship with the store owner through the agent manning the cash register. Registering for a university or college course, getting a haircut, reserving a hotel room, ordering lunch are all examples of contracts being formed.

A great deal of the law related to contracts was created through common law precedents. Statutes do affect certain categories of contracts, with the extent of statutory control varying among provinces and territories. For example, the common law approach to contracts requires that certain elements be present to constitute a legally binding agreement. There is no common law requirement that contracts must be in writing to be enforceable. Nevertheless, statutes in most provinces and territories do require that certain types of contracts have a written component; contracts for the purchase of real estate, insurance contracts, and agreements where a third party becomes obligated to cover someone else's loan payment obligations are all examples of contracts that require some written evidence of the agreement before courts will enforce them.

Courts will not enforce all agreements. As a starting point, they look for a common *intention to be legally bound* between the people who have entered the agreement. If friends, or family members make casual agreements, like me agreeing to take out the garbage if my spouse does the dishes, a court would normally *presume* that neither of us was intending to have the courts become involved if we failed to live up to our obligations. On the other hand, if the parties are strangers, or if the agreement is being set up in a business context, a judge would *presume* that the parties intended to be legally bound. A judge would have to be convinced, through evidence presented in court, that this was not so.

The three core elements that a judge would expect to find in a contract are:

(1) an *offer*;
(2) *acceptance* of the offer; and
(3) *consideration*.

An *offer* is nothing more than a tentative promise of an exchange. For example, "I offer to sell you my fishing boat for $7,500." Sometimes, you can make an offer without even saying anything. The context will be enough for the person you are hoping to contract with to get the message, the *communication* of your offer. At the start of this section, I mentioned selecting a loaf of bread from the shelf in your local convenience store and taking it to the cash register. If you place it on the counter, the cashier will likely assume that you're offering to purchase the bread for the price marked on the wrapper. You could reinforce this communication of an offer by holding out enough money to cover the purchase price.

The second element, *acceptance*, is also a pretty straight-forward concept. Often, it simply requires saying, "I accept", "Yes", or something equivalent to show that you do want to buy my fishing boat for $7,500. The cashier in the convenience store accepting the cash offered for the bread and allowing you to leave with your purchase would also be a pretty clear indicator of this element.

If a person tries to change the terms of the agreement in response to an offer, this is negotiation, or a *counter-offer*, and does not satisfy the acceptance requirement to form a contract. For instance, replying to my boat offer by saying, "I'll give you $7,500 if you include the trailer and motor," just puts a new offer on the table. Now, I'm in a position to accept, reject, or make a further counter-offer.

The *consideration* element usually falls into place during the offer, or negotiation stage. *Consideration* in this context has a special meaning. It is not the concept of being thoughtful. For contracts, *consideration* is a mutual promise that something of value will be exchanged. I promise to give you my boat. You promise to give me $7,500 in exchange. Or, you promise to pay the store $2.59 in exchange for their promise to supply a loaf of bread. Judges, in most circumstances are not interested in measuring whether the exchange of something of value is fair. Parties entering into contracts are free to make a bad deal. A court will enforce the agreement on the terms the parties have set.

The contract is formed as soon as all three elements are in place. Either party to the contract is then in a position to ask the court for help if the other party to the contract fails to do what he or she has promised. You show up with $7,500 and I refuse to turn over the boat. You could sue for breach of contract. You paid $2.59 for a loaf of bread you had every reason to expect would be fit to eat and discover that it is full of mould when you open it at home. It may not be worth your while to sue for the $2.59 if the store fails to provide a remedy, but from a strict legal perspective you may have that right.

There are people who could use the common law concept of *lack of capacity* to avoid having the promises they have made in a contract enforced against them in court. People who are *minors*, those who are *impaired by alcohol or drugs* and people who are *mentally incapacitated* at the time they enter into the agreement could all raise the issue of lack of capacity as a defence to a claim based on their failure to pay for items that would be classified by a judge as *non-necessary* for a person in their situation.

The list of items that a court might classify as non-necessary is potentially huge. Precedents related to necessary items, that all these individuals could be compelled to pay for, have been limited to basic meals, shelter and essential articles of clothing. Anything else, including cars, computers, concert tickets and my fishing boat are far more likely to be classified as non-necessary.

Due to provincial and territorial statutes, people under the age of 18 are generally considered to be *minors* for contract purposes. A minor could weasel out of having a contract for non-necessaries enforced against the minor even if he or she appeared to be 25 years of age. This is a completely one-sided protection. If a minor wishes to enforce the terms of a contract against an adult with whom he or she has contracted, a court would assist the youth in this regard. An adult cannot use the fact that the adult was foolish enough to contract with a minor as an excuse for failing to live up to the adult's contractual promises.

The common law situation is a little more complicated for someone who is claiming to have been drunk or mentally incapacitated at the time of entering into the contract. This individual would have to convince a judge that the level of impairment or mental incapacity at the time of entering the contract was so great that he or she didn't know what was going on. In addition, the judge would have to be convinced that the person the drunk or mentally incapacitated individual was dealing with should have reasonably been aware of this state of diminished capacity. Thirdly, the person who was drunk or mentally incapacitated would have to attempt to get out of the contract as soon as he or she regained sobriety or mental capacity. A lack of evidence of any of these three elements and a judge will conclude that the contract is binding despite the claim of diminished capacity.

A *breach of contract* occurs when someone has failed to do what he or she agreed to do under the terms of the contract. This is what entitles another party bound under the terms of the contract to sue. Because of a common law concept called *privity*, it is only people who were parties to the contract who are entitled to sue using the breach as the cause of action.

Say, for example, you paid several hundred dollars for front row seats to a rock concert. Both you and your date take a night off work and rent a car to get to the venue. This is costing you big bucks. Sadly, the lead singer for the headline act has serious drug problems and never makes it to the concert. You are furious and decide you'll sue. Clearly, the concert you paid for wasn't delivered. A contract has been breached! When you phone the ticket agent to demand a refund, the response is straightforward: "Hey, it's not our fault those losers didn't show, sue the band." Can you?

You can't sue the band for breach of contract. Why? You never entered a contract with them. Your contract was set up through a ticket agent. This *agent* is probably selling tickets on behalf of a concert promoter. This concert promoter would have a contract with the band, but you don't. Your only recourse is to sue the party that you have a contract with for failing to provide the concert you purchased. The concert promoter could, in turn, sue the band if the terms of their contract allow. You cannot jump the promoter and sue the band directly. *Privity* is blocking this route.

What *remedy* will a judge provide if a person can successfully sue for a breach of contract? The usual remedy is *damages*, financial compensation for the monetary loss that flows from the breach. However, in the area of contract law, a judge will not just let a victim of a breach sit back and allow the losses to pile up. A victim of a breach of contract is expected to *mitigate* his or her damages before suing.

A couple of simple examples should clarify the way the concept of mitigation works. I agreed to sell you my fishing boat for $7,500. Before I turned it over, I found someone else who was prepared to pay me $9,000 and now I'm refusing to give you the boat. I am breaching the contract. You decide to sue. Can you wait until the fishing season is over and try and get financial compensation for losing a whole season of fishing due to my refusal? No. The concept of mitigation would require you to make reasonable efforts to find an alternative boat to purchase to minimize your loss. Assume, after making the effort you find a similar boat, but have to pay $8,500. A court would allow you to sue for the difference between what you had to pay for the alternative boat and what you should have been paying if I had followed through with my part of the original deal. You're entitled to $1,000, plus, perhaps, a small amount to compensate you for extra expenses incurred securing the second deal (*e.g.*, gas money for driving around looking at other boats).

Working in a post-secondary institution, students will often come around and ask me what would happen if they were to move out of their apartments before their leases expire, or without giving the full notice period required for terminating a lease in our provincial landlord-tenant statute. I explain that this would, of course, be a breach of their rental contracts and would entitle a landlord to sue for the unpaid portion of the rent. However, I also point out that a landlord, as a victim of the breach, has a common law duty to mitigate the loss. Practically, this means the landlord would have to make a reasonable effort to find another tenant to move in and cover the unpaid rent. If the landlord is successful in finding an alternative tenant, the loss suffered as a result of the breach would be greatly reduced and it may not be worth suing at all. If the landlord makes no effort, or a really half-hearted effort to mitigate, a judge would take this into account before making any financial compensation order against the original tenant.

Of course, this discussion of common law contract principles has just provided an introduction to a very complicated area of law. Statutes, particularly at the provincial and territorial level, alter many of the more generalized statements. This is especially true of *consumer protection legislation*, which is aimed at leveling the contractual playing field between sophisticated business people and the average consumer, who may be vulnerable due to limited knowledge of legal rights and obligations.

PROPERTY ISSUES

Many civil lawsuits arise because of disputes over property. Questions of owner-ship, possession, sales, rentals, insurance and rights to use other people's proper-ty may have to be resolved in court if they can't be resolved by agreement. Canadian law divides property into three different categories, *real, personal* and *intellectual,* with a myriad of federal and provincial or territorial statutes and distinct common law principles being directed at each.

Real property is land and *fixtures* that are permanently attached to the land. A house or an office building is considered part of the real property on which it is located because it is attached in such a way that it could not be easily removed without causing damage. A toilet, once installed, or a carpet that is glued or sta-pled to the floor would also be considered fixtures, and hence part of the real property.

Personal property includes a wide variety of articles with some level of in-trinsic value. Legally, these items are also known as *chattels* or *goods.* A car, a boat, a plane, a chair, a desk and this book are all personal property. The person-al property category also includes documents that have value because of what is written on them. For example, a cheque, an I.O.U. or a promissory note to repay a loan, fit into the personal property category. A sub-category label used for the-se documents is *choses in action.*

Intellectual property involves the ownership of ideas or business concepts. Because of federal statutes like the *Patent Act, Trade-marks Act* and *Copyright Act* it is possible to claim and register ownership of an invention, business iden-tity features or creative work, including literature, art and computer software.

In each of the provinces and territories, statutes require that the owners of re-al property register their ownership interest in a local public registration system. Other people claiming rights to the real property, like a bank that has made a loan to the purchaser and has a mortgage contract allowing for seizure if pay-ments are missed, would also have to register these interests. Due to a variety of statutes, utility companies, municipal governments who are owed property taxes and even workers or material suppliers who haven't been paid for work done on real property, could register *liens* against the title. These liens are said to "run with the property", which means they can be enforced against future owners. Because of the complexity of laws affecting real property, the purchasing pro-cess can be a real legal quagmire. The expert assistance of a lawyer or specially trained law clerk is essential. For someone hoping to work in the field, special-ized courses and training will be needed to muddle through the legal morass.

Landlord and tenant law is another specialized niche in the larger real proper-ty picture where statutes created at the provincial or territorial level have a big impact on the contractual freedom of the parties. Many terms, like the notice period to terminate a lease, when a landlord could enter a tenant's unit and the process to be followed if a tenant stops paying the rent, or a landlord cuts off the heat are dictated by statute. In some provinces and territories there are strict guidelines on the rent that can be charged and how often, and under what circumstances it could be raised.

Many contracts related to personal property are also affected by statute. The most significant might be the *Sale of Goods Act*. The first *Sale of Goods Act* was really a compilation of the common law principles that had been developed around this area of the law in England in the 1800's. The original English statute was so good that Canadian provinces "borrowed" it, practically word for word and very little has been changed in the past 120 years. The statutes cover sales of *goods* for money. Contracts for services are not covered, nor sales of land, nor barter arrangements. The statutes imply certain terms, like when *title* to the goods passes from vendor to purchaser, that the goods should be free from any third party claims to their ownership and the quality of goods the purchaser should be able to expect. The Act also provides remedies for breached terms, including the rights of a vendor who hasn't yet been paid. So many day-to-day transactions are covered by the *Sale of Goods Act* that both business people and consumers benefit from a working knowledge of this law.

The federal statutes that allow for the ownership of *intellectual property* have some similar features, but their distinctions are more important. To a large extent, the statutes have overridden the few common law precedents that existed before the Canadian government became active in intellectual property lawmaking. Today, common law in this area largely deals with statutory interpretation and application, though the tort of *passing off* has significance in the area of protection for business identity features.

The *Patent Act* gives an inventor, or someone to whom the inventor has sold the plans, a government-granted monopoly to produce or profit from an invention for a limited period of time. The invention could be a machine, a process or a "composition of matter". The plans for making the invention are registered in a public filing system and, in return, the owner of the invention gets a head start for a significant period of time (20 years for most inventions), during which he or she can make money from the idea. After this protection period expires, it can't be renewed. Anyone else could then use the registered plans to profit from the invention.

The registration process is complicated. The applicant will usually hire a qualified *patent agent*, who must check currently registered patents to ensure no one else has already registered a similar plan. The invention must really be new to get protection. In addition, Canadian patent protection only protects the registrant from others in Canada who may try to profit from the registrant's idea. Because of a lack of treaties among countries providing recognition to Canadian patents abroad, a person wanting worldwide protection for the ownership of an invention must apply in dozens of countries. This process can be complex, time-consuming and expensive. An inventor without money or financial backing may find it easier to sell the idea to a business with more resources before starting the process.

The federal *Trade-marks Act* allows businesses to register business identity features, like a distinctive name, drawing, design or colouring pattern that has been used in association with their products and services. You can't get protection for a mark if it is "confusingly similar" to one another business is using. Before the mark can be registered, the applicant must advertise in a special journal and anyone can object to the registration if they can prove prior use. The registration protects the exclusivity of the symbol for an initial 15-year period, and unlike patent protection, *Trade-marks Act* protection is renewable. However, if you register a mark and then stop using it to identify your product or service, others could apply to end your exclusive right to use. Canadian trademark registration has no effect beyond Canada's borders. If you wish to secure trade-mark protection in order to do business in other countries, you would have to apply in each of these countries.

Common law does play a part in protecting business identity features, under a tort called *passing off*. This tort allows a business with an established reputation to sue anyone who tries to profit by confusing consumers into thinking a competitive product is affiliated with the established business. Since the *Trade-marks Act* prohibits anyone from getting the exclusive right under that statute to use common words like "Canadian" or "Blue", the beer businesses that have sold products under those names for years would be able to use the tort of *passing off* to challenge a competitor who tried to profit by using similar labelling.

You might wonder why so many different companies are able to market beers using names like "Ice" and "Honey". The words are too common to warrant exclusive use under the *Trade-marks Act* and none of the businesses have used the label long enough to develop the *established reputation* that is required to take advantage of the tort of *passing off*. In a situation like this, they're forced to compete by making a better beer, or selling at a lower price, rather than by claiming legal ownership of the name.

The *Copyright Act* gives legal ownership rights to the creator of original artistic, literary or scientific works. The range of creative work that merits protection is quite broad, from paintings to textbooks, original photos and computer software. The protection is automatic, as soon as the work is created, the statute provides ownership rights. It lasts for the life of the creator, *plus* 50 years, so the family of the creator could continue to profit from the work after his or her death. Though not technically necessary, it is possible to register the ownership of your work with the federal agency responsible for the statute. This may make it easier to prove ownership if a dispute arises.

The federal intellectual property statutes provide criminal penalties for people who violate others' ownership interests. The statutes also give the owners the right to sue, with a variety of civil remedies at their disposal, including *damages*, or financial compensation for losses suffered as a result of encroachment and *injunctions*, ordering the violators to discontinue any illegal use. Because of the civil remedies provided, the police do not spend a great deal of time or energy enforcing these statutes. Criminal charges in this area are rare, but civil lawsuits to enforce intellectual property interests are relatively common. It can be costly and time consuming for intellectual property owners to hire their own lawyers and use the civil litigation processes to protect their ownership interests. An example of a simple copyright infringement lawsuit, called *Glanzmann Tours Ltd. v. Yukon Wide Adventures* has been included in Appendix 5 at the end of this book.

FAMILY LAW

Marriage may be founded in love, but it is surrounded by law. Even long-term cohabitation arrangements that don't include marriage can have diverse legal ramifications. Federal and provincial or territorial statutes and common law all figure in the mix.

The federal government has enacted the *Civil Marriage Act*, which simply defines marriage as "… the lawful union of two persons to the exclusion of all others". The federal *Marriage (Prohibited Degrees) Act* prevents you from marrying people you are related to "lineally" or through adoption. In other words, you can't marry your brother, sister, mother, father, child or grandparent.

Provincial and territorial statutes set out the process you must follow to become married, including the issuance of marriage licences and the recording of married status once the ceremony has been performed by the individuals legally permitted to provide that service.

Provincial and territorial statutes also specify who, as a parent or guardian, could be required to provide financial support for a child. The obligation to provide financial support is based on the relationship and is not dependent on having custody of the child or access visits if the family is no longer together.

While most people realize they have a legal obligation to provide financial support for their children, many are surprised to find that provincial and territorial statutes may also make them responsible for a parent in need. If your mother or father becomes destitute, governments expect you to do your share before social benefits kick in.

The federal *Divorce Act* provides the legal basis for a lawsuit to end a marriage. *Marriage breakdown* is the key concept and a marriage is considered to have broken down if:

(1)   the husband and wife intentionally live separate and apart for one year or longer; or

(2)   either the husband or wife commits *adultery*; or

(3)   either the husband or wife subjects the other to intolerable physical or mental cruelty.

The *Divorce Act* also contains provisions that allow a husband or wife to ask for financial support for self and/or the children of the marriage and to ask the court to decide who gets custody and access to the children once the family has split. If a married couple have separated, but have not yet divorced, or if the couple have been involved in a long term relationship but never married, they are entitled to apply under provincial or territorial family law statutes to have custody, access and support issues resolved by a judge.

When deciding custody and access issues, judges will focus on what is in *the best interests of the child*, not, primarily what the parents may want. This perspective is emphasized in the statutes and in the common law precedents. There are some statutory guidelines, including the importance of a child continuing to have ongoing contact with both parents, unless, of course, there is some real risk of harm. As a result, the willingness of a custodial parent to facilitate access by the non-custodial parent is seen as a positive.

When judges are asked to resolve issues of financial support, they balance the *need* of the person requesting support with *the ability to pay* by the person who is being asked to provide the support. Lifestyle expectations that have developed while the family has been together enter into the picture, but a great deal of the uncertainty in terms of child support has been eliminated through the establishment of *child support guidelines* that have become regulations under the federal *Divorce Act* and provincial and territorial family law statutes. These regulations set up tables that base support on the income of the paying party and the number of children for whom support will be paid. The guidelines are established using economic studies of the spending patterns of families in the province or territory in which the family resides.

As discussed back in Chapter 2, according to the *Constitution Act, 1867* (section 92, enumerated power 14), property issues are a matter of provincial responsibility. When a family splits and has to decide who will get possession of the family home, cars, boats, a cottage and other property, provincial or territorial law will provide the guidelines. Most of these statutes start from the premise of an equal division and then list factors that should be considered in altering the balance. For example, if one of the former partners will have custody of the children, it may be appropriate for that person to remain in the home or to share a larger portion of the value of the property if it is sold.

Not all families need the courts to resolve custody, support and property division issues when they split. Often, with expert legal assistance the parties can arrive at a contractual agreement on how these issues will be settled. If the parties do divorce, the judge can incorporate the separation agreement as part of the court order terminating the marriage. In other circumstances, the parties may live according to the terms of the agreement without having to involve the courts at all.

CHILD WELFARE

Provincial and territorial statutes allow child protection workers and police officers to remove a child from a home setting if the child fits a statutory definition of *a child in need of protection*. The statutes require anyone who becomes aware that a child is suffering from physical, mental or emotional abuse, or that the child's parent or guardian can no longer provide for the child to report this to a local Children's Aid Society or the police. There are quasi-criminal penalties for failure to report.

Since Canadian criminal law does not apply to anyone under the age of 12, child welfare legislation also allows for the removal of a child from his or her home setting if the child is engaging in criminal activities that endanger the child or others. The idea is to allow for alternative forms of supervision if the parent or guardian is unable to discourage the child from continuing to engage in harmful behaviour.

If the child protection workers determine that a child should be kept out of the home setting for a significant period of time, or permanently, an application must be made to have a judge review the appropriateness of the removal and any plans for the child's care. The child's parent or guardian would receive notice of the court hearing and would be entitled to be present, to be represented by a lawyer and to provide any evidence available to challenge the plan of the child protection agency.

Again, the emphasis in court would be on the *best interests of the child*. The goal is to provide care that will best ensure the physical, mental and emotional well-being of the child. Statutes require that judges give consideration to the child's cultural and religious background and that any placements are made with a view to ensuring that the child is not cut off from his or her heritage. If a child can be kept in his or her home, or that of a family member with societal support and supervision, this is encouraged. Frequently, parents or guardians will agree to a supervision or placement plan prior to the court hearing.

KEY TERMINOLOGY

acceptance	an unconditional positive response to a contract offer
agent	someone authorized to enter into contracts on behalf of another
breach of contract	failing to comply with the terms of an agreement
capacity	having the maturity and mental capabilities to enter into a binding agreement
chattels	personal property with intrinsic value, also known as "goods"
child in need of protection	child who has been neglected or subjected to physical, mental or emotional abuse
choses in action	documents that have value due to financial commitments written on them
consideration	a promise that something of value will be exchanged
consumer protection laws	laws that are intended to protect consumers from questionable business practices
contracts	agreements that courts will help enforce
counter-offer	an alternative proposal of an offer made during contract negotiations
damages	financial compensation ordered as a result of a lawsuit
fixtures	goods that are permanently attached to real estate, becoming part of the realty
goods	personal property having intrinsic value, also known as "chattels"
intellectual property	a bundle of rights, including ownership in relation to business concepts, inventions and creative works
intention to be legally bound	a desire to enter into a binding contract

lien	a legal claim to some of the value of a piece of property
minors	people who are under the age of majority set by a province or territory
mitigate	keep the damages as low as possible
non-necessary	not a necessity for a particular person
offer	a tentative promise of an exchange
passing off	an attempt to have people falsely believe that a particular product is affiliated with an established brand
patent agent	an expert who could assist a person applying for patent protection for an invention
personal property	goods or chattels and choses in action
privity	the requirement that there be a direct contractual relationship between people involved in a lawsuit for breach of contract
real property	land and fixtures permanently attached
remedy	a solution a judge will order to resolve a lawsuit

STATUTES MENTIONED

Civil Marriage Act, S.C. 2005, c. 33

Copyright Act, R.S.C. 1985, c. C-42, as am.

Divorce Act, R.S.C. 1985, c. 3 (2nd Supp.), as am.

Marriage (Prohibited Degrees) Act, S.C. 1990, c. 46, as am.

Patent Act, R.S.C. 1985, c. P-4, as am.

Sale of Goods Act, R.S.O. 1990, c. S.1, as am.

Trade-marks Act, R.S.C. 1985, c. T-13, as am.

CASE MENTIONED

Glanzmann Tours Ltd. v. Yukon Wide Adventures, [2012] Y.J. No. 42, 2012 YKSM 3 (Sm. Cl. Ct.)

TEST YOURSELF

1. You have invented a clever device that can reduce gas consumption on an average car by as much as 30 per cent. If you want to protect your ownership of this invention, you should:

   (a) register under the *Trade-marks Act*;
   (b) contact a patent agent to assist you;
   (c) do nothing, you have automatic *Copyright Act* protection;
   (d) take advantage of the common law concept of passing off.

2. You hope to market your device under the name, GUZZLER MUZZLER. Protecting the ownership of this name is:

   (a) best accomplished by registering it as a trademark;
   (b) automatic under copyright legislation;
   (c) what the *Patent Act* is for;
   (d) unnecessary, it's a stupid name and no one else would want it.

3. You entered into a contractual agreement to buy a house in your community. When you moved into the house, you discovered that the previous home-owner had stripped the house of everything, including the toilets, sinks and light fixtures, leaving gaping holes in each room. When you complained, the previous owner said that there was no mention that these were to be part of the transaction in the contract for the purchase of the house, so he has done nothing wrong. Is this correct? Why or why not?

4. (a) This is a small research assignment. Go to the legal collection in your library, or on the website for provincial or territorial statutes in the jurisdiction where you live and find the name of the statute that dictates how property is divided between spouses when there is a divorce in your province or territory.

   (b) Why isn't property division covered in the federal *Divorce Act*?

5. Find the name of the agency that is responsible for child welfare or child protection services in your community.

Chapter 7

Administrative Law

ADMINISTRATIVE DECISION MAKERS

Many legal decisions affecting the lives of Canadians are made by government officers, boards, agencies and tribunals, rather than by judges. The decision-making positions and the criteria the decision makers will use are established by statute. Administrative decision makers seldom have the range of discretion that can be exercised by a judge, nor are they likely to have the breadth of legal training that we expect of our judges. Nevertheless, within the sphere of their power, or *jurisdiction*, administrative decision makers can have a significant impact on the lives of Canadians. Entitlement to social assistance, immigration and refugee claims, timing of release from prison and whether or not you qualify to drive a motor vehicle are all administrative decisions that are made by someone other than a judge.

COMPARING ADMINISTRATIVE DECISION MAKERS AND COURTS

Most administrative decision makers lack the job security and independence judges enjoy. After a judge is appointed, he or she will likely stay in the position until retirement and any review of job performance will be conducted by a panel of other judges, rather than by politicians. People sitting on administrative boards, tribunals and commissions have much less security. Appointments may be for a relatively short fixed term, until a specific purpose is achieved, or "at the pleasure" of the government that made the appointment. This would mean that termination could occur at any time and could be influenced by politics, rather than performance.

The people appointed as administrative decision makers may be appointed because of special expertise, but appointments may also be used as a form of reward for people who have been active in supporting the political party in power at the time the appointment is made. When the party in power changes, dismissals may occur right away, or retirement replacements will reflect a different political climate and perspective. There is probably more of an expectation from everyone involved with administrative boards and tribunals that decisions may be coloured by the policies of the government of the day.

While our courts operate as an adversarial system, where judges sit back and wait for the parties to present the evidence on which they will base their decisions, some administrative decision makers take a much more inquisitorial role, digging for evidence and actively participating in the questioning of witnesses to a much greater extent. Some boards, tribunals and commissions have in-house staff to conduct investigations and gather evidence that will be used in reaching a decision.

Administrative decision-making is usually done without all the formal trappings of a courtroom. Even if lawyers are present, neither they nor the decision makers will be wearing the gowns that are seen on judges and on lawyers in superior levels of court. Lawyers and agents will bow when they enter and leave a courtroom to show respect for the judge and the system of justice. This isn't expected in most administrative settings. While lawyers and agents appearing in court will always stand to speak, administrative hearings may be conducted much more informally, with everyone seated throughout the proceeding.

The rules of evidence are often greatly relaxed by administrative tribunals, with statutes commonly allowing the administrative decision makers to base their decisions on any evidence they consider reliable. Some administrative tribunals will require sworn evidence, while for others requiring an oath is optional. Hearsay and opinion evidence that a court would never hear because of an adherence to strict rules of evidence could be admitted in an administrative process. Tribunals are expected to use the civil standard of a preponderance of evidence, or a balance of probabilities when reaching a decision.

Administrative tribunals seldom require parties to provide advance disclosure of the evidence they will be using at a hearing to opponents. This sort of procedural streamlining allows tribunals to schedule hearings more quickly, but may also create surprises that prompt requests for adjournments to properly process new information and prepare a response.

Administrative decision makers are generally not required to follow precedents set in previous tribunal decisions. This can add a real element of unpredictability to this area of the law for lawyers, agents and their clients.

All Canadian courts, whether exercising civil or criminal jurisdiction have written rules of procedure that dictate the form of documents that should be used, notifications that must be given to other parties, methods for ensuring witnesses show up for court, the timing of various steps in the process and other pertinent directions to ensure consistency, efficiency and fairness. Only four provinces, Alberta, British Columbia, Ontario and Quebec have statutes that set out procedural parameters for administrative tribunals. Even in these jurisdictions, the procedures apply to some, but not all provincially created tribunals. Other tribunals are entitled to set their own procedures. Lawyers, agents and affected parties have to scramble to understand the idiosyncrasies of each in order to satisfy procedural requirements and ensure an effective presentation of submissions.

Unlike the court system, there is no consistent right to appeal administrative decisions. The governing statute may specify the rights and procedures related to reviews or appeals, or may attempt to prevent any appeal or review by inserting a *privative clause*. These clauses stipulate that the decision of a particular board or tribunal is final and not subject to appeal or review. Obviously, this is an attempt by government to minimize cost and complexity and to streamline a particular decision-making process.

Some statutes simply direct a discontented party back to the administrative body that made the original decision to request a review. Other statutes provide comprehensive rights to appeal to a supervisor, another tribunal or to a designated level of court. For example, the decisions of many federal boards and tribunals can be appealed to Federal Court.

Most of the legal rights contained in sections 7 through 14 of the *Canadian Charter of Rights and Freedoms* were created with criminal justice processes in mind. Nevertheless, it is obvious that rights like the right of a party or witness to an interpreter, contained in section 14, would also apply in government-created tribunals. Section 7 of the *Charter* protects people from being deprived of "… life, liberty and security of the person … except in accordance with the principles of fundamental justice". It is logical that this would necessitate an adherence to the principles of fundamental justice in tribunals that could affect a person's income, employment situation or release from prison, among others.

PRINCIPLES OF ADMINISTRATIVE LAW

Administrative decision-makers are given specific spheres of jurisdiction in statutes. They are generally free to exercise their power without interference or review from the courts unless they step beyond the bounds of the statutory powers or act unreasonably or unfairly.

Privative clauses will not prevent a court from reviewing an administrative decision if a judge can be convinced that the decision maker acted outside the scope of his or her jurisdiction. Inventing powers that he or she hasn't been given in an enabling statute, considering factors that are not within the mandate or failing to consider factors that should have been considered before a decision was made could all open the door for someone who has been affected by a decision to ask a court to intervene. Refusing to make a decision at all, when that is clearly the statutory function of the administrator, is also considered a legitimate reason for the courts to get involved. Most often a judge will order that the matter be properly reconsidered by the erring commission, board, tribunal or agent, rather than substituting his or her own decision.

Canadian courts have consistently required publicly funded bodies that make decisions that affect individuals to provide *procedural fairness* to the people affected. This common law principle of procedural fairness includes two primary elements, a *right to be heard* and a *right to an impartial decision maker*.

The right to be heard does not always require the type of hearing that one would expect in a court setting. Sometimes, submissions can only be made in writing. What the right to be heard does require is notification that a decision will be made and an opportunity for a person who will be affected by a decision to present his or her side of the story. This usually includes an opportunity to challenge any submissions that may be made by a person or organization with an adverse interest. In most circumstances, an affected party will be entitled to be represented by a lawyer or agent when presenting his or her own submissions and when mounting a challenge to contrary evidence.

The right to an impartial decision-maker requires that there be no apparent bias or conflict of interest on the part of the person or persons who will be making the decision. Decisions should be made in good faith and not for frivolous or irrelevant reasons. This issue can often be addressed by supplying a written rationale for the decision that is ultimately made.

While some administrative officers, boards and tribunals have been exercising their assigned jurisdictions for years, others are established to achieve more short-term goals or may be replaced or eliminated when government policies and priorities shift. Regardless of the permanence of individual administrative decision-making bodies, experts suggest that there may be as many as 1,500 separate federal, provincial or territorial boards, commissions or other agencies making legal decisions that could affect the lives of Canadians at any given point in time.

Let's take a little closer look at a couple of examples of administrative decision-makers that operate at the federal, provincial and territorial levels.

PAROLE BOARD OF CANADA

The Parole Board of Canada is assigned tasks under two federal statutes, the *Corrections and Conditional Release Act* and the *Criminal Records Act*. Both statutes have been recently amended by the federal government. Most people are aware that this is the body that decides whether or not an inmate will be released from prison prior to the expiry of his or her sentence. The *Corrections and Conditional Release Act* sets the parameters for arriving at those decisions when a federal prisoner is involved. The Board also makes early release decisions affecting inmates in territorial jails and contracts with eight of the 10 provinces to deal with these issues in relation to provincially incarcerated prisoners. The Board, through its regional offices, is involved with over 15,000 parole applications each year.

The *Criminal Records Act* allows a person with a limited criminal record acquired in the past to apply for a *record suspension*, if a significant period of time has passed since the last involvement with the criminal justice system. A record suspension could be useful for securing certain types of employment, may allow for international travel that would otherwise be restricted by the host country and is generally sought by individuals seeking a fresh start with a clean slate. Close to one in 10 Canadians have a criminal record of some sort and many of these people could benefit from a record suspension. However, with the federal government recently restricting the availability of record suspensions and significantly increasing the cost of the application process, the number of people applying has plummeted from over 20,000 per year to fewer than 4000. Decisions on whether a person has met the statutory requirements to qualify for a record suspension are made by the Parole Board.

The Parole Board of Canada operates out of five regional offices. As many as 40 full-time and another 30-40 part-time board members deal with the applications for conditional release from prison and pardons. A full-time Parole Board member earns in the vicinity of $130,000 per year, with part-timers being paid approximately $650 for each day their services are required.

By statute, Parole Board members are appointed by *order-in-council*. What does this mean? Even though there is an application process involving screening for appropriate background, knowledge of the criminal justice system and aptitude for the job, this just gets you on a list of potential candidates. The final decision on selecting members of the Parole Board is made by the federal Cabinet. Cabinet is composed of politicians exclusively from the party with the most seats in the House of Commons. Meetings are held behind closed doors, without opposition scrutiny or input. The press does not have access. Some people claim that there is an element of political patronage in these appointments and in appointments to many other administrative decision-making positions.

When the Parole Board of Canada deals with parole and other forms of conditional release applications, the *Corrections and Conditional Release Act* requires that they make protection of society their number one consideration. The Act stipulates that Board members should only grant parole if:

(1) the offender will not present an undue risk to society before the end of his or her sentence; and

(2) the release of the offender will contribute to the protection of society by facilitating re-integration as a law-abiding citizen.

The government is clearly suggesting that, whenever possible, the supervised, gradual re-integration afforded by parole is better for the ultimate protection of society than simply locking a prisoner in a cell until the end of the sentence, then unleashing him or her, unsupervised, into a society that may no longer be familiar and is unlikely to be welcoming. At the same time, Parole Board of Canada members are being cautioned not to create a risk for society by releasing someone who is likely to re-offend while on parole. The only real way for Board members to satisfy the statutory requirements is to engage in a process of risk assessment and Board policy manuals tell the members the sort of factors they should consider and the type of available evidence that may be relevant in this process. Parole applications are usually assessed by a panel of two or three Board members.

The right to apply for parole set out in the *Corrections and Conditional Release Act* isn't available for most prisoners until they have served at least a third of the sentence they were given by a judge. For people convicted of murder, a range of violent offences and some drug charges, the sentencing judge will have specified the number of years to be served in jail before a parole application can be made. For example, if a person has been convicted of first degree murder, he or she will have received a *life* sentence. This literally means that the individual will be under correctional supervision of some sort for the rest of his or her life and will not even be entitled to apply for parole until at least 25 years have been spent in jail (some prisoners may be able to apply to court to have this ineligibility to apply reduced after serving at least 15 years). Having the right to apply for parole is no guarantee that it will be granted. Many first time applicants are refused and will face a waiting period before they can re-apply.

In order to complete the paper component of an application for parole, a prisoner, with the assistance of a case management officer, or inmate liaison officer in the jail, must prepare a *release plan*. This would detail the specifics of living arrangements and employment prospects if released and any community-based treatment programs that would be available. A parole officer is assigned to check the details of the plan with the community contacts like prospective employers and housing supervisors.

In making an initial assessment of the application, Parole Board of Canada members could access a range of documents from a printout of the offender's criminal history, to the judge's reasons for the sentence imposed, victim impact statements used at sentencing and the full correctional institution file on the applicant. The longer the inmate has been incarcerated the longer and more detailed an institutional file will be. It could contain all institutional infractions, classification reports, records of participation in treatment and counselling programs and mental health assessments if any have been done.

Parole Board members may also have access to criminological statistics to help them assess the *recidivism risk* of inmates with certain characteristics. A recidivism risk is a risk that the person will commit another criminal offence. The Statistical Information on Recidivism Scale is one risk assessment tool that has been used by corrections personnel in Canadian institutions and may be found in an inmate's institutional file. The scale lists 15 personality factors and assigns positive or negative points depending on whether or not, from a statistical perspective, the characteristic tends to show a high or low risk of re-offending. For example, if an inmate's criminal record shows more than five previous convictions for break and entry, statistics demonstrate that this is an individual committed to a life of crime with a high risk of re-offending on release. This would generate negative points on the risk assessment scale. Conversely, from a statistical perspective, someone who is in jail for homicide presents a very low risk of re-offending after release. This actually earns the person being assessed positive points. Being 50 or more at the time of a first conviction merits positive points, showing it's highly unlikely this person will re-offend, while a first conviction as a teenager garners negative points, indicating a young person on a bad track. Totals generated after going through all the factors on the scale are then used to assess the statistical likelihood of the individual re-offending if released. An assessment tool like this could become one more piece of the puzzle for Parole Board members required to assess the risk presented by any particular applicant.

Parole Board Members may reject an application for parole if the paperwork alone demonstrates the lack of an appropriate release plan or simply too great a risk to society if the offender is released. Far more often, a hearing is scheduled for the offender in the institution where he or she is incarcerated. Prior to the hearing, the inmate will be notified of the date of the hearing, told of his or her right to be represented by a lawyer or an agent at the hearing and given an opportunity to go over the institutional file and other information that the Board will take into account.

Parole Board of Canada hearings tend to be much more inquisitorial than a session in court. Members conducting the hearing will question the applicant and his or her lawyer or agent to challenge aspects of a release plan or to investigate what the inmate has done by way of programs or preparation to increase the confidence of the Board that he or she will not create a risk to society if released. Victims and other members of the public may apply to attend parole board hearings and victims can submit written impact statements, or audio or visual tapes for the consideration of the Board in arriving at their decisions.

The applicant will be provided with reasons for a Parole Board decision. If the inmate is granted parole, a number of conditions will be automatic, including requirements to obey the law, keep the peace, report regularly to a parole officer and stay in a designated geographic area. Special conditions can be added by the Board, including abstention from alcohol or drugs, limits on contact with victims or their families and a requirement that the person reside in a designated halfway house. Any failure to follow the conditions can result in the Board revoking parole and returning the offender to jail.

Decisions of the Parole Board of Canada can be appealed to an internal Appeal Division of the Board. The appeal panel would be made up of board members who had not been involved in the original decision.

If someone were to claim that the Parole Board had acted outside its jurisdiction, or incorrectly interpreted the law that controls the Board, a common law application for judicial review could be made to the Federal Court.

Hearings are less common when the Parole Board processes applications for record suspensions under the *Criminal Records Act*. There is a prescribed application form that must be completed and the applicant is told exactly what supplemental documentation the Board will require in order to assess the application. The applicant is expected to gather these documents and submit them with the prescribed form.

If the request is for a record suspension from a summary conviction charge, section 4 of the *Criminal Records Act* stipulates that the Board *may* issue a record suspension if the offender has not been convicted of any other offence for a period of five years from the time any penalty imposed for the charge expired. Evidence of the penalty imposed by the court, when it was completed, and a printout of the offender's record, are all required to process this type of request. Recent data on the Parole Board website indicates that these requests take an average of about six months to process.

If the request is for a record suspension from an indictable offence, the process becomes a little more complex. It says that the Board *may* grant a record suspension if the person has not been convicted of an offence for ten years from the expiry of the original penalty and "has been of good conduct". In order to assess the "good conduct" component the Board will want the names and addresses of reputable personal references and time to check on their support of the applicant's claim. The Board's website suggests 12 months to process these requests, increasing to 24 months if the Board is proposing to refuse the request.

It is only if the Board proposes to refuse to grant a record suspension that the possibility of a hearing arises. The *Act* requires the Board to notify the applicant of the intended refusal and allow a reasonable time for the applicant to make additional written submissions, "… or, if the Board so authorizes, orally at a hearing held for that purpose". Again, an applicant could expect the hearing to be inquisitorial with Board members directing questions on the "good conduct" issue. If the record suspension application is ultimately refused, the applicant has to wait at least a year to re-apply.

This statute does not provide for appeals. A request for a common law judicial review by the Federal Court would require a substantial error in applying the law by the Board or a jurisdictional problem.

PROVINCIAL AND TERRITORIAL HUMAN RIGHTS TRIBUNALS

Each province and territory has a human rights statute, designed to protect individuals from discriminatory actions initiated or potentially controlled by employers, landlords, retail merchants and others they encounter in their daily activities. Typically, the statutes list prohibited forms of discrimination, including age, colour, race, religion, marital or family status, sex, sexual orientation, mental or physical disability and others that may be targeted in some jurisdictions and not in others.

The human rights statutes also create human rights boards or commissions that may be assigned several functions, including a public educational role, an obligation to investigate complaints of discriminatory actions, a mediation function to try to resolve problems without the need for a formal hearing and the power to establish tribunals to resolve disputes that are more hotly contested in a court-like forum.

When formal hearings become necessary, the multi-faceted roles of these boards and commissions characteristically make it necessary to appoint *ad hoc* decision makers to conduct the hearings, rather than employing full-time adjudicators. Frequently, these tribunals receive input, not only from the person who filed the complaint and the party compelled to respond, but also from lawyers or agents representing the board or commission, who may take an active position on the case and present evidence gathered by the commission's own investigators. To maintain an appearance of impartiality, it is important that the people chosen to make the decisions not work in the same office as the board or commission's legal counsel and investigators. College or university professors, retired judges or other members of the community with a sound grasp of legal principles and procedures may be chosen as *ad hoc* decision-makers. Some provinces appoint hearing officers to more permanent positions.

Human rights hearings are often quite formal, with witnesses providing sworn evidence, the entire procedure being recorded and the parties having the right to be represented by a lawyer or agent throughout. Statutes that provide the power for these tribunals customarily stipulate that the decisions that are made have the same force as court orders and can be filed with a designated provincial or territorial court. Orders can then be enforced using civil law enforcement methods, like sale and seizure of property or garnishment. Though potential remedies differ among jurisdictions, it is common for human rights adjudicators to be able to order that financial compensation be paid, training programs be instituted, discriminatory practices cease or that workers be re-hired or promoted.

Some of the human rights statutes designate a court to which tribunal decisions can be appealed. Even without a specific mention, directing that tribunal orders can be filed as a court order of a particular court may well open the door to the same appeal process that would be available for the orders of the named court.

TRIBUNALS DESIGNED TO COMPENSATE VICTIMS OF CRIME

Most Canadian provinces have statutes that create administrative boards with responsibility for providing financial compensation for people who have been injured through the actions of criminals. The existence of these tribunals recognizes that civil lawsuits against criminals may often not be a very realistic remedy for victims to secure compensation for harm that has been caused to them. Firstly, the criminal who caused the harm may never be caught, or even identified. Secondly, criminals make notoriously bad defendants in civil cases. Frequently, the perpetrator has no assets or significant (honest) income in the first place. There's the additional problem that if the perpetrator of the crime is located and sent to jail, he or she is unlikely to be earning enough money making licence plates, or sewing mail bags to be able to pay any judgment awarded.

All of the statutes limit claims to compensation for physical injuries or death. Damage to property is not covered. Nor, in most circumstances is there compensation for damages caused to mental health. There are also strict caps placed on the amount of compensation that can be awarded. These vary greatly from province to province, with Alberta's *Victims of Crime Act* limit of $110,000 being the top of the scale and Prince Edward Island's $15,000 (in an act of the same name) representing the lower end. None of these limits come close to what a civil lawsuit might generate for serious physical injuries, but of course this is an effort on the part of governments to provide some compensation when civil lawsuits are simply not practical. The funding for the compensation funds comes from a variety of sources, including "surcharges" that are added to fines that are imposed by criminal courts in the respective provinces.

KEY TERMINOLOGY

balance of probabilities	civil standard of proof — more likely than not
jurisdiction	legal responsibility based on geography or division of legislative powers
order-in-council	cabinet decision
privative clause	a provision in a statute that purports to prevent a court from reviewing the decisions of administrative tribunals
procedural fairness	a process that enables an effected party to make submissions to a decision-maker before decisions are made
recidivism risk	the likelihood of someone committing another criminal offence
record suspension	the possibility of having a criminal record separated from records that could harm a person's ability to get a job or travel abroad
right to be heard	includes a right to reasonable notice that a decision will be made and a right to make submissions to the decision-maker prior to that decision
right to an impartial decision-maker	a right to have decisions made by someone who is unbiased

STATUTES MENTIONED

Canadian Charter of Rights and Freedoms, Part I of the *Constitution Act, 1982*, being Schedule B to the *Canada Act 1982*, c. 11

Corrections and Conditional Release Act, S.C. 1992, c. 20, as am.

Criminal Records Act, R.S.C. 1985, c. C-47, as am.

Victims of Crime Act, R.S.A. 2000, c. V-3, as am.

Victims of Crime Act, R.S.P.E.I. 1988, c. V-3, as am.

TEST YOURSELF

1. (a) You apply for a part-time job in a local bar. The boss interviews you and asks if you're married and if you have any kids. He explains that he finds singles more reliable for late night shifts. Is the boss violating any law by asking these types of questions? Briefly explain.

    (b) If you feel the boss is violating a law, what, if anything could you do about it? Briefly explain.

2. A 65-year-old and a 23-year-old are both applying for parole. The 65-year-old was convicted 15 years ago of second degree murder after she killed her spouse. This was her first offence. The 23-year-old was sent to jail four years ago for a violent robbery. He had over 30 prior convictions for break and entry, with his record starting shortly after his 15th birthday.

    If the Parole Board bases its parole decisions on the Statistical Information on Recidivism Scale, which of these offenders is more likely to be granted parole? Why?

3. (a) Do the administrators at your college or university need to follow the principles of procedural fairness before kicking someone out of school for cheating on exams? Briefly explain why or why not.

    (b) What procedural safeguards, if any, are in place at your institution to protect the rights of students who could face expulsion or other forms of academic discipline?

Chapter 8

Criminal Law — The Big Picture

BASIC CRIMINAL LAW PRINCIPLES

In Canada, criminal behaviour is considered an offence against all of society and not just the individual victim. As a result, the police, who are often society's investigative representatives, and the prosecutors, who act as society's agents in the court process, may continue an investigation and prosecution of a criminal charge even if the victim is unable, unwilling or uninterested in going ahead.

Anyone can report an incident involving criminal behaviour to the police, or directly to a judge or a justice of the peace. If the police investigate and develop *reasonable and probable* grounds for believing that the behaviour fits within the wording of a criminal statute, an allegation may be brought to a judge or justice of the peace (J.P.) in the form of a document called an *information.* This is the document commonly used to start the criminal justice process in motion. Someone with personal knowledge of a crime could by-pass the police and *swear* the information directly before a judge or J.P. Once the document has been sworn to be true and accepted by the judge or justice of the peace as a legitimate allegation, the named individual has been formally *accused* of committing a crime.

Everyone accused of committing a crime is entitled to have his or her guilt or innocence determined by a judge or jury in *open court*, following a fair trial. The open court concept, with members of the public being able to attend and observe the proceedings, is intended to prevent the types of injustices that occur in countries where "justice" is carried out, literally, behind closed doors. A large number of common law principles have been developed to ensure fairness and many of these have been enshrined in statutory form in the *Canadian Charter of Rights and Freedoms*, which is Part 1 of the *Constitution Act, 1982*.

It is a fundamental principle of our criminal justice system that an accused person is *presumed to be innocent* until his or her guilt is proven *beyond a reasonable doubt* in court. The *onus*, or legal responsibility for proving that someone has committed a crime is always on the prosecutor, representing society. The prosecutor must call witnesses who have enough evidence to prove to the judge or jury that the behaviour of the accused fits the description of the alleged crime as it is laid out in a statute. If the evidence is not sufficient to prove guilt beyond a reasonable doubt, the accused person must be *acquitted.*

The accused person is normally entitled to face his or her accusers in court and to challenge any allegations through *cross-examination* and through the opportunity to present evidence that would raise a reasonable doubt about guilt.

Cross-examination is a style of questioning designed to test the powers of observation, memory and/or truthfulness of a witness.

The accused person can never be forced to testify in court, but if he or she does decide to give evidence, the prosecutor can cross-examine the accused and any other witness called by the defence.

Because of the contest-like nature of our criminal justice proceedings, with each side being able to present evidence that will be considered by the judge or jury and to challenge the accuracy of the evidence being presented by the other, our system of justice is called an *adversarial system.* As discussed in Chapter 4, the judge serves as an independent arbiter between the prosecution and the defence, ensuring that the process will be fair by enforcing common law and statutory rules of evidence and procedure.

While an accused person could choose to act as his or her own advocate in court, the complexity of evidentiary rules and procedure, and the likelihood that the prosecutor will be a trained legal expert makes it practically important that an accused person have the guidance of his or her own lawyer or trained paralegal.

CONSTITUTIONALLY PROTECTED CONCEPTS

The *Canadian Charter of Rights and Freedoms*, found in Part 1 of the *Constitution Act, 1982*, is designed to protect individuals in Canada from actions of the various levels of government that might limit the listed rights and freedoms, considered to be of fundamental importance to people in our democratic society. Governments cannot create laws which ignore these rights and freedoms, nor can government employees and agents like police officers, customs officers, meat inspectors or taxing authorities operate without respecting the boundaries they set.

People working in the criminal justice system tend to focus on the "Legal Rights" enshrined in sections 7 through 14 of the *Canadian Charter of Rights and Freedoms,* which capture crucial criminal justice concepts. Other portions of the *Constitution Act, 1982* provide the context that emphasizes how fundamentally important constitutional protections are. Subsection 52(1) of the *Constitution Act, 1982*, is a useful place to start:

> **52.** (1) The Constitution of Canada is the *supreme law* of Canada, and any law that is inconsistent with the provisions of the Constitution is, to the extent of the inconsistency, *of no force or effect.* (Emphasis added.)

In other words, there are no Canadian laws more important than the legal protections found in the constitution. To support this preeminence, the *Constitution Act, 1982*, provides a range of potential remedies for individuals whose constitutional rights have been violated. Subsection 24(1) says that anyone whose rights, "… have been infringed or denied may apply to a court … to obtain *such remedy as the court considers appropriate and just in the circumstances*". This makes the range of potential remedies as broad as the imagination of the judge who is asked to help. In criminal cases, judges have used this remedy to stop trials, force investigators to turn over relevant information and to reduce sentences imposed upon people who are convicted of offences.

Subsection 24(2) focuses more on evidence that has been gathered, "... in a manner that infringed or denied any rights or freedoms ... ." Such evidence would be excluded from use in a trial, if letting it in, "... would bring the administration of justice into disrepute". Constitutionally protected rights and freedoms cannot be ignored by police or other government investigators with impunity. They must recognize legal limits in conducting investigations.

Section 8 of the *Charter* protects everyone from *unreasonable searches*. Courts have interpreted this to mean that in situations where someone has an expectation of privacy, a government agent must get a *warrant*, a court order authorizing an encroachment on this privacy. The only exceptions made are for real emergency situations, when it isn't practical to get a court authorization to act.

Section 9 prevents government agents from *arbitrarily* detaining or imprisoning anyone. In other words, a person can only be arrested or even stopped for investigative purposes if there is a good legal reason for doing so. Section 10 follows this up by making it clear that if someone is stopped or arrested by a government agent, he or she is entitled to be promptly told the reason and to be allowed to consult with a lawyer if he or she chooses. The person is also entitled to be brought before a judge or justice of the peace to make sure that the government agent has not made a mistake.

If someone in Canada is charged with an offence, section 11 of the *Charter* provides a lengthy list of rights for the accused person. These include the right to be presumed innocent, the right not to be denied reasonable *bail* if the person has been locked up and the right to a public trial by an independent and impartial judge within a reasonable time. If the charge involves a potential sentence of five years or more, the accused person can also choose a jury trial. Section 14 allows for an interpreter if the accused person requires such services and section 12 protects everyone from "... any cruel or unusual punishment".

There is no doubt that these *Charter* sections capture many of the common law principles that developed in relation to criminal justice prior to this part of the constitution being enacted in 1982. Just in case some common law principles were missed, section 7 ensures everyone a right to, "... life, liberty and security of the person and the right not to be deprived thereof except *in accordance with the principles of fundamental justice*".

What are these *principles of fundamental justice*? While the courts have expressed them generally as societal values, common law principles of criminal justice are clearly an important component. It is this seemingly vague section which captures important criminal justice concepts like the *right to remain silent* and the right of an accused person to get *disclosure* of any evidence the prosecution has gathered that could be used in the trial, well in advance of the court hearing.

Charter protections are not absolute. Section 1 makes it clear that they are "... subject only to such *reasonable limits* prescribed by law as can be demonstrably justified in a free and democratic society". For example, provincial statutes enable police officers to randomly stop drivers of motor vehicles to check for sobriety, fitness of the vehicle, proof of insurance and proper licensing. Courts have said that this process may well be a violation of section 9 of the *Charter*, which protects people from arbitrary detention. Nevertheless, the Supreme Court of Canada has also ruled that the practice is *demonstrably justified* for investigative tactics like seasonal "ride checks" because of the pressing and important societal concern with impaired drivers (*R. v. Ladouceur*, [1990] S.C.J. No. 53, 56 C.C.C. (3d) 22 (S.C.C.)).

The full text of the *Charter* sections that make up Part 1 of the *Constitution Act, 1982*, have been included as Appendix 3 at the end of this book.

CRIMES AND QUASI-CRIMES

Federal Offences

As has been previously stated, there are no common law crimes. (I should probably admit here that this is a bit of a little white lie. A judge's power to punish someone for "contempt of court" is a common law concept, but I can't think of any others). In order for behaviour to constitute a crime, it must fit within the wording of a criminal statute. The power to enact criminal laws was given to the federal government in section 91, enumerated power 27 of the *Constitution Act, 1867*. The primary federal statute dealing with criminal law is, of course, the *Criminal Code*. Over 800 sections in length, this massive statute lists several hundred different criminal behaviours and provides penalties for violators. Offences against society in this statute cover a very broad spectrum of human depravity as well as the alphabet, from abandonment and abduction to witchcraft and wounding. The *Code* also contains a great deal of criminal procedural law.

Other federal statutes, like the *Controlled Drugs and Substances Act*, focus on particular niches of criminal behaviour, while some statutes like the *Immigration and Refugee Protection Act* include a few specific criminal charges, for offences like smuggling humans, buried in a large statute whose primary function is to set up an administrative scheme for the efficient processing of immigration and refugee applicants.

Statutes like the *Youth Criminal Justice Act* and the *Canada Evidence Act* are important criminal procedural laws, but contain almost no charging sections at all, except in relation to people who violate procedural requirements (like the prohibition against publishing the names of youth who are dealt with under the *Youth Criminal Justice Act*).

People who are ultimately convicted of federal offences end up with a *criminal record*. The Royal Canadian Mounted Police (RCMP) operate the Canadian Police Information Centre (CPIC), which provides a central computer based system for recording and accessing this information. Access to criminal records is tightly controlled, but police and courts do make use of these records. Individuals can, of course, access their own records through the police and many employers or volunteer organizations will request that applicants submit copies of their criminal records, or proof that there isn't one.

Provincial and Territorial Offences

Enumerated power 15 in section 92 of the *Constitution Act, 1867* allows provinces to enforce their laws through, "The Imposition of Punishment by Fine, Penalty, or Imprisonment …". Territories have been granted the same power by the federal statutes that set out their legislative jurisdiction. The result is that, while provinces and territories cannot technically create *crimes*, they have a wide range of statutes imposing penalties for behaviours that have been labelled, *quasi-criminal*, or like crime.

Not surprisingly, while the names of the statutes may vary, there is a great deal of common ground among the types of behaviour being controlled by provincial and territorial legislation. They all have statutes to manage motor vehicle traffic on public highways, hunting and fishing regulations, controls over the sale of liquor, protections for consumers and the environment and trespass restrictions. Ontario's *Trespass to Property Act*, which is included in Appendix 4 at the back of this book, is an example.

The court processes used to assess guilt or innocence in relation to these offences is the criminal process, requiring proof beyond a reasonable doubt, onus of proof on a prosecutor, representing society and the other key elements of criminal justice. Provinces and territories do add procedural rules of their own for processing both provincial and municipal offences. For example, many have established set fines and streamlined processing for people who are prepared to enter guilty pleas to common types of offences, like speeding, failure to wear a seat belt and other motor vehicle offences. Each province and territory, of course, has the power to create their own penalty limits for particular types of behaviour. Speeding in Prince Edward Island is not necessarily going to result in the same fine as the exact same behaviour in Quebec or Alberta.

People who are convicted of provincial offences do not have a *criminal record*, though provincial and territorial ministries of transport use this information for licensing purposes and do keep records of provincial convictions related to the operation of motor vehicles. Insurance companies can, and do access provincial driving records. As a result, convictions affect insurance rates.

Municipal By-Laws

Municipalities receive all of their law-making power from the provincial and territorial governments. While there are some distinctions in the range of matters downloaded to municipalities in each jurisdiction, there are also common patterns. Municipalities will impose fines for people who violate parking, property maintenance and pet ownership restrictions. They usually require that businesses secure licences to operate and control where they can locate, the types of signs they can display and hours of operation. Violators are prosecuted by municipal lawyers, by-law enforcement agents and/or the local police service.

Convictions require proof beyond a reasonable doubt and the provincial or territorial legislation that provides procedural detail for the prosecution of provincial offences is drafted to cover municipal by-law enforcement as well.

ACTUS REUS AND *MENS REA* ELEMENTS

Actus reus, an illegal action or omission of some sort is always an element of a criminal or quasi-criminal offence. The statute will specify what the illegal act or omission might be. For example, section 210(2)*(b)* of the *Criminal Code* states that everyone who, " ... is found, without lawful excuse, in a common bawdy-house ..." is guilty of an offence. You may have to go to section 197 to learn that a "common bawdy-house" is a place "... kept or occupied ... for the purpose of prostitution ...", but if you are found in one and you aren't there to deliver the newspaper or the mail, or to check the gas meter you could be convicted of committing this crime.

Would the prosecutor have to prove that you were there *intentionally*, or perhaps *recklessly*, or *negligently* to secure a conviction? In other words, is it necessary for the prosecutor to prove a *mens rea*, or mental element in order for a judge to convict? There doesn't seem to be anything in the wording of the charging section to require this, though it does suggest that if you have a "legal excuse" for being there, you won't be convicted.

In 1978, in the case of *R. v. Sault Ste. Marie (City)*, the Supreme Court of *Canada* ruled that there are three types of offences:

(1)   true criminal offences — *mens rea* is a necessary element;

(2)   strict liability offences — proof of the *actus reus* is enough, but accused can avoid conviction by showing due diligence;

(3)   absolute liability offences — *actus reus* is enough, no loopholes.

For offences that fall into the first category, requiring a prosecutor to prove a *mens rea* element, the statute itself usually contains words that make the need for this element clear. Subsection 265(1) of the *Criminal Code*, which defines assault, makes it a crime if someone applies force "intentionally". Subsection 279(1) says that it is illegal to kidnap someone "with intent". The infanticide section 233 makes it illegal for a mother to cause the death of her newborn "by a wilful act or omission". Even section 219 specifies that someone commits criminal negligence if in doing or omitting to do anything he or she "... shows wanton or reckless disregard for the lives or safety of other persons". Many of these offences carry the risk of significant prison sentences if someone is convicted, so requiring the prosecutor to not only prove a wrongful action but also criminal malice or contempt for the effect of the actions on others does not seem unreasonable.

The second and third categories of offences are often said to be more of a regulatory or public welfare nature. They are aimed at stopping certain behaviours, regardless of whether or not the individual accused intends harmful consequences or is criminally reckless. Imposing speed limits, prohibiting the sale of certain drugs, curbing the discharge of pollution into the air or water and making it illegal to sell food that hasn't been properly refrigerated, all provide examples of federal, provincial or territorial offences that would fit into the strict or absolute liability categories.

Courts have long been reluctant to penalize the morally innocent. As a result, most offences that don't require a *mens rea* component are categorized by judges as strict, rather than absolute liability offences. This allows an accused person to avoid a conviction if he or she can show that all reasonable care was taken to avoid the offence, but that it happened despite this *due diligence*.

In fact, judges have made it clear that it would be a breach of the principles of fundamental justice, protected in section 7 of the *Charter* if a person without any real moral fault could be sent to jail. This would seem to limit the use of the absolute liability categorization of offences to charges against corporations, or charges that involve a maximum penalty of a fine, without any risk of jail time even for defaulting on the payment of the fine.

SUMMARY AND INDICTABLE CATEGORIES

All criminal and quasi-criminal charges are categorized as either *summary* or *indictable* offences. The categorization affects the entire criminal justice process that will be used for the offence, from arrest, or alternatives to arrest through the court hearing to sentencing.

Summary offences are often thought of as including the less serious charges, though in reality they include all municipal and provincial or territorial offences, regardless of the severity of penalty attached. Federal offences labelled as summary by the government in Ottawa do tend to involve a lower range of potential penalties than federally created indictable charges. The criminal justice process is streamlined for all summary charges. People accused of committing summary offences will seldom be arrested and taken into custody at the time of their first contact with the police. They will not be subject to fingerprinting and identification photos prior to appearing in court. Jury trials are not an option. Summary offence trials are held before a judge alone in the provincial or territorial court of criminal jurisdiction.

Indictable offences can only be created by the federal government and this label does suggest that federal politicians have decided that the offences so labelled should be considered the most serious of criminal charges, with substantial potential penalties attached. People facing these charges can be required to provide fingerprints and identification photos and are more likely to be arrested and spend some time in custody prior to their court hearing. Consequently, indictable charges also tend to include the widest range of procedural protections for an accused person, including the possibility of choosing a trial by jury.

Unfortunately, for people trying to understand the criminal justice process, indictable charges are not all treated the same. Sub-categories of indictable charges are created by sections 553 and 469 of the *Criminal Code*. As we shall discuss in the next chapter, offences listed in section 553, which include very common charges like *theft and fraud under $5,000*, are treated very much like summary offences from a procedural perspective. In contrast, section 469 lists a small group of rare, but very serious charges like *murder, piracy* and *treason* that can only be dealt with by the superior court of justice in each province or territory.

Dozens of federal offences involve a choice. Such charges are commonly known as *hybrid* or *dual procedure offences*. Because the statutory sections that describe the penalties for these charges provide an option, prosecutors have the discretion to treat these charges as either *summary* or *indictable*. A prosecutor will announce his or her choice, prior to the accused person being asked to enter a plea (of "guilty" or "not guilty") to the charge. Before the prosecutor has announced his or her choice, police officers are allowed to use all the processes they could use with someone facing a straight *indictable charge*, including asking the accused person to provide fingerprints and identification photos.

The *Criminal Code* section which sets out the penalties available for someone convicted of theft of property worth less than $5,000 provides an example of a *hybrid offence*:

> **s. 334** ... everyone who commits theft
>
> > *(b)*   is guilty
> >
> > > (i)   of an indictable offence and is liable to imprisonment for a term not exceeding two years, or
> > >
> > > (ii) of an offence punishable on summary conviction, where the value of what is stolen does not exceed five thousand dollars.

Subclause (ii), which allows the option of treating *theft under* as a summary conviction offence, does not mention the potential sentence if the charge is dealt with in that manner. Those in the know quickly discover that section 787 of the *Criminal Code* provides a general penalty for *summary* conviction charges. This section applies any time the federal government has not specified another penalty for one of these offences:

> **787.(1) General Penalty** — Unless otherwise provided by law, everyone who is convicted of an offence punishable on summary conviction is liable to *a fine of not more than five thousand dollars or to a term of imprisonment not exceeding six months or to both.* (Emphasis added.)

The provincial and territorial statutes that provide procedures for dealing with the quasi-criminal offences created by provincial, territorial or municipal governments also specify general penalties that will apply when nothing else is specified in the statute that establishes the offence. Some of these allow for fines similar to the $5,000 limit in the *Criminal Code*, but tend to avoid attaching the imprisonment option outlined in the federal statute.

KEY TERMINOLOGY

acquitted	found not guilty
actus reus	the criminal act or omission
adversarial system	our trial system — involving a contest between the parties, with a judge acting as an independent arbitrator
arbitrarily	without a legitimate legal reason
bail	a process for releasing someone who has been arrested from custody pending his or her trial
beyond a reasonable doubt	the criminal standard of proof — requires the prosecutor to present enough convincing evidence to eliminate reasonable doubts in order to secure a conviction
CPIC	Canadian Police Information Centre — a central computer based data bank containing criminal records of members of the public
criminal record	a record of convictions for federal criminal offences
dual procedure offence	also called "hybrid", Crown has choice to use summary conviction or indictable process
hybrid offence	also called "dual procedure", Crown has choice to use summary conviction or indictable process
indictable offence	the more serious federal offences, usually involve a greater potential penalty and more procedural protections for the accused person
information	the document that starts the court process for most criminal and quasi-criminal charges
mens rea	the mental element that may be required to convict someone of a criminal offence, could involve intention or recklessness
no force and effect	a law that is invalid, cannot be enforced
onus	the legal responsibility for proving something
presumed innocent	an assumption that an accused person is innocent until proven guilty in court

principles of fundamental justice	common law principles of justice preserved by s. 7 of the *Canadian Charter of Rights and Freedoms*
quasi-criminal	sharing many of the same characteristics as criminal charges, created by a province, territory or municipality
reasonable and probable grounds	the standard of belief required of a police officer to apply for a warrant or to lay a criminal charge
reasonable limits	restrictions on rights protected by the *Canadian Charter of Rights and Freedoms*
summary offence	all provincial, territorial and municipal charges and less serious federal charges
warrant	a court order authorizing a search, seizure or arrest

STATUTES MENTIONED

Canada Evidence Act, R.S.C. 1985, c. C-5, as am.

Canadian Charter of Rights and Freedoms, Part I of the *Constitution Act, 1982*, being Schedule B to the *Canada Act 1982* (U.K.), 1982, c. 11

Controlled Drugs and Substances Act, S.C. 1996, c. 19, as am.

Criminal Code, R.S.C. 1985, c. C-46, as am.

Immigration and Refugee Protection Act, S.C. 2001, c. 27, as am.

Trespass to Property Act, R.S.O. 1990, c. T.21, as am.

Youth Criminal Justice Act, S.C. 2002, c. 1, as am.

CASE MENTIONED

R. v. Ladouceur, [1990] S.C.J. No. 53, 56 C.C.C. (3d) 22 (S.C.C.)

TEST YOURSELF

1. Which level of government (federal, provincial or territorial, or municipal) is responsible for creating each of the charges listed below.

    Murder —

    Trespass —

Speeding —

Possession of Marijuana —

No overnight parking —

Fishing out of season —

Excessive noise —

Failure to provide necessaries of life to a child —

Failure to report child abuse —

2. Which of the charges listed in question one do you think are likely to be *indictable* charges? Explain why you chose these charges.

3. Which of the charges listed in question one do you think are likely to require proof of a *mens rea* component to secure a conviction? Why?

EXTRA CHALLENGE: Review the "legal rights" outlined in sections 7 through 14 of the *Canadian Charter of Rights and Freedoms*, found in Appendix 3 at the back of this text.

4. Make a note of anything contained in those sections that you don't understand so you can ask your instructor for clarification.

5. Which of the *Charter* rights do you feel will be of most importance to you, or the people with whom you will be working in your future career? Provide a reason for each choice.

Chapter 9

Criminal Law — Charging and Compelling Appearance

ARREST POWERS

An arrest involves interfering with someone's freedom. Canadian society considers this a serious matter. Section 9 of the *Canadian Charter of Rights and Freedoms* makes it clear that it should not be done "arbitrarily". This obviously means that there should be a valid legal reason for the arrest. The *Criminal Code* is the key statute providing legal justifications for arrest. Sections 495 and 31 provide specific arrest powers for *peace officers*, while sections 494 and 30 outline narrower arrest powers that could be exercised by anyone.

When discussing the *Criminal Code* arrest powers, it is important to realize that the broader powers apply to *peace officers*. This term is defined in section 2 of the *Code* and includes not only police officers, but customs officers, corrections officers, fisheries officers and Canadian Forces military police as well. It also includes a justice of the peace, sheriff, the mayor of a municipality and the pilot of an aircraft while it is in flight. Private security personnel do not have the same arrest powers as peace officers.

Obviously, peace officers are entitled to arrest someone if a judge or justice of the peace has issued a *warrant* for that person's arrest. A warrant is a court order that is issued under the authority of Part XVI of the *Criminal Code*. A judge or justice of the peace usually makes this kind of order if an accused person is facing a criminal charge, but can not be located, or if the accused has failed to attend court to face a charge, or has escaped from custody. The order directs any peace officer in the jurisdiction (usually within the province or territory where the judge or justice of the peace sits) to arrest the named individual and bring that person to court. In order for the warrant to be used in another province or territory, a copy of the warrant could be taken to a judge within that jurisdiction to be *endorsed*. This extends the effect of the order. If a warrant is originally made by a *superior court judge*, it would be valid Canada-wide, without any endorsement.

Sections 495 and 31 of the *Criminal Code* provide peace officers with arrest powers when a judge or justice of the peace has not yet been involved with the case and there is no warrant for the individual's arrest. Under section 495, a peace officer can arrest someone if the officer has reasonable grounds for believing the person has committed or is about to commit an indictable offence. The reasonable grounds could be based on convincing information received from someone else. If the officer actually finds someone in the act of committing a criminal offence, whether or not it fits in the indictable or summary categories, he or she can also arrest, though for summary or hybrid charges, or even indictable charges that fit in section 553, alternatives to arrest must be considered.

The case report of the recent Supreme Court of Canada decision, *R. v. Burke* has been included as one of the cases in Appendix 5 at the end of the book. It is a useful illustration of judges ensuring that peace officers treat restrictions on their power of arrest under section 495 seriously.

Section 31 of the *Criminal Code* allows peace officers to be proactive. An officer is authorized to arrest anyone he or she reasonably believes is about to join, or renew a *breach of the peace*. The officer can also arrest anyone he or she has witnessed committing a *breach of the peace*. The term, *breach of the peace* is not defined in the *Criminal Code*, but common law has stipulated that it would include actions that could result in actual or threatened harm to someone, or to that person's property in his or her presence. The section could be used to stop riots or any other disturbance that might result in assaultive behaviour. After being initially arrested, a person might be released without charge, or could face any number of charges under specific sections of the *Criminal Code*, depending on the behaviour involved. The concept, *breach of the peace*, is simply a justification for an arrest; it is not a *Criminal Code* charge by itself.

Section 30 of the *Criminal Code* allows *everyone* who witnesses a breach of the peace to step in and break it up and to *detain* people involved for the purpose of handing them over to a peace officer. This is not to encourage vigilantism, and as stated in section 30, members of the public are cautioned that they can use "... no more force than is reasonably necessary to prevent the continuance or renewal of the breach of the peace ...". I, for one, am more likely to dial 911 than to get into the middle of the action, but it is easy to understand the rationale for including an interventionist protection like this for members of the public who may be a little braver at trying to stop harm from being done.

Section 494 of the *Criminal Code* authorizes *anyone* to arrest a person he or she finds committing an *indictable* offence. The trickiest part of this, of course, is that very few members of the public are likely to be able to make the distinction between criminal offences that would be classified as summary or indictable. This can be challenging enough for experienced police officers.

The section also authorizes someone in lawful possession of property, or a person authorized by the owner of property (private security personnel, for example), to arrest an individual he or she finds committing an offence in relation to that property. The section was amended in 2012 to extend the time frame a little. It now allows for arrests of people who have "recently" committed an offence in relation to property. For these property offences, there is no need to decide if the potential charge would fit the summary or indictable category.

You or I, or other members of the public, are also authorized by section 494 to arrest a person we have reasonable grounds to believe has committed any criminal offence *and* is being freshly pursued by people with authority to arrest. This gives members of the public the power to assist police officers, or someone whose purse has just been stolen, in the arrest of the fleeing perpetrator.

Anyone other than a peace officer who makes an arrest must turn the person arrested over to an officer "forthwith", according to section 494(3).

Provincial and territorial statutes that provide quasi-criminal procedures to be used in relation to municipal and provincial or territorial offences generally limit powers of arrest to situations where a person who is being charged with an offence refuses to provide any identification or attempts to escape.

ALTERNATIVES TO ARREST

Subsection 495(2) of the *Criminal Code* says peace officers *shall not* arrest someone facing summary, hybrid, or section 553 indictable charges unless the arrest is necessary to identify the person, preserve evidence, or to prevent the continuation of the offence or commission of an additional offence. Similarly, provincial and territorial procedural statutes limit the number of circumstances in which a person should be arrested for quasi-criminal charges. If everyone is presumed to be innocent and has a right to a fair trial before guilt can be established, it would seem reasonable to restrict the use of the intrusion on freedom created by an arrest. The only question that arises is how do police officers ensure that someone will show up in court to face a charge if the person is not going to be kept in custody prior to the time of his or her first court appearance?

Most people facing federally-created summary conviction, hybrid or section 553 indictable charges are simply given a document called an *Appearance Notice*. Police officers carry multiple copies of these and can complete them on the side of the highway, at someone's front door or at the scene of an altercation in front of a tavern. The form used is pre-printed and has spaces for the identity of the accused, a brief outline of the charge(s) and a notification of the time and place that the accused must initially show up in court. If a charge fits the indictable or hybrid category, the document might also give a time and place that the accused must attend, prior to the first court appearance, to provide fingerprints and have identification photos taken. There is a warning on the form notifying the accused that if he or she fails to attend the first court appearance, or fingerprinting session, an additional charge of *failure to appear*, under s. 145 of the *Criminal Code* can be added. In addition, the accused is warned that a *warrant* for his or her arrest will be issued by the judge.

The accused person will be asked to sign the Appearance Notice, but this is simply to provide the police officer with a handy form of proof that the accused was appropriately notified of the time and place of the initial court appearance. Even if it is not signed, the document is valid and the officer can testify that the notice was provided to supply evidence necessary to support a charge for failure to appear.

Since these forms are intended to be used by officers in situations where they may not have easy reference to the appropriate statute, the description of the charge on the Appearance Notice does not have to be in the exact wording of the charging section. In fact, the document is simply intended to get the accused to court to face criminal or quasi-criminal charges and it is not improper if the eventual charge is different, or if additional charges are added by the time the accused person appears in court.

The officer will take his or her own copy of the completed Appearance Notice to a judge or a justice of the peace to have it *confirmed*, prior to the first court appearance by the accused. This procedural step gives the Appearance Notice the power of a court order, compelling the accused to appear in court. Once it is done the accused could be validly charged with failure to appear.

A police officer who investigates an incident that results in a criminal charge may initially take an accused person into custody, even if the charge is not one of the more serious indictable offences. This could occur for a number of reasons, including the need to diffuse a volatile situation, to allow time to secure evidence or to complete the proper identification of the accused. Once these short-term concerns have been addressed, an *officer in charge* of the police lock-up facilities could use an *appearance notice* or one of the alternative forms available to release the accused and assure the individual's attendance for the first court appearance.

A *Promise to Appear* is accurately named. An accused person would have to sign this document, promising to show up at the time and place designated for the first court appearance. If the accused refuses to sign, he or she will not likely be released prior to a bail hearing in front of a judge or justice of the peace. This form can be used for the same range of offences covered by an appearance notice (summary, hybrid and section 553 charges), plus indictable charges with maximum sentences up to five years in length.

A *Recognizance* adds an extra measure of security that the accused person will show up for the first court appearance. An accused asked to sign a *recognizance* will also be promising to pay a set charge of up to $500 if he or she fails to appear. If the accused person lives more than 200 kilometers from where he or she has been arrested, he or she may additionally be required to actually deposit up to $500 in cash or valuable property with the police before being released. Not having the money to put up could result in being kept in custody until a bail hearing can be held.

If a person has been arrested pursuant to a *warrant* and the officer in charge is still willing to consider a release, it is likely that a document called an *undertaking* will be attached to the *recognizance*. The undertaking could include requirements that the accused remain in the general area, report to the police on a regular basis, refrain from any contact with alleged victims, avoid consumption of alcohol or drugs and other similar restrictions.

Provincial and territorial procedural statutes and regulations stipulate the forms that will be used in each jurisdiction to notify an accused of a provincial, territorial or municipal charge and to assure attendance at a court hearing. Although officially bearing a variety of titles in different jurisdictions, these quasi-criminal charging forms are commonly referred to as *tickets*. The forms are similar in format to federal appearance notices. In addition, tickets often provide the option on the form of signing a "guilty" plea and paying a set fine, rather than making any court appearance.

All of the forms described above are used when police have been in contact with the accused person at an early stage in the investigation, have made a preliminary assessment of charges that will be laid and wish to provide the accused person with a notice to get the person to court to face criminal or quasi-criminal charges. None of these are the documents that officially set out the actual charge or charges the accused will face in court and trigger the court process. After any of these forms have been given to an accused, police must still prepare the document called an *information*, which was mentioned briefly in Chapter 8. This is the document that officially starts the court process in motion.

The *information* will be drafted by consulting the specific wording of the appropriate charging section, or sections, in the *Criminal Code* or other statute. On the *information*, the "informant" will be swearing that he or she has personal knowledge or reasonable and probable grounds for believing that the named accused has committed the specified offence. Once it is prepared, the *information* must be taken to a judge or justice of the peace, who has responsibility for assuring that the informant has knowledge of each of the required elements of the charge. The informant will *swear* to this knowledge before the document is accepted and signed by the judge or justice of the peace. At this time, the judge or justice of the peace will also *confirm* the validity of copies of the appearance notice, promise to appear or recognizance that was given to the accused.

There are circumstances in which police officers may investigate an offence and develop reasonable and probable grounds for believing a crime, or quasi-crime has been committed without having any contact with the potential accused. This may occur because they have not yet been able to locate the person, or persons they plan to charge. In situations like this, the procedural steps are reversed. Officers will draft an *information* and have it sworn before a judge or justice of the peace. They will also ask the judge or justice of the peace to issue a *summons*. A *summons* is a court order, requiring the accused person to show up in court at a designated time and place to face the charge outlined in the *information*. The *summons* will then have to be *served* on the named accused when he or she can be located. Or, it could be validly served on the accused by leaving it at his or her known residence with anyone who appears to be at least 16 years old.

BAIL ISSUES

If an accused person has been arrested and is not released by the arresting officer or the officer in charge of the lock-up, he or she will be entitled to be brought before a judge or a justice of the peace for a *bail* hearing. Section 503 of the *Criminal Code* requires that this occur within 24 hours, or if a judge or justice of the peace is not available in that time frame, as soon as possible.

This probably relieves the need for people who have been locked up to make use of the ancient common law protection that has been enshrined in clause (*c*) of section 10 of the *Canadian Charter of Rights and Freedoms*: "Everyone has the right on arrest or detention ... to have the validity of the detention determined by way of *habeas corpus* and to be released if the detention is not valid". Since the time of ancient Rome, this concept has been used to protect citizens from the arbitrary actions of state agents, like police officers. If these agents lock a person up, the person has a right to be brought before an independent decision-maker (judge) to have the validity of his or her incarceration assessed.

The procedure that will be followed at a bail hearing is set out in section 515 of the *Criminal Code*. Interestingly, the section calls the process *judicial interim release*, rather than bail. This title is actually a good description of what is going on. A judge or justice of the peace will consider the appropriateness of ordering that an accused person be released from custody during the interim period between his or her arrest and the first court appearance scheduled to deal with the charge.

The section makes it imperative that an accused *shall* be released on the giving of an *undertaking*, a simple written promise to show up in court, unless the prosecutor can *show cause* why the person should be kept in custody or more complex release requirements added. Because of the *onus*, or responsibility being placed on the prosecutor, many people also call a bail hearing a *show cause hearing*.

Subsection 515(10) outlines justifications that could be established by the prosecutor for keeping the accused in custody. The first is commonly called the *primary ground*, "where the detention is necessary to ensure his or her attendance in court ...". Professional criminals quickly learn that if they are ever convicted of a charge of failure to appear, the prosecutor will always make a big issue of this at future bail hearings. It provides ready evidence that it may not be safe to release the accused from custody again.

Clause (*b*) in section 515(10) provides a second justification for keeping an accused locked up. This one is commonly referred to as the *secondary ground*, "where the detention is necessary for the protection or safety of the public ... including any substantial likelihood that the accused will, if released from custody, commit a criminal offence or interfere with the administration of justice ...". A risk of interference with the administration of justice could include evidence that the accused has threatened potential witnesses or has attempted to destroy evidence.

There is a clause (*c*) to subsection 515(10). It allows for a detention order if it's necessary "... to maintain confidence in the administration of justice". This clause directs a judge to consider matters like the seriousness of the charge and whether firearms were used. It also suggests a judge consider the "apparent strength of the prosecution's case". It would seem a little tough for a judge to determine this without turning a bail hearing into a mini trial and most bail hearings are pretty streamlined affairs.

Before a judge or justice of the peace decides to continue keeping the accused locked up, he or she would have to consider the possibility of release using alternative orders, outlined in section 515, that include escalating conditions and guarantees attached to ensure the accused person's appearance. These range from *undertakings* with conditions attached, through *recognizances* that involve promises to pay sums of money to actual deposits of cash to guarantee attendance.

If the accused person has no money or personal assets to put up for bail guarantees, a judge may be prepared to let someone else act as a *surety*. This could be a relative or friend of the accused who is willing to pledge his or her own assets as a guarantee of the future attendance of the accused. Unlike in the United States, Canadian law does not allow private lenders to act as professional bail bondsmen.

If an accused is charged with murder, treason or piracy, all of which require special treatment because of their inclusion on the short list of the most serious indictable charges set aside by section 469 of the *Criminal Code*, a bail hearing that results in the release of the accused cannot be held by a justice of the peace or a provincial court judge. The accused will have to wait until a justice of the superior court of criminal jurisdiction in the province or territory is available to conduct a bail hearing. For these charges, detention in custody pending trial is the norm, rather than the exception. In fact, section 522 of the *Criminal Code* stipulates that for one of these charges, the accused will have the *onus* of convincing a superior court justice that he or she should be released, rather than the responsibility of justifying custody or other restrictions resting on the prosecutor.

Since a *presumption of innocence* is both a common law and constitutionally protected principle of fundamental justice in our criminal justice system, this kind of *reverse onus*, placing responsibility on the accused, is exceptional and courts will only support it if they consider it a reasonable limit for special circumstances. In addition to the most serious indictable charges listed in section 469, which receive special treatment throughout the criminal justice process, section 515(6) of the *Criminal Code* lists several other special circumstances in which the *onus* will be on the accused to justify his or her release at the bail hearing. This list includes a situation where the accused is alleged to have committed a new offence when he or she was already on bail for a previous charge. It also covers people who are not ordinarily resident in Canada and are alleged to have committed a serious indictable offence, people who are alleged to have committed the offence in question in order to benefit a criminal organization and people who are alleged to have committed an act of terrorism. Offences alleged to have been committed with firearms, explosives or other prohibited weapons also trigger this special treatment. Judges, including justices of the Supreme Court of Canada, have ruled that shifting the responsibility to the accused is reasonable in some of these listed circumstances.

In fact, the approach to bail taken in section 515 of the *Criminal Code* would appear to be pretty consistent with the constitutional protection added to the concept of bail by clause (*e*) of section 11 of the *Canadian Charter of Rights and Freedoms*. It states that a person charged with an offence has a right, "not to be denied reasonable bail without just cause".

ARRAIGNMENT PROCESS

An accused person's *first appearance* in court to face a criminal or quasi-criminal charge is also called an *arraignment*. The purpose of the arraignment is to formally present the accused person with the allegations of criminal behaviour that society is making against him or her. This will be accomplished by reading the *information* containing those allegations.

Subsection 800(2) of the *Criminal Code* stipulates that a defendant facing a summary conviction charge may either attend his or her arraignment "… personally or by counsel or agent". In other words, the accused may not need to show up as long as it has been arranged that a lawyer or non-lawyer agent will attend on the defendant's behalf. The section goes on to state that a judge does have the discretion to require personal attendance by the defendant at the arraignment. Most provincial and territorial statutes establishing the procedure for municipal, provincial or territorial offences contain similar provisions.

Individuals facing indictable charges must appear personally. They are, of course, entitled to appear with a lawyer, but the lawyer can't appear instead of the accused. Non-lawyer agents are not entitled to represent a defendant in relation to an indictable charge.

If an accused does not show up to face the charges and neither a lawyer nor an agent is there to explain, a judge will check to ensure that the accused was given proper notice of the time and place of the arraignment. If that can be established, the judge will *adjourn* or postpone the arraignment and issue an *arrest warrant*. This would authorize any police officer in the province or territory to take the accused into custody to ensure his or her attendance in court.

Most accused people will make their first court appearance in the *provincial court* of criminal jurisdiction. The only exception is for people charged with one of the most serious of *indictable* charges, listed in section 469 of the *Criminal Code*. The entire process for these charges, including the arraignment, falls within the jurisdiction of the *superior court* for the province or territory.

If a person has been charged with a *hybrid* offence, the prosecutor will be asked to choose whether the case will be dealt with as a summary conviction or an indictable matter immediately after the charge is read. This choice is entirely within the prerogative of the prosecutor and cannot be challenged by the defendant or overturned by the judge.

The arraignment process generally differs for *summary* and *indictable* charges, primarily because a person facing an indictable charge is usually entitled to choose, or *elect* the court in which he or she would like the trial to be held. That choice will most often be made at the time of the arraignment in the provincial court. The accused can opt to stay in the provincial court, or go to the superior court, where there are two additional choices: trial by judge alone or by judge and jury.

People being arraigned for a summary conviction charge or for one of the less serious indictable charges listed in subsection 553 of the *Criminal Code* have no choice of court. Their entire court process will be held in the provincial court where the arraignment takes place. As a result, once the charge has been read, the accused will be asked to enter a plea.

If the accused person chooses to enter a plea of "not guilty", the judge will then ask the prosecutor and the defence lawyer or agent how long they expect the trial to last. Answers will depend on the complexity of the allegations and the number of witnesses that will likely have to testify. Once the judge has this information, he or she will check for a suitable time frame on his or her trial calendar and propose a date for the trial to be held at some point in the future. Both the prosecutor and defence counsel may be asked to comment on their own availability and the availability of the key witnesses before the trial date is set.

If the accused enters a plea of "guilty" there will be no need to set a trial date to determine guilt or innocence. The judge may proceed immediately to the *sentencing* stage of the hearing, or may set a date in the near future to listen to submissions from the prosecutor and defence counsel on their views of the appropriate sentencing range for this particular accused and this offence. The judge may want to consider a *pre-sentence report* prior to imposing a sentence. This type of report is usually prepared by someone working for the provincial or territorial probation services unit. The compiler of the report will seek information about the offence and the offender from victims, members of the community, the offender's employer or school counselor, or anyone else who can furnish useful background detail. Both the prosecutor and the offender's lawyer or agent will receive a copy of the pre-sentence report prior to the sentencing hearing, so they can have an opportunity to comment on the contents. After receiving any input the judge feels is appropriate, he or she will decide on the sentence that will be imposed. This becomes a court order.

When the defendant is being arraigned on an indictable charge that does not fit within the lists of offences covered by sections 553 or 469 of the *Criminal Code*, he or she will be asked to make an election, or choice of court, immediately following the reading of the charge. If the defendant chooses to stay in the provincial court, the process will follow the same steps as described above for a summary conviction charge from this point on.

If the defendant chooses a trial in superior court, with a judge alone, or a judge and jury, there will be an extra step in the process before the matter is sent on to the superior court. The provincial court judge who accepted the election will check his or her calendar for the time needed to schedule a *preliminary inquiry*. This is a hearing during which the prosecutor will have to call some of the witnesses who would eventually be expected to testify during the trial. The defence lawyer will have an opportunity to cross-examine after each witness testifies for the prosecution. During the preliminary inquiry the provincial court judge will assess the evidence to make sure that the prosecution has enough proof to establish a *prima facie case* against the accused. What this means is that the prosecutor must be able to produce some evidence of each of the required elements of the crime, as it is described in the statute. At this stage, the provincial court judge is not looking for proof beyond a reasonable doubt. Rather the judge is ensuring that the prosecution has enough evidence to make it worthwhile to send the case on to the superior court for a trial.

Very few cases are *dismissed*, or thrown out following the preliminary inquiry, but it does provide a procedural protection for the accused and can furnish an opportunity for the defence lawyer to assess the quality of the witnesses and the evidence that has been compiled by the prosecution. Sometimes an accused will re-elect and return to the provincial court to enter a "guilty" plea following this preview of the strength of the prosecution case.

CHOICE OF COURT

There are both strategic and practical reasons why a defendant might choose one court over another when entitled to an election in relation to an indictable charge.

Strategically, an initial choice of a trial in superior court with a judge and jury can be legitimately used as a delaying tactic to postpone the trial. Because this choice would require the scheduling of a preliminary inquiry in the provincial court before the case could be sent on, this could result in a delay of several months. Once the decision is made to proceed to superior court, a court date must be set far enough in advance to allow for the selection of a jury. In addition, jury trials tend to require a larger block of time due to the need for the judge to assess the admissibility of evidence without the jury in attendance and the added need for the judge to explain a wide range of procedural matters to the jurors. All these factors result in delays which could work to the advantage of the defence. Evidence might go missing. Memories could fade and the overall strength of the prosecution case might be diminished by the delay.

There is also the strategic advantage for the defence of getting a preview of the prosecution's witnesses and the strength of the case that must be met during the preliminary inquiry. The delay could also give the defence more time to gather evidence to respond to the prosecution case and to research the applicable law and potential defences. If the accused is not in custody and is working, he or she could gather the resources to pay for effective legal representation, or to cover any eventual fine if that is part of a sentence in the event that the defendant is convicted.

If the accused is in custody awaiting trial, he or she may not be in favour of delay and may choose to be tried before a judge alone or in the provincial court simply because the process will be quicker.

An accused who does not qualify for *legal aid* may also choose a quicker route to trial simply because he or she cannot afford expert legal help through the delay and additional court time required for a preliminary inquiry and jury selection process.

Some lawyers will recommend that if a client's best defence strategy is based on technical legal points, it may be better to present the evidence and make these points in front of a highly trained legal expert like a judge alone, rather than in front of a jury.

On the other hand, if a defence is based on working on the sympathy of the people assessing the case, some defendants might receive a more sympathetic audience from a jury than from a judge who hears hundreds of these tales over the course of a career.

A choice of a superior court judge over a provincial court judge, or vice versa may be done on the advice of a defence lawyer who knows the track record of the respective judges or perhaps, the sentencing tendencies of these judges in the event of a guilty plea or a conviction following the presentation of evidence.

KEY TERMINOLOGY

adjourn	postpone, set over to a later date
appearance notice	document used by police officers to get an accused person to court for a first appearance on a summary, hybrid, or s. 553 *Criminal Code* offence
arraignment	first appearance in court to face a criminal charge
arrest	interfere with someone's freedom by preventing freedom of movement
arrest warrant	court order authorizing police officers to arrest a named individual
bail	a process for releasing someone who has been arrested from custody pending his or her trial
breach of the peace	actions that could result in actual or threatened harm to someone, or to a person's property in the person's presence
confirmed	judge or justice of the peace will review and endorse an appearance notice, promise to appear or recognizance issued by a police officer
detain	prevent someone from going where he or she wants to go
dismiss	court order eliminating a criminal or quasi-criminal charge against an accused person
elect	to make a choice
endorse	a local judge re-affirming the effect of a court order made in another jurisdiction
failure to appear	didn't show up at the time and place appointed for an appearance in court or for fingerprints and photos
first appearance	also called an "arraignment", initial time in court to face a criminal or quasi-criminal charge
habeas corpus	the right to be brought before a judge to have the validity of incarceration assessed
hybrid offence	also known as a "dual procedure" offence, can be treated as a summary conviction or indictable offence — at the discretion of the prosecutor

indictable offence	the more serious federal offences, usually involve a greater potential penalty and more procedural protections for the accused person
information	the document that starts the court process for most criminal and quasi-criminal charges
judicial interim release	the name used for the "bail" process in the *Criminal Code*
justice of the peace	an administrative officer appointed by the province to perform a variety of functions in the criminal justice process
legal aid	a scheme to provide expert legal representation for people who fall below the limits of a financial means test and face serious legal consequences in court
officer in charge	the police officer in charge of the local lock-up, given extra release powers in the *Criminal Code*
peace officer	defined in the Interpretation section of the *Criminal Code* — includes police officers, correctional officers, customs officers and others
preliminary inquiry	a process during which the prosecutor is required to produce enough evidence to convince a provincial court judge that an indictable case is worth sending on to a superior court for trial
pre-sentence report	background information to assist the judge at the time of sentencing someone who has been convicted of an offence — usually prepared by a probation officer
presumption of innocence	a fundamental principle in the criminal justice system — an accused person is assumed to be innocent until a court decides otherwise
prima facie case	this is what a prosecutor has to establish at a preliminary inquiry to convince a judge to send the case to superior court for trial — some evidence of each of the elements of the charge as described in the charging statute
primary ground	the necessity to keep an accused person locked up or otherwise restricted with bail conditions to ensure that he or she will show up in court to face a criminal charge

promise to appear	a document used by an officer in charge of a lock-up to release someone facing a relatively minor charge who is prepared to sign a promise to attend court for a first appearance
recognizance	a document used by an officer in charge of a lock-up to release someone facing a relatively minor charge who is prepared to deposit up to $500 or commit to paying that amount to secure release pending a first appearance
secondary ground	the necessity to keep a person locked up or otherwise restricted with bail conditions to ensure he or she won't commit another offence or interfere with the administration of justice
sentencing	the process of determining the appropriate punishment for someone who has been convicted of a criminal or quasi-criminal offence
show cause hearing	another name for a "bail" hearing — prosecutor must convince a judge or justice of the peace that the accused person should be kept in custody or that restrictions be placed on release
summary offence	all provincial, territorial and municipal charges and less serious federal charges
summons	a judge's order that an accused person attend court to face a criminal or quasi-criminal charge
surety	a family member or friend who is prepared to pledge money or property to secure an accused person's release from custody and to guarantee that the accused will attend court to face a charge
undertaking	a signed promise that an accused person will attend court to face charges, could include conditions that must be followed during the period of release from custody
warrant	a court order authorizing a search, seizure or arrest

STATUTES MENTIONED

Canadian Charter of Rights and Freedoms, Part I of the *Constitution Act, 1982*, being Schedule B to the *Canada Act 1982* (U.K.), 1982, c. 11

Criminal Code, R.S.C. 1985, c. C-46, as am.

CASE MENTIONED

R. v. Burke, [2009] S.C.J. No. 57, 2009 SCC 57 (S.C.C.)

TEST YOURSELF

Describe the appropriate PROCEDURE (arrest, appearance notice, warrant, *etc.*) to ensure that each of these accused persons appear in court to face their charges:

1. A student is caught spray-painting swear words on a professor's office door.

2. A 20-year-old woman is charged with shoplifting a pair of nylons from a department store and given an appearance notice. She has now failed to appear for her first court date.

3. A young woman has been spotted in Peterborough, Ontario. Police believe that she is the subject of a warrant that was issued in Victoria, British Columbia in relation to a failure to appear on a charge that arose out of a logging protest (she had chained herself to a tree).

4. A 15-year-old cyclist is stopped by a police officer for speeding down a local hill at high rate of speed. He refuses to tell the officer his name and simply rides away.

5. A middle-aged professor is spotted by a police officer failing to stop at a stop sign at an intersection close to the university/college.

   The officer is unable to catch the incredibly athletic professor before he turns into the driveway of a house in a local neighbourhood and goes inside. When the officer knocks on the door, no one answers.

6. Police are in pursuit of a suspect in a purse-grabbing incident that occurred on a downtown street, in broad daylight. The suspect ran into a nearby church and the door now seems to be locked.

EXTRA CHALLENGE

7. A young man is one of three suspects in a sexual assault. Police do not yet have enough evidence to a lay a charge, but would like to bring him in for questioning.

Chapter 10

Criminal Law — Trial Issues

JURY TRIALS

Clause 11(*f*) of the *Canadian Charter of Rights and Freedoms* provides the right to a trial by jury for anyone charged with an offence that has a maximum penalty of five years or more. An exception is made for members of the armed forces who are tried under military law in a military hearing. That procedure provides for a panel of adjudicators.

Any Canadian law involving potential jail time of five years or more would be a federally created indictable offence. No provincial, territorial or municipal offence would fit the criteria, nor would federal offences that are categorized as summary conviction matters. There are still a wide range of offences that do qualify for jury trials from assault and criminal negligence causing bodily harm, through break and entry of a home to trafficking in a controlled substance and on to homicide in all its manifestations. Despite the large number of opportunities for defendants to choose a trial by jury, only a relatively small percentage of Canadian criminal trials involve jurors in the decision-making process. Accused persons simply don't exercise their right to elect this mode of trial very often.

Despite the rarity of jury trials in Canada today, the concept enjoys a lengthy history in our justice system and involves an interesting body of law that differs in practice from some of the American jury trial principles that are often portrayed in popular media. For example, while Canadian jurors are expected to be impartial decision-makers who will base their final assessment of the guilt or innocence of the accused solely on the evidence they hear during the trial, Canadian lawyers are not permitted to go through a lengthy questioning process to determine if the jurors have been influenced in advance by reports of the incident they may have seen or heard on television or radio. Canadian judges do not expect jurors to be hermits without an interest in current events. Rather, jurors are simply asked if they can impartially assess the case on the evidence presented at trial, rather than pre-judging the matter. Jurors are trusted to answer honestly.

Canadian prosecutors, defence lawyers and the accused are not allowed to communicate with potential jurors, directly or indirectly, outside the courtroom. Lawyers are not permitted to conduct surveys or interview neighbours or employers of potential jurors in an attempt to assess the jurors' views on issues that may be relevant at the trial.

Section 626 of the *Criminal Code* gives provinces the right to set the qualifications for jurors in their jurisdiction. As a result, the criteria for jury qualification may vary from province to province. Nevertheless, there is common ground. Jurors will usually be selected in a form of random draw from lists that are initially compiled for other purposes, like the enumeration lists of people who have registered to vote in municipal elections or tax assessment lists.

The statutes also commonly disqualify certain individuals from jury duty, including people who are mentally incompetent, police, judges, lawyers, and others professionally employed in the justice system. Eliminating people with specialized legal training is intended to prevent these individuals from exercising too much of an influence on other jurors. Juries are supposed to be composed of the "peers" of the defendant, made up of a cross section of local residents, not legal experts.

It is illegal to ignore a *jury summons*. The document has the effect of a court order, requiring attendance to be part of a jury panel, from which jurors for a particular trial can be selected. A warrant could be issued for the arrest of someone who ignores the summons.

Judges have the right to excuse potential jurors from jury duty pursuant to section 632 of the *Criminal Code*. Jurors will be excused if they have a personal relationship with the accused, the judge, one of the lawyers or a potential witness in a trial. Judges also have the discretion to excuse jurors if sitting on the jury will cause personal hardship to the juror. This could include a range of difficulties from a parent without a practical ability to secure child care for young children to someone with restrictive health problems or a self-employed individual with no one to cover the business during a prolonged trial. Employers and educational institutions are expected to make accommodations so that people who have been summoned for jury duty will be able to serve.

Section 19 of the *Canadian Charter of Rights and Freedoms* guarantees a defendant the right to a trial in either English or French, Canada's two official languages. This may create a special challenge for court personnel in gathering a panel of potential jurors in parts of the country where one language is much more prominent than the other.

Once a panel of potential jurors has been compiled, the selection of the 12 jurors required for a particular trial will proceed with both the prosecutor and defence lawyer being able to challenge the inclusion of individual jurors whose names are drawn from a box held by the *clerk* of the court. An unlimited number of challenges can be made for one of the *causes* listed in section 638 of the *Criminal Code*. Most of the *causes*, like an inability to speak the official language of the trial or to physically act as a juror, will be addressed in a survey of the entire panel conducted by court officials in advance of the actual jury selection hearing. It is more likely for one of the lawyers to raise the issue of a potential juror being biased toward the prosecution or the defence. Canadian judges do not allow lengthy questioning to test for such bias and will usually pre-screen the questions that can be asked. After the first two jurors have been chosen for the trial, they will be the ones who assess whether or not the challenge for cause is legitimate and if the potential juror challenged should be excluded from the panel.

The prosecution and defence are both allowed a limited number of *peremptory challenges* of potential jurors, 20 for murder trials and 12 for most other charges. The lawyers do not have to provide any reason at all for these challenges and the challenged jurors will usually be eliminated from the panel without being asked any questions. Lawyers will develop their own rationale for the use of these peremptory challenges. In some types of cases, they may want to eliminate as many older jurors as they can, in other types of cases, they may decide to limit the number of male or female jurors selected or jurors who are frowning.

Once a panel of 12 jurors has been selected, it will become their responsibility to sit as the *triers of fact*, responsible for determining whether or not the evidence that will be presented at trial is sufficient to prove beyond a reasonable doubt that the accused committed the crime alleged. The judge will provide any legal instruction they require, but it will be up to the jury to decide guilt or innocence. As was recently pointed out by the Supreme Court of Canada in a case called *R. v. H. (W.)*, even appeal court judges are expected to give great deference to jury decisions.

In Canada, the jury's decision must be unanimous. If the 12 cannot agree on a verdict after a concerted effort to reach unanimity, the judge may be forced to dismiss the jury and start the trial all over again with a new panel of jurors.

MENTAL FITNESS TO STAND TRIAL

If an accused is mentally disordered to the extent that he or she would be unable to understand the court procedure, the potential consequences of the trial, or to communicate effectively with a lawyer, a judge could rule that the person is *unfit to stand trial*. While section 672.22 of the *Criminal Code* makes it clear that judges are to *presume* that each accused is fit to stand trial, a prosecutor, defence lawyer or the judge can all raise the issue of lack of the appropriate mental capacity.

In order to assist in arriving at a decision, the judge has the power to order that the defendant be given a psychiatric assessment and the trial will be adjourned until this can be done. Frequently, individuals who are found to be mentally disordered will be admitted to a mental health facility under the authority of the provincial or territorial mental health laws. The judge will intermittently review the person's status and if he or she regains sanity to the extent of being able to understand the trial process, the trial can resume.

TIME LIMITS

Subsection 786(2) of the *Criminal Code*, which applies to *summary conviction offences*, states that, "No proceedings shall be instituted more than six months after the time when the subject-matter of the proceedings arose ... ." Provincial and territorial procedural laws affecting municipal, provincial and territorial charges include similar provisions. What do they mean? Since the document that actually "institutes" criminal procedures is the *information*, an *information* must be sworn within six months of the alleged date of the summary conviction offence. If the investigation is not far enough along to lay a charge, or if the evidence of an offence has not come to light before the six-month time limit expires, it is too late to prosecute someone for a summary conviction offence.

Except in the case of a charge of treason, under sections 46-48 of the *Criminal Code*, which has its own unique limits, there are no specific time limits for proceeding on *indictable offences*.

Clause 11(*b*) of the *Canadian Charter of Rights and Freedoms* states that "Any person *charged with* an offence has the right to be tried within a reasonable time." (Emphasis added.) This is designed to ensure that the prosecution keeps the case moving along *after* a charge has been laid against a defendant. Unreasonable delays by the prosecution after making an allegation of criminal behaviour against the individual have resulted in judges granting a *stay*, or stoppage of the trial process under this section.

Clause 11(*d*) of the *Charter*, which assures a person charged a "fair" hearing and the "principles of fundamental justice", preserved by section 7 of the *Charter*, might provide an accused person with an avenue for challenging a charge that was laid a long time after evidence of an indictable offence came to light. This sort of delay might harm the ability of the defendant to gather evidence that could assist in his or her defence and could be seen as affecting the fairness of the trial. However, many prosecutions have been allowed to go ahead where the police simply did not have sufficient evidence to proceed with a charge against a defendant until 10, 15 or even 20 years after the offence was alleged to have occurred.

QUICK OVERVIEW OF EVIDENCE ISSUES

At a criminal trial, the prosecutor will make an *opening statement* to provide an overview of the case that will be presented against the accused person. When the defence lawyer's time comes, he or she may also make an opening statement, focusing on the aspects of the evidence that the judge or jury will hear that may be helpful to the defence. Both are also likely to make *closing statements*, after all the evidence has been presented, to draw the judge or jury's attention to the pieces of evidence that were most supportive of their respective positions. Nothing that the lawyers say is considered to be *evidence* on which the judge or jury can base its decision.

Evidence is information that can be considered by the judge or jury in coming to a decision about the guilt or innocence of the defendant. Evidence is almost always presented to the court through the oral testimony of witnesses. Even when it is something physical or visual, like a knife, or photo of a crime scene, the context that makes the evidence *relevant* will have to be explained by a witness.

Information presented to the judge or jury during the trial should always be *relevant*. Courts want to decide cases based on evidence that has *probative value*, or tends to prove or disprove one of the key issues. What are the key issues in most criminal trials?

(1) *ACTUS REUS* — Did the accused person do one of the activities prohibited by the *Criminal Code* or other statute?

(2) *MENS REA* — IF intention is a necessary element of the offence, do the accused person's actions tend to demonstrate the required intent?

(3) IDENTITY — Is it clear that this accused person did the prohibited activity?

(4) CREDIBILITY — Are the witnesses believable?

During a criminal trial, the prosecutor has the *onus* of proving that the accused person committed the crime. As a result, the prosecutor will call his or her witnesses first. When all of the prosecution witnesses have testified, the defence lawyer could make a motion, asking the judge to rule that the evidence presented is not sufficient to prove the case beyond a reasonable doubt. If that motion is successful, the defendant will be acquitted. If it is not, the defence lawyer may then call witnesses to refute the testimony of the prosecution witnesses or to lay the basis for a defence.

The lawyer or agent who calls a witness to testify is usually not allowed to ask *leading* (suggestive) questions of that witness. As a result, it is necessary for the lawyer to meet with the witnesses before the trial to discuss the type of questions that will be asked and the potential answers the witness can provide.

A witness can go over prepared notes, or a transcript of his or her prior testimony (*e.g.*, testimony provided at a preliminary inquiry), before going into court to testify. Once the witness takes the stand, he or she is expected to testify from memory. Most witnesses cannot use notes to refresh their memory in court. If a witness wants to use notes to refresh his or her memory, he or she must ask the judge's permission. The judge will only grant permission if the witness is someone who works in a profession in which it is normal business practice to make notes as part of an investigation and if it is clear that the notes being referred to were made at the time of the event recorded, or shortly thereafter. Using these criteria, police and forensic investigators are usually granted permission to refer to notes made during their investigations.

After each witness has testified for the prosecutor or defence lawyer or agent who called the witness, the opposing lawyer or agent is entitled to *cross-examine* the witness to challenge the truthfulness or accuracy of what was said. The lawyer or agent can and will use leading questions to suggest alternatives to the witness during a cross-examination. If the witness has relied on notes, the opposing lawyer is entitled to look at those notes and could use discrepancies between what has been recorded and the testimony of the witness to challenge the value of the witness's account of events.

When a witness is testifying in court, the opposing lawyer can *object* to the type of question being asked, or challenge the *admissibility* of the type of evidence the witness is being asked to present. When an objection is made, a witness should wait until the judge rules on the issue before answering.

Perhaps the most common type of objection will occur when one of the lawyers is simply challenging whether or not a particular piece of testimony is relevant. Even if evidence is relevant, judges have discretion to exclude evidence if the unfairness or prejudice it would cause the accused outweighs the probative value. For example, if Dan Jones is on trial for the sexual assault of Vera Waters, a jury might find it very relevant that Dan had four prior convictions for sexually assaulting other victims. Nevertheless, if they were allowed to hear that evidence, they might focus more on that than the fact that the prosecutor may not have enough evidence to prove, beyond a reasonable doubt, that Dan committed this assault. As a result, Dan might be wrongfully convicted because of past behaviour, rather than because of convincing evidence that he committed this particular crime.

Most witnesses are not allowed to express an opinion when they testify. They are called to court because they have seen or heard something that is relevant. Exceptions are made for *expert* witnesses, if the expert opinion that they can provide will help the judge or jury in arriving at a decision. Before an expert is allowed to express an opinion, the judge will assess:

(a)   if the expert really does have special knowledge that would assist the judge or jury in reaching a just decision; and

(b)   if the subject matter is one that really requires an expert evaluation.

Pathologists and forensic analysts are examples of experts who testify despite the fact that they were not in attendance when a criminal incident occurred. They may not have seen or heard what happened, but they can use their scientific expertise to study the evidence that has been left behind and provide a helpful opinion as to how it got there, who left it, at what time and under what circumstances. The judge or jury may not be able to work out any of these details without the guidance of the expert in explaining the relevance of the evidence that has been gathered.

Hearsay evidence creates special problems and a judge must decide if it can be used in a trial. Evidence of an out-of-court statement that the prosecutor or defence wants to use to prove the truth of what was said is usually NOT admissible. The court generally wants to hear from the person who made the original statement, not just from someone who has heard what was said. If the original statement maker cannot be cross-examined in court, there is no way of testing the truthfulness of what was said at the time the out-of-court statement was made.

There are important exceptions that will allow for the admission of hearsay statements when the circumstances would tend to show that it's likely that the contents of those original statements are trustworthy and the original speaker is not available. Examples would include dying declarations by a victim who spoke, knowing he or she was about to die. Judges are inclined to let these in, operating on the premise that the deceased would be unlikely to lie in these circumstances. Judges have also made exceptions for the out-of-court statements of very young sexual assault victims, who may be considered too young to testify in court, but whose out-of-court allegations to responsible adults have a ring of truth and provide a necessary evidentiary link.

Out-of-court confessions by the accused are also admissible. The rationale for this hearsay exception is that the person who is alleged to have made the original statement is in the courtroom and available to refute what is reported to have been stated previously if he or she chooses to do so.

DEFENCES

In its broadest context, a *defence* could be anything that results in the acquittal of an accused person. If the prosecutor cannot provide evidence that convinces a judge or jury that the accused person acted in a way that provides all of the elements of the *actus reus* and *mens rea* (if required) of a crime or quasi-crime, then that defendant must be acquitted. The simplest defence is a justifiable claim that the prosecutor has not proven all of the elements of the offence beyond a reasonable doubt.

Subsection 8(3) of the *Criminal Code* states that, "Every rule or principle of the common law that renders any circumstance a justification or excuse for an act or a defence to a charge continues in force … except in so far as they are altered by or are inconsistent with this Act or any Act of Parliament." This statutory provision recognizes that judges have created common law defences to criminal charges and that these can only be changed through the specific wording of a statute.

For years, judges have grappled with the defence of *intoxication*. It is fairly easy to understand that someone could be so drunk that he or she may be incapable of forming the intent to commit a crime, apparently providing a defence related to the *mens rea* element of some offences. Nevertheless, judges have been reluctant to allow people who voluntarily and recklessly became drunk to use this as an excuse for their behaviour. In an attempt to address this issue, the federal government added section 33.1 to the *Criminal Code*. It states that for crimes that include an element of assault, or interference with the bodily integrity of someone else, "It is not a defence … that the accused, by reason of self-induced intoxication, lacked the general intent or voluntariness to commit the offence …".

The resulting state of our law seems to be that someone could raise extreme intoxication as a defence to a criminal charge that requires proof of a *specific intent*. A charge like first degree murder would be an example. Not only does this charge require a wrongful killing, section 231(2) of the *Criminal Code* also specifies that the defendant's actions would have to be "planned and deliberate". It is certainly conceivable that evidence could be produced at a trial that would raise a doubt about a drunken defendant being capable of the required "planning and deliberation". Nevertheless, the defendant could still be convicted of manslaughter, because that charge only requires the general intent of committing a wrongful action that causes death and the drunkenness defence would be precluded by section 33.1. Similarly, if an accused were charged with robbery, contrary to clause 343(c) of the *Criminal Code*, which prohibits assaulting someone *with intent to steal*, evidence of extreme drunkenness could provide a defence related to the capacity to form the intent to steal. The accused may still be convicted of common assault. This charge only requires the general intent of an intentional application of force and section 33.1 makes it clear that intoxication will not be a valid defence to that charge.

Intoxication is considered a *partial defence*. In a small number of cases, it may provide a defence to very serious criminal charges, but the accused person will not get off the hook entirely. He or she is likely to be convicted of a *lesser and included offence* that incorporates some of the same elements of the original charge, but not a specific type of thought process that would suggest a fully operating mind.

Automatism is another common law defence that has caused problems for judges. Expert witnesses have testified that some individuals have committed criminal actions while in an unconscious or involuntary state, caused by blows to the head or sleepwalking. The Supreme Court of Canada has accepted the validity of this evidence and the defence in *R. v. Bleta* and *R. v. Parks*. If successful, this defence results in a full acquittal since an action done involuntarily must have been done without fault.

There are a number of statutory defences included in the *Criminal Code*, including the defence of *mental disorder* in section 16, *compulsion by threats* in section 17, *defence of person* or *defence of property* in sections 34 and 35 and *provocation* in section 232.

Section 16 of the *Criminal Code* removes the criminal responsibility of a person who suffers from a mental disorder (defined in section 2 as a "disease of the mind"), "... that rendered the person incapable of appreciating the nature and quality of the act ... or of knowing that it was wrong". There are, obviously, people suffering from mental disorders who wouldn't qualify to use this defence. A judge or jury would have to hear convincing evidence from mental health experts who would be prepared to say that the defendant was so mentally disordered at the time of the crime as to be incapable of comprehending that the behaviour was wrong. If the defence is successful, the accused person is neither acquitted nor convicted; he or she is labelled as being *not criminally responsible*.

Such a finding allows for a variety of appropriate *dispositions*, or court orders, affecting the future of the person so labelled. Dispositions must take into account the mental condition of the individual and the benefit of reintegration into society, if possible, but also must consider the need to protect the public if the individual poses a danger. A *Review Board*, including mental health experts, is established in each province to assist the judge in deciding how to deal with the individual. The disposition could allow for a *discharge*, a form of release into the community with a wide variety of possible conditions attached to the release. Alternatively, the disposition could require that the person be locked up in a mental health facility. Periodic reviews of the status of the individual are required, but if he or she is assessed to be a continuing danger, the use of this defence could result in the person being held involuntarily in a mental health facility for a significant period of time. At the time of writing the updates to this edition, the federal government has proposed an increased review role for judges and more limited options to deal with the most potentially dangerous individuals who are judged to be not criminally responsible.

Section 17 of the *Criminal Code* provides a defence for someone who commits a crime while being threatened with death or bodily harm. It must be reasonable to believe that the threat will be acted upon and the person who is doing the threatening would have to be present when the crime was committed. The use of the defence is very strictly limited. The section specifies that it is *not* available for a long list of charges that include murder, sexual assault, robbery, arson, hostage taking and assault with a weapon.

There is also a common law defence of *duress* that is similar to the statutory defence. It also requires a real, immediate threat of physical harm. Judges will not allow defendants to successfully employ this defence if there was an avenue of escape available.

The *defence of person* section in the *Criminal Code* (section 34) makes it clear that a person can use force to defend himself or "another person". The key is that the responding action must be "reasonable in the circumstances". Subsection 34(2) lists a number of factors that can be taken into account in deciding on the reasonableness of the response. They include the attributes of the parties involved and the history of their interactions, as well as the availability of other methods of response.

Section 35 of the *Criminal Code* provides a defence for someone who needs to take action to prevent someone from unlawfully entering onto, removing or damaging property. Again, the action taken in response must be reasonable in the circumstances.

There is a controversial partial defence provided in section 232 of the *Criminal Code*. Murder can be reduced to manslaughter, "… if the person who committed it did so in the heat of passion caused by sudden provocation". The provocative act would have to be, "… of such a nature as to be sufficient to deprive an ordinary person of the power of self-control …". Reading the cases in which this defence has been considered can be a fascinating study in human nature and is necessary to grasping the way in which judges have dealt with the defence. In fact, statutory defences generally are best understood in the context of their real life applications.

YOUTH CRIMINAL JUSTICE ACT

The federal government has created the *Youth Criminal Justice Act* to provide special procedures for youth between the ages of 12 and 17 who are charged with any federal offence. Provinces and territories have established parallel procedural protections for youth facing quasi-criminal charges created by provinces, territories or municipalities, in some cases narrowing the range of special procedures to apply only between the ages of 12 and 15.

The *Youth Criminal Justice Act* starts with both a Preamble and a Declaration of Principle to clarify the context of the legislation and to guide decision-makers using the statute. Clause 3(1)(*b*) is part of the Declaration of Principle and contains this statement, "the criminal justice system for young persons must be separate from that for adults and emphasize the following ... fair and proportionate accountability that is consistent with the greater dependency of young persons and their reduced level of maturity". Rehabilitation and reintegration of the young person are emphasized and the statute makes it clear that serious offences should be treated differently than less serious offences.

The use of "extrajudicial measures", diverting youth accused of less serious offences away from the courts and involving the broader community in seeking solutions to getting young people back on the right track, are emphasized in the statute. In the years since the statute's implementation in 2003, statistics show that more youth are being dealt with outside the courts, using community-based programs rather than court-imposed penalties. Judges, police and correctional personnel who work with youth have all expressed their support of this approach. Fewer charges are being laid for less serious offences in the first place and for the cases that get to court, fewer sentences involving custody are being used.

Under the Act, young persons over 14 are not transferred to adult court if they are facing the most serious of charges, like murder and aggravated sexual assault, though they do face the same penalties as adults. Because of the *Charter* guarantee of the choice of a jury trial for any offence that carries a maximum penalty of five years or more, the composition of the courts designated in each province as *youth courts* includes superior court judges who can supervise jury trials if an accused youth chooses this option.

For other offences, one of the primary procedural protections provided for youth by the *Youth Criminal Justice Act* is a range of sentencing options that attempt to minimize the time spent in custody and emphasize rehabilitation and reintegration of young persons into the community as productive citizens. Young persons who do end up in custody are kept separate from adult offenders whenever possible. All custodial sentences are followed by a period of community supervision. Names of youth charged with criminal offences are not published to reduce the negative effect such public labelling can have on the future development of a young person.

KEY TERMINOLOGY

actus reus	the criminal act or omission
admissibility	the issue of whether or not evidence can be used during a trial — judge decides
automatism	acting while in an involuntary or unconscious state
challenge for cause	one of the reasons listed in the *Criminal Code* for keeping someone off a jury
closing statement	a last attempt to convince a judge or jury by a lawyer acting on behalf of one of the parties at a trial
compulsion by threats	a potential defence for some criminal charges for someone who has been threatened with physical harm
credibility	whether or not a witness can be believed
cross-examine	challenge the testimony of a witness called by an opponent in a trial with probing and leading questions
defence	a rationale for a defendant's actions that eliminates or reduces liability
defence of mental disorder	suffering from a mental condition that renders a person incapable of knowing that what he or she is doing is wrong
defence of person	protecting yourself or another from harm
defence of property	protecting property from harm
discharge	a special form of sentencing that may include a period of probation but will enable the offender to claim he or she has not been convicted of a criminal charge
duress	a defence based on being forced to act through threats of physical harm
evidence	information that can be considered by a judge, jury or administrative tribunal in making a decision
expert witness	a witness with special knowledge or training, whose opinion would be helpful to a judge, or administrative tribunal in making a decision

extrajudicial measures	remedies provided outside the courtroom
hearsay evidence	out of court statements being presented by someone other than the person who initially made the statement
hybrid offence	also known as a "dual procedure" offence, can be treated as a summary conviction or indictable offence — at the discretion of the prosecutor
identity	identifying who committed a criminal offence
indictable offence	the more serious federal offences, usually involve a greater potential penalty and more procedural protections for the accused person
intoxication	a partial defence to some criminal charges based on being so impaired that the person is unable to form a specific intent
jury summons	a court order requiring a person to attend court for possible selection as a juror
leading question	a form of question that suggests the answer
lesser and included offence	another, less serious charge that includes many of the same elements
mens rea	the mental element that may be required to convict someone of a criminal offence, could involve intention or recklessness
not criminally responsible	a possible trial outcome for someone suffering from a mental disorder that renders that person incapable of knowing that what was done was wrong
object	ask a judge to rule that certain evidence should not be admissible, or that certain conduct by an opposing advocate is inappropriate
onus	the legal responsibility for proving something
opening statement	an initial oral presentation by an advocate representing one of the parties, outlining the key points in the case that will be presented on behalf of that party
opinion evidence	an expert's point of view on an evidentiary issue

partial defence	an explanation of an accused person's behaviour that may result in a conviction for a lesser and included offence rather than for the more serious offence charged
peremptory challenge	being able to keep a potential juror off the jury panel without having to provide a reason
provocation	a wrongful act or insult that is enough to deprive an ordinary person of self-control
relevant	having probative value with respect to an issue of importance in a trial
self defence	acting to protect oneself from serious bodily harm
specific intent	a particular mental element to a crime required by the wording of the charging statute
summary offence	all provincial, territorial and municipal charges and less serious federal charges
trier of fact	the judge or jury required to make a decision about what happened and whether or not it fits the elements of a crime, guilty or not guilty
unfit to stand trial	suffering from a mental disorder to such an extent that the person would not be able to understand what is happening during a trial or to instruct a lawyer providing representation
youth court	the court designated in each province to deal with charges under the *Youth Criminal Justice Act*

STATUTES MENTIONED

Canadian Charter of Rights and Freedoms, Part I of the *Constitution Act, 1982*, being schedule B to the *Canada Act 1982* (U.K.), 1982, c. 11

Criminal Code, R.S.C. 1985, c. C-46, as am.

Youth Criminal Justice Act, S.C. 2002, c. 1, as am.

CASES MENTIONED

R. v. Bleta, [1964] S.C.J. No. 31, [1965] 1 C.C.C. 1 (S.C.C.)

R. v. Parks, [1992] S.C.J. No. 71, 75 C.C.C. (3d) 287 (S.C.C.)

R. v. H. (W.), [2013] S.C.J. No. 22, 2013 SCC 22 (S.C.C.)

TEST YOURSELF

1. Ida is accused of torturing and killing two neighbourhood dogs. She is facing criminal charges. Duty counsel (a lawyer provided under the legal aid scheme to assist people who are unrepresented) has spoken to her and tells the judge at Ida's arraignment that Ida seems incapable of understanding the charges she is facing. Ida has told the lawyer that she knows the lawyer is from Planet B-12, like the evil animals who keep trying to brainwash her. She is insisting the lawyer stay away from her. What should the judge do in this situation? Why?

2. Alf was caught handing out apples containing pins and candy laced with arsenic to children on Halloween. He has repeatedly told the police that he is the Devil and has told them that their courts can't put the Prince of Darkness on trial. He insists that he doesn't need a lawyer. He is equally insistent that he knows that what he has done is against "the world's laws, but, of course, such nonsense does not apply to me". The police have charged him under several sections of the *Criminal Code*, including administering a noxious substance and attempted murder. What, if anything, can the courts do with Alf? Briefly explain.

3. Alf believes he can exercise a kind of mind control over members of the public. Would he be entitled to a jury trial with respect to his charges? Why or why not?

4. If Alf were entitled to a jury trial, could the prosecutor exclude a potential juror who has listed his occupation as "warlock". If so, on what basis? If not, why not?

5. If Alf is put on trial, would a police officer be able to tell the court about Alf's out-of-court statements where he stated that he knew that what he was doing was against the world's laws? Provide the rationale for your answer.

6. Would any of your answers from questions 2 through 5 change if Alf was only 16 years old? Briefly explain.

Chapter 11

Criminal Law — After Conviction

GENERAL SENTENCING PRINCIPLES

Once a person has been convicted of a criminal or quasi-criminal offence, judges are responsible for imposing an appropriate sentence. Canadian juries do not get involved in the sentencing process, except in relation to a conviction for second degree murder, when a jury can recommend (but not set) a period of parole ineligibility.

Statutes do provide sentencing guidelines for judges. Most penalties are set out in the statutes that define the crimes and quasi-crimes, expressed as a maximum penalty that a judge can impose for a particular offence. Rarely, the statute will also specify a minimum penalty. Judges have discretion to set the penalty within these limits, taking into account the circumstances of the offence and the degree of responsibility of the offender.

Section 718 of the *Criminal Code* provides a list of possible objectives to be obtained when a judge chooses a particular sentence. These include denouncing the conduct, deterring this offender or others and simply separating offenders from society. Promoting a sense of responsibility in offenders and rehabilitation are also listed. All are set in the context of the fundamental purpose of contributing, "… to respect for the law and the maintenance of a just, peaceful and safe society …".

Judges are told by the federal government to consider non-custodial sentences in clauses 718.2(*d*) and (*e*) of the *Criminal Code*, "an offender should not be deprived of liberty, if less restrictive sanctions may be appropriate in the circumstances; and … all available sanctions other than imprisonment that are reasonable in the circumstances should be considered for all offenders …".

Judges are provided with a list of *aggravating* circumstances, which could justifiably increase the severity of a sentence in relation to a particular charge. These are laid out in clause 718.2(*a*) of the *Criminal Code* and include evidence that the offence was motivated by prejudice or hatred, based on race, colour, religion, sexual orientation, disability or similar factors. Abusing your spouse or child, or abusing a position of trust in relation to the victim, can also attract more severe sanctions, as will committing a crime that could be considered terrorism or of benefit to a criminal organization.

The importance of common law precedents in sentencing is emphasized in clause 718.2(*b*) of the *Criminal Code*, "a sentence should be similar to sentences imposed on similar offenders for similar offences committed in similar circumstances".

Judges are expected to conduct a sentencing hearing as soon as practicable after someone is convicted, or enters a guilty plea. Adjournments will be made so the prosecutor or a defence lawyer or agent can properly prepare submissions, or to allow a probation officer to prepare a *pre-sentence report*, providing a summary of background information on the offence and the offender.

During a sentencing hearing, a judge may take into account any evidence the judge considers relevant and many rules of evidence, particularly, the rules against the use of hearsay evidence, will be relaxed during a sentence hearing. Once the person has been convicted, a judge can and will consider the prior convictions of the offender and these often influence the sentence that will be imposed for the new conviction. Judges also consider *victim impact statements* that have been prepared and if the victim wishes to read his or her statement in court, rather than simply providing a written version, this will be permitted.

SENTENCING ALTERNATIVES

Jail

Most penalty limits in federal statutes are expressed in terms of maximum jail time. For indictable offences, maximum jail times tend to be expressed as 2, 5, 7, 10, 14 years or "life". For federally created summary conviction charges, maximum jail sentences might be as long as 18 months, but the general penalty section 787 sets the most common summary maximum at six months.

Statutory requirements for minimum periods of incarceration are rare; but recently the federal government has added more of these to the statutes for which they are responsible. Mandatory minimum sentences are found in sections related to the use of a firearm in the commission of an offence, for trafficking in firearms and for people with more than one conviction for impaired driving, among others. First degree murder convictions require the imposition of a jail sentence, specified as "life", without eligibility for parole before 25 years of the sentence has expired. Second degree murder convictions also result in life sentences, but limits on parole eligibility could be set between 10 and 25 years by the sentencing judge.

If there is no minimum period of incarceration set out in a statute, a judge could exercise discretion to impose a fine, probation or another alternative form of sentence, subject to the common law parameters established for particular offences.

If an accused who is eventually convicted has been denied bail and kept in pre-trial custody, a judge is permitted to take this into account at the time of sentencing, reducing the jail time imposed. The convicted individual may be given credit for the time actually served in pre-trial custody since he or she would not have been entitled to participate in institutional programs in the lock-up and would not have qualified for early release credit in relation to that period.

If a judge is considering imposing jail time in relation to convictions for more than one offence at a particular hearing, the judge has the discretion of ordering that the sentences be served either *concurrently* or *consecutively*. Concurrent sentences run at the same time. So, if an accused were convicted of both theft and possession of stolen property arising out of the same incident and received concurrent sentences of five months and three months for the respective charges, the actual sentence would be five months, with the three month sentence running at the same time. By way of contrast, if an accused entered guilty pleas at one hearing to four different break and entries, all of which occurred at different times and places, a judge may decide to impose consecutive sentences of three months for each charge. These would run one after the other, so that the actual sentence would be four times three, or 12 months.

Section 732 of the *Criminal Code* enables a judge to impose an *intermittent* jail sentence on an offender if the sentence is for 90 days or less. This most commonly enables convicted individuals who are gainfully employed or pursuing an education to serve their jail time on weekends.

Most people sentenced to jail are told by the judge exactly how long their sentences will last, whether it is 20 days or 20 years. The sentence establishes a *warrant expiry date*, the end of the time when the convict will be under the supervision of correctional services personnel. Through the provisions of statutes like the federal *Corrections and Conditional Release Act*, a convict will also be able to predict his or her *parole eligibility dates*, when he or she will be entitled to apply to the Parole Board for various types of early release into the community with correctional supervision.

People who are labelled as *dangerous offenders* at the time of sentencing are given *indeterminate* sentences. This means the individual does not have a set warrant expiry date and does not know when the jail sentence will end. A *dangerous offender* will only be released from custody if and when the Parole Board can be convinced that he or she is no longer a danger to the public. According to section 761 of the *Criminal Code*, the first review of this status by the Parole Board need not occur until the dangerous offender has served at least seven years.

The application to have a convict labelled a dangerous offender is made by the prosecutor at the time of sentencing if the person has been convicted of a serious personal injury offence that carries a potential sentence of more than 10 years. The full criteria for dangerous offender status are laid out in section 753 of the *Criminal Code*. Dangerous offenders constitute a threat to the life or safety of others, demonstrated through persistent, aggressive behaviour or a particularly brutal act that shows a lack of restraint and concern for victims. When the application is made, a judge can order that the individual be remanded and assessed by mental health behavioural experts before a decision is reached.

The *Criminal Code* provides another special status for individuals who are labelled as *long-term offenders*. According to section 753.1 of the *Criminal Code*, these are individuals who would be appropriately sentenced to more than two years in jail for their crimes and because of the substantial risk of reoffending after release if their behaviour is not controlled, require a lengthy period of community supervision when the jail sentence expires. Community supervision for up to 10 years can be tacked on to any jail sentence imposed. The section was designed to control the behaviour of sex offenders, particularly pedophiles. Experts say that most of these individuals respond to medication and on-going treatment programs. Long-term community correctional supervision can reduce the recidivism risk by ensuring that the offenders continue to take the medication. Of course, the way the Code is worded, the use of this status is not restricted to sex offenders. It could be used for any violent offender who requires on-going community supervision following a jail term.

Conditional Sentences

Due to the high cost of sending members of society to jail, some years ago the federal government added section 742.1 to the *Criminal Code*. For many offences that do not require a minimum jail term, a judge sentencing a person to less than two years imprisonment could order that the sentence be served in the community *if* the judge is satisfied that such a sentence will not endanger the public. Recently, the federal government seemed to lose confidence in the ability of judges to exercise discretion in this regard by adding a long list of charges for which conditional sentences are NOT an option. These include importing and trafficking drugs, offences committed with weapons, terrorism offences and offences committed for the benefit of criminal organizations.

The judge can impose a large number of conditions on the way time will be spent in the community, under a *community supervisor*, a community-based corrections worker. Conditions often include severe restrictions on leaving a residence, other than for work, tight controls on drug or alcohol consumption and restrictions on visitors. In *R. v. Wu* the Supreme Court of Canada made it clear that this is imprisonment without incarceration; it is not a form of probation.

Suspended Sentences

If there is no minimum jail term required for an offence, clause 731(1)(*a*) of the *Criminal Code* allows a judge to suspend imposing jail time and release the individual on a term of probation instead. If the terms of the probation order were violated, the offender could be sent to jail.

Probation

This is by far the most commonly used sentencing option. Probation can be combined with a fine, or a jail sentence of less than two years. Probation can last for up to three years and can include up to 240 hours of community service.

According to section 732.1 of the *Criminal Code*, every probation order contains a requirement that an offender, "keep the peace and be of good behaviour". In addition, he or she must notify a probation officer of any change of name, address or employment. There are lots of optional conditions of probation available, including a requirement that the offender report to the probation officer on a regular basis, abstain from drugs, alcohol or the possession of weapons, remain in the jurisdiction, undergo treatment programs or any "... other reasonable conditions the court considers desirable ... for protecting society and facilitating the offender's successful reintegration into the community".

There is a double whammy hammer available for enforcing probation orders. Section 733.1 of the *Criminal Code* makes it a hybrid offence to fail to comply with the terms of a probation order and under section 732.2 if anyone commits an offence while on probation, the probation order can be revoked and another sentence can be imposed for the original charge.

Fines

The majority of provincial, territorial and municipal offence penalties are expressed in terms of maximum fines and each province and territory provides procedural consequences, including jail time if fines are not paid.

Section 734 of the *Criminal Code* allows a judge to impose a fine in lieu of other punishments, except where a minimum jail term is specified, or in addition to other sanctions. The general penalty section for summary conviction offences, section 787, sets a $5,000 maximum for individuals. It, of course, applies when a federal statute does not specify another fine limit for a particular offence. Section 735 increases the fine limit substantially for "organizations". This could include corporations, partnerships, trade unions and other groups organized for a common purpose. The summary conviction fine limit for organizations is $100,000. There is no dollar limit on the fines that can be imposed for indictable offences. Fines for indictable offences are "in the discretion of the court".

Subsection 734(2) of the *Criminal Code* makes it clear that a judge should be satisfied that an offender is capable of paying a fine, or working it off through a *fine option program* before a fine is used as a form of punishment. Provinces and territories are given the discretion to set up *fine option programs*, if they choose. Where they have been established, these programs allow offenders to work off their fines by performing work that is beneficial to the local community. Credit is given at the provincial or territorial minimum wage rate for the number of hours of work performed.

If an offender requests a reasonable period of time in which to pay a fine, a judge will usually grant this request with periods from 30 days, up to six months being quite common.

Generally, fines collected are paid to the provincial or territorial governments, though in some provinces and territories, municipalities benefit if they are given responsibility for enforcing the laws locally. Provinces and territories are given the discretion to set enforcement policies, including the power to refuse the renewal of hunting and fishing or driving licences if there are unpaid fines. Provinces and territories can also file orders to pay fines with civil courts and use the range of civil remedies, including garnishment of wages to collect unpaid fines.

Despite the availability of the range of enforcement tools, time to pay and the requirement that a judge satisfy him or herself of the offender's ability to pay, before imposing a fine, a disturbing number of offenders are incarcerated in Canada each year for refusal to pay fines. Subsection 734(5) of the *Criminal Code* provides a formula for determining the number of days an offender must serve if he or she is in default. Offenders are given proportional credit to reduce the time if they can pay a portion of the fine.

Discharges

If there is no minimum penalty specified for an offence and it doesn't carry a 14-year or life maximum, a judge may consider an *absolute* or *conditional discharge*. This is a very beneficial outcome for the offender because despite his or her guilty plea or a finding of guilt, section 730 of the *Criminal Code* makes it clear that the effect of the discharge is that, "… the offender shall be deemed not to have been convicted of the offence …". This could be of particular use to someone for whom a conviction would have serious future ramifications, perhaps barring entry into a profession like policing or preventing entry into the United States for an international trucker, professional entertainer or athlete.

According to section 730, a judge can only consider a discharge if it is "… in the best interests of the accused and not contrary to the public interest …". Judges have used these provisions to limit the use of the discharge to situations where the offender was of previous good character, truly in need of a break in terms of the future ramifications of a conviction and in relation to charges where deterrence of this offender and others was not really a concern in sentencing. There are no set rules limiting the use of discharges to first time offenders who have committed relatively minor offences, but this is the practical reality.

If a judge imposes a *conditional discharge*, there will be a period of probation imposed before the discharge becomes effective. The offender will be expected to keep his or her nose clean during the probation. An *absolute discharge* is effective from the date of sentencing. There are no probation conditions attached.

Restitution Orders

In addition to any other sentence imposed, a judge can order an offender to pay compensation to a victim for the replacement value of damaged property or for loss of income if the offender has caused bodily harm. If bodily harm was caused to a family member of the offender, causing this person to move out, compensation can be ordered for the moving expenses incurred. Section 741 of the *Criminal Code* allows for the restitution to be paid out of any money found on the accused at the time of arrest and also allows the victim to file the order with a civil court to enable the use of civil remedies to enforce payment if it isn't done promptly.

Prohibition Orders

In addition to any other sentence imposed for an offence committed with a weapon, trafficking, importing or producing a controlled substance or any offence involving violence and carrying a maximum penalty in excess of 10 years, section 109 of the *Criminal Code* states the judge *must* impose a 10 year ban on possessing a firearm, cross-bow, ammunition, explosives or a restricted weapon. The 10 year prohibition applies to a first offence. Any subsequent convictions in the categories of concern draw a lifetime prohibition.

Section 110 of the Code gives the judge the discretion to impose the same type of prohibition for up to 10 years for any type of crime of violence, even if the maximum sentence for the offence is less than 10 years.

SENTENCES FOR YOUNG PERSONS

In addition to specific encouragement that less serious offences involving youth should be handled outside the court system, the *Youth Criminal Justice Act* provides youth court judges with a range of sentencing options that exceeds those available for adult offenders. Some of the sentencing alternatives are unique to the youth system, while others are simply designed to operate within different parameters.

Part 1 of the *Youth Criminal Justice Act* establishes the principles for the use of *extrajudicial measures*, designed to keep youth who accept responsibility for their actions out of court. Clause 4(*c*) of the Act stresses that, "extrajudicial measures are presumed to be adequate to hold a young person accountable for his or her offending behaviour if the young person has committed a non-violent offence and has not previously been found guilty of an offence ...". Clause 4(*d*) immediately emphasizes that even if a young person has been found guilty of a previous offence, that does not preclude the use of extrajudicial measures if they are adequate to hold a young person accountable in particular circumstances.

Police officers dealing with youth are directed to consider whether or not a simple *caution*, or a community program designed to discourage the young person from future offences might be sufficient. Provinces are given the authority to establish community programs for this purpose. In fact, provinces can establish community based programs to set up an array of extrajudicial sanctions that can be used, depending on the type of offence that is alleged to have been committed. Youth must willingly participate in this form of diversion or the matter will go to court.

In some provinces or territories, prosecutors may be made responsible for the *caution* programs and directing the youth towards out-of-court diversionary programs.

If a matter goes to court and a young person enters a guilty plea, or is found guilty, youth court judges can consider sentences ranging from nothing more than a *reprimand* to custody. Many sentencing options that are also available to judges sentencing adults are part of the mix, including absolute and conditional discharges, restitution and prohibition orders.

Fines are limited to a maximum of $1,000 and must be based on the young person's ability to pay. The Act specifically discourages imposing fines that are simply going to be paid by a parent or guardian. Probation orders are limited in length to two years, as opposed to three for adults, but otherwise work in much the same way as adult probation orders.

Provinces are invited to establish *intensive support and supervision programs* that would allow for intensive rehabilitative programming without placing the young person in custody. Federal funding is available to encourage provinces and territories to buy in. If a province or territory sets up the program, a judge can then use this as a sentencing alternative.

Custodial sentences are expected to be a last resort and the *Youth Criminal Justice Act* requires that a custodial sentence be followed by a period of mandatory community supervision. Maximum penalties that would be faced by adults according to the statutes that create the offences are not the maximum penalties that youth face. For the majority of charges, the custody and supervision combination could only run for a maximum of two years. If a charge carries a maximum *life* sentence for an adult, a custody and supervision order for a youth could run for a maximum of three years, unless the offence is one that is labelled as a *presumptive offence* in the *Youth Criminal Justice Act*.

First or second degree murder, attempted murder, manslaughter, aggravated sexual assault or three serious violent convictions by a young person are listed as *presumptive offences* and receive special treatment in the Act. If a young person is at least 14 (provinces or territories are entitled to choose 15 or 16 as the lower limit) and is convicted of one of these presumptive offences, he or she will be facing the possibility of the regular adult sentence. The *Youth Criminal Justice Act* states that this will happen unless the youth or his lawyer convinces the youth court judge otherwise. However, a Supreme Court of Canada case, *R. v. B. (D.)*, ruled that this type of *reverse onus*, placing the onus on the accused, violates section 7 of the *Charter of Rights and Freedoms*. As a result, the onus is on the prosecutor to convince the youth court that an adult sentence is appropriate, despite the wording of the *Youth Criminal Justice Act*. The accused youth or his lawyer would be able to challenge this type of application to encourage the judge to use the youth sentence range for this particular offender, regardless of his or her age. A youth sentence for first degree murder would be a maximum of 10 years, with six years in custody and four years of supervision. For second degree murder, a youth sentence maximum would be seven years, with four years custody and three of supervision.

CORRECTIONAL FACILITIES

The Canadian Centre for Justice Statistics, the Correctional Service of Canada and Public Safety Canada regularly compile statistical and summary information on crime and punishment in Canada. Some of this information is accessible on federal government websites. A quick search reveals a great deal about the corrections component of the Canadian criminal justice system.

The federal, provincial and territorial governments spend over four billion dollars per year on corrections, with about 75 per cent of that being spent on custodial, or lock up facilities. The Correctional Service of Canada operates over 50 prisons, and the provinces and territories combined operate slightly more than 100 additional jail facilities.

Twenty times as many people sentenced to jail in a particular year are sent to a provincial or territorial facility, as opposed to a federal institution. In fact, more than half of the jail sentences imposed each year run for 30 days or less, with roughly 80 per cent of jail sentences amounting to less than six months. In addition, provincial institutions house as many people on pre-trial remand as they do sentenced offenders. Because of restrictions on sentence length and the requirement for separate custodial facilities for young persons, provinces also operate all the primary youth detention centres. On any given day in Canada, there are roughly 38,000 prisoners in custody, with about 37 per cent of those inmates in federal institutions. Another 120,000 or so Canadians would be under correctional supervision in the community.

Federal institutions are where prisoners serve custodial sentences in excess of two years. Prisoners are categorized according to security classification based on escape risk, potential danger to the public, and danger to other inmates. The largest percentage of federal prisoners is housed in medium security facilities. Far fewer inmates require maximum security accommodation, with a portion of those prisoners needing the extra security of *protective custody* to guard them from attacks by other inmates. One federal institution has a *special handling unit* for prisoners presenting an exceptional security risk. *Solitary confinement* is used as a punishment for prisoners who break institutional rules and is usually accommodated in a small unit in each prison. Minimum security facilities are used for the transitional return to the community and a small number of federal facilities serve both medium and minimum security clientele.

It is far more common for provincial or territorial jails to accommodate a mixture of security classifications within one institution. Provinces and territories set their own criteria for classifying prisoners and assigning them to appropriate incarceration facilities.

Women represent a very small proportion of Canadian prisoners. Five small regional facilities accommodate the majority of federal female inmates. Most fit the medium or minimum security classifications. Three federal institutions that also house male prisoners have designated units to accommodate female prisoners requiring maximum security. British Columbia has the Burnaby Correctional Centre for Women that holds women of all security classifications and is a facility operated jointly by the federal and provincial governments.

COMMUNITY SUPERVISION

The vast majority of people convicted of criminal or quasi-criminal offences never spend a day in jail. While some of these convictions are handled with a fine and nothing more, a large number result in some period of probation. Where community supervision orders do not create a risk to public safety, they could replace sentences that would otherwise have resulted in jail time and most offenders who do go to jail are released on parole or some other form of controlled reintegration prior to the expiry of their sentences. All of these offenders require supervision by corrections personnel, parole or probation officers, or community supervisors.

Probation and community supervision orders will contain terms and conditions imposed by the sentencing judge. The Parole Board can establish the parameters of the forms of early release that they control. Correctional facility supervisors can set limits on temporary absence permits and dictate whether or not an inmate requires an institutional escort.

There is no doubt that all the forms of community supervision are considerably cheaper than incarceration. Custodial services eat up three quarters of correctional budgets, even though there are three times as many convicted criminals under some form of correctional supervision outside our jails on any given day. It costs taxpayers close to $360 per day to house the average inmate in federal penitentiary and about $171 per day in provincial jails.

Society experiences additional savings if people convicted of crimes or quasi-crimes are able to continue employment and provide financial support for family members while under some form of community supervision.

KEY TERMINOLOGY

absolute discharge	a sentence which enables the offender to claim he or she has not been convicted of a criminal offence, this one is effective as soon as the judge makes the order
aggravating circumstances	factors related to the offence that could justify a judge imposing a more severe penalty
caution	a warning not to get involved in criminal behaviour again, could include a warning against associating with certain individuals or being in certain locations
community supervision	a sentence served in the community with conditions attached and a community correctional worker monitoring compliance
concurrent sentence	a sentence that is served at the same time as a sentence for another offence
conditional discharge	a sentence that includes a period of probation, but if that is completed successfully it would allow the offender to claim that he or she has not been convicted of a criminal offence
consecutive sentence	a sentence that will be added on to another sentence and served after the initial sentence expires
dangerous offenders	a label attached at the time of sentencing to convicts who have committed particularly violent offences, showing a lack of regard for others, carries an indeterminate sentence
extrajudicial measures	remedies provided outside the court process
fine option program	provincially or territorially initiated programs that allow offenders to work off their fines
indeterminate sentence	a sentence with no set expiry date, used for dangerous offenders who will only get out of jail when the Parole Board is convinced they are no longer a danger to society
intermittent sentence	a sentence which can be served on weekends — can't be longer than 90 days

long-term offenders	special label given to violent offenders who will need a long period of supervision in the community (up to 10 years) after their jail sentences expire
parole eligibility dates	the dates at which offenders sentenced to jail will become eligible to apply for various types of supervised release into the community
pre-sentence report	background information to assist the judge at the time of sentencing someone who has been convicted of an offence — usually prepared by a parole or probation officer
presumptive offences	list of serious offences that will require a youth to face an adult sentence unless the youth court is convinced that it would be inappropriate
protective custody	special security provided for a prisoner who may be targeted by others
reprimand	verbal denunciation of a youth's criminal actions
reverse onus	placing the responsibility to prove a defence or a sentencing element on the accused
solitary confinement	prison punishment involving isolation from others
special handling unit	a specially designed prison unit with extra security for the inmates that pose the greatest risk of escape or danger to others
victim impact statement	a written submission to a court by a victim, describing the way in which an offence has impacted on the victim and his or her family
warrant expiry date	the date on which a prison sentence imposed by a judge expires and correctional supervision of a convict ends

STATUTES MENTIONED

Criminal Code, R.S.C. 1985, c. C-46, as am.

Corrections and Conditional Release Act, S.C. 1992, c. 20, as am.

Youth Criminal Justice Act, S.C. 2002, c. 1, as am.

CASES MENTIONED

R. v. B. (D.), [2008] S.C.J. No. 25, [2008] 2 S.C.R. 3 (S.C.C.)

R. v. Wu, [2003] S.C.J. No. 78, [2003] 3 S.C.R. 530 (S.C.C.)

TEST YOURSELF

1. Last month, 14-year-old M. broke into the local arena with his 19-year-old brother, Zach. They were intent on stealing hockey equipment and game sweaters from the local junior team's storage room. As they were stuffing skates into a large equipment bag, they were surprised by a female security guard. Zach attacked her with a skate, swinging it by the laces and smashing it several times into the woman's head. The guard suffered large gashes on her face and a skull fracture. She was knocked unconscious. M. aimed a kick at the security guard after she fell, but missed. The whole attack was caught on a video camera, installed for security purposes. Neither young man was aware that they had triggered a silent alarm when they entered the equipment room. They were captured by police, who responded to the alarm as they tried to leave the arena with their stolen goods.

   Police have charged both Zach and M. with break and entry, theft over $5,000 and aggravated assault. The last of these charges is the most serious and carries a maximum penalty of 14 years. Investigation of the brothers shows that Zach has a lengthy youth record for break and enter and four previous assault convictions. These are his first charges as an adult. M. has no previous convictions and has been in the care of the Children's Aid Society since he was 10. He was living in a group home when his brother picked him up for this "outing". The boys' father is currently serving a penitentiary sentence for trafficking in narcotics. Their mother is in a treatment facility due to a heroin addiction.

   (a) Will the two young men be tried together? Why?
   (b) Assume that both Zach and M. are convicted of all of the charges they are facing and that you are the judge who will be sentencing each of them. Describe the sentence you will be imposing on each, listing the factors you have taken into account and your complete rationale.
   (c) If either of the sentences you have imposed will involve custody, explain where the sentence will be served.

EXTRA CHALLENGE

2. Investigate whether or not a FINE OPTION program is available in your community.

Chapter 12

Trends in the Canadian Justice System

VIDEOS AND VIOLENCE

The horrific taser-related death of Robert Dziekanski at the Vancouver Airport in April 2007 triggered outrage at the behaviour of the four RCMP officers who confronted the confused, Polish-speaking visitor and the controversial weapon they used. Why? Because an airport bystander recorded the incident on his camera phone and we have all been able to view the resulting record of the incident on television. Thank goodness, neither Commissioner Thomas Braidwood, who led an inquiry into the incident, nor members of the public, had to rely solely on the recollections of the police officers involved. Police accounts were self-serving distortions of what is clearly depicted on the video. For many Canadians, this was their first exposure to the thuggery and contempt for the truth exhibited by a nasty segment of our law enforcement community.

It should be obvious to people planning a career in the investigation and enforcement side of the Canadian justice system that video technology is here to stay and is likely to become an ever more important tool for recording events accurately and reducing the need for judges to resolve "he said-she said" controversies that arise in so many trials and administrative hearings. You could look up an interesting example of the use of video evidence by Justice David Paciocco in *R. v. Parker*, a 2013 Ontario Court of Justice case.

Video records could logically result in an increase in the number of "guilty" pleas. Video was used extensively to prosecute charges in relation to criminal activity that occurred during the Vancouver Canuck riots and G20 Summit in Toronto. At the same time, the technology may act as a useful control on the actions of overzealous enforcement or investigation activities that reflect badly on the individuals whom society arms, but relies upon to act with restraint and integrity in performing an important public function.

Many Canadian police services already equip their vehicles with video cameras and in a *Globe and Mail* article Vancouver Police Chief Jim Chu predicted that within the next few years, "Officers will be wearing body cameras". Such cameras are already in use in Britain and Australia and have been used in pilot projects in Canada.

ALTERNATIVE DISPUTE RESOLUTION INITIATIVES

Conflict is a natural part of human interaction and, to a large extent, laws are designed to minimize and regulate potential conflict situations. Courts and administrative tribunals have long been considered forums which allow the parties to articulate their perspectives on conflicts in which they are immersed. After listening to the parties, the court or tribunal will impose a society-sanctioned solution designed to end the conflict. However, civil, criminal and administrative systems of justice have tended to rely on an adversarial approach to conflict resolution. When this approach predominates and solutions are imposed, someone usually wins and someone else loses.

There is an increasing tendency throughout the justice system to offer alternatives that will increase the possibility of a win-win outcome, with mediators nudging and encouraging parties toward a consensual solution to their conflicts and community-based diversion and healing programs replacing court imposed punishments. Business contracts often include a mediation clause, which requires the parties to negotiate to reach a common ground before asking a court to impose a solution. Some contracts will name a third party arbitrator, or panel of decision-makers who are given the power to impose a solution, circumventing recourse to the public court system altogether. This is done to avoid the delays that can be caused by civil justice procedural steps and the clogged schedules of busy courts.

Family laws, including the federal *Divorce Act* and various provincial and territorial family statutes, require families that have fractured to consider or use the services of family mediators to seek solutions to property division, support and custody disputes before scheduling an appearance in court. The aim is to increase cooperation, tone down the animosity and to reserve court time for only the most contentious of problems. Since many families that split will have some form of continued interaction into the future, encouraging cooperation from the outset is seen as setting the proper tone.

Civil procedure has always been structured to encourage out-of-court settlement, but many of the procedural steps that in the past were optional have become compulsory. This includes settlement conferences and pre-trial meetings with judges who become very pro-active in directing the parties to narrow the issues that have to be resolved in court and in describing likely outcomes if matters are not solved by agreement. Judges can help encourage a reasonable approach to settling disputes by ordering parties who have been uncooperative to pay the legal expenses of opponents who have taken a more conciliatory approach.

On April 25, 2013, the *Globe and Mail* reported on a trio of task forces composed of legal professionals who work in the civil justice system. The task forces had all published recent studies recommending systemic changes like making court forms much more user-friendly, so more litigants could realistically represent themselves. They also encouraged broader use of legal insurance schemes to reduce the impact of the shockingly large lawyer bills that discourage people from using the courts to resolve civil disputes. In addition, the task forces felt the system should allow judges to become even more interventionist in a "triage" approach, pushing simpler matters into compulsory mediation and settlement conferences, avoiding trials whenever possible.

The *Youth Criminal Justice Act* recognizes that a youth record and a court-imposed penalty may not be the best way to deal with all young people who have come in conflict with the law. Part 1 of the Act directs police and prosecutors to consider *extrajudicial measures*. These could include the simple use of warnings and cautions or more comprehensive community-based programs established to structure appropriate sanctions. If a young person accepts that he or she has done something wrong, rectification could be achieved through meetings with or formal apologies to victims, by repairing damage done, or providing volunteer labour for community projects. Some communities have established mentoring programs to link youth with positive role models who can provide counselling and guidance.

When the *Youth Criminal Justice Act* became law in 2003, one of its stated goals was to reserve the most serious forms of intervention for the most serious crimes. The new emphasis on extrajudicial measures seems to be helping to achieve this goal. Statistical returns show fewer youth cases are being dealt with in court overall, with a significant reduction in the number of cases that involve minor, non-violent charges.

Section 717 of the *Criminal Code* allows provinces to establish *alternative measure* programs to divert adult offenders from court. This has not been used as extensively as the extrajudicial measures prescribed for youth, but has met with success in some communities where local groups have been proactive in encouraging provincial participation and in securing funding to establish these diversion programs. Initiatives like these require financial commitments from government.

RESTORATIVE APPROACHES TO CRIMINAL JUSTICE

Section 19 of the *Youth Criminal Justice Act* provides that a police officer, prosecutor or a judge could convene a *conference* for the purpose of assisting in any decision making that could be done under the Act. This could include decisions on extrajudicial measures, bail, sentences or community reintegration plans. The *conference* is a meeting of community representatives that could include the family of the accused youth, the victim and the victim's family and/or various community elders or social activists interested in community-based solutions aimed at positively re-integrating offenders back into the community.

The inclusion of the conferencing concept in the *Youth Criminal Justice Act* is recognition of *restorative approaches* to criminal justice that have been gaining some momentum across Canada and around the world. Judges, prosecutors and police officers, prompted by concerned members of the general public, have come to recognize that an impersonal criminal justice system, where there is little opportunity for an accused to be confronted with the impact of his or her actions on victims, family members and the broader community, has shortcomings. Punishments that involve sending the offender off to jail, cutting ties with the community and immersing him or her in an environment with other criminals, does little to heal the offender or the community. There is a real risk that when a custodial sentence expires, an offender may return to the community with fewer positive community ties than prior to the departure and an increased chance of re-offending.

Healing circles that were part of justice remedies in some First Nations communities prior to the arrival of Europeans have provided a model for this restorative approach. Members of the conference or healing circle confront the accused with the effect his or her crime has had on others and collectively work out treatment, educational, counselling or compensatory schemes designed to heal the harm that has been caused to the community and re-integrate the offender in a positive way. Rather than sending the offender to a remote prison setting, remedies are developed and implemented locally.

Where justice system personnel have been prepared to buy into the technique, it has met with considerable success. The youth justice system in New Zealand was able to drastically reduce the number of youth in custodial facilities and the astronomical costs associated with the incarceration culture, while boasting significant reductions in recidivism rates. Canadian communities, from tiny Sparwood, British Columbia and Hollow Water, Manitoba to rapidly expanding urban centres like Calgary, have used restorative approaches to justice successfully. A five-year Collaborative Justice Project in the Ottawa area produced positive results. A restorative approach was used in cases of serious, bodily injury crimes. The results demonstrated that both victims and offenders were more satisfied with the restorative approach to justice than a control group that was tracked through the regular court-based system. Offenders were kept out of jail and there was a reduction in recidivism over a three-year follow-up period. With the powerful combination of reduced criminal justice costs and lowered recidivism rates, look for this trend to spread, especially if we can elect some politicians who don't simply recycle failed approaches involving questionable notions of retribution and deterrence. Tired "tough on crime" agendas are usually a sign of unimaginative politicians pandering to voter ignorance.

DISTURBING FEDERAL GOVERNMENT INITIATIVES

Many people working in the criminal justice system have criticized the federal government for creating new restrictions on the use of conditional sentences, creating many more mandatory minimum jail sentences, limiting the use of sentence reduction credit for pre-trial custody and delaying parole eligibility. Even more insidious are changes that have eliminated or greatly reduced the use of "pardons" for Canadians who have made efforts to positively improve their lives. Pardons have been changed to less accessible; more delayed "record suspensions" involving increased application fees. Mr. Justice Melvyn Green of the

Ontario Court of Justice recently wrote: "A policy of punishment, incapacitation and stigmatization has replaced one premised on the prospect of rehabilitation, restoration and reform." Justice Green went on to state: "Draconian penalties will never address the rewiring and therapy necessary to make damaged persons, if not whole, then at least productive and responsible participants in the community we share." (*Globe and Mail*, May 3, 2013, p. A4.)

Justice Green, like many other social commentators has pointed out that while many U.S. states are moving away from failed policies that resulted in high incarceration rates, with no reduction in crime, Canada's federal government seems to be moving in the opposite direction.

CRIMINOLOGICAL TRENDS

As Benjamin Disraeli once said, "There are lies, damned lies and statistics". Any time you see criminal justice statistics, it is wise to ask yourself, "Who has gathered this information, who is reporting it and why"? There is no doubt that certain people or groups can benefit from criminal justice trends. If you sell car alarms or insurance, it may help sales if statistics show that car theft is on the rise. Of course, if you were to investigate current crime rate statistics, you would find that this is not so. As a result, people in this line of work might find it more fruitful to publish the total number of cars stolen annually, which can look quite shocking, even though the rate of auto theft is experiencing a decline.

If you are a police chief, petitioning politicians to increase funding so that you can hire more officers, statistics that show lower crime rates may not serve your purpose. However, if you could highlight more focused data demonstrating that gang-related crime is up, the chance of wrangling financing for a special unit targeting gangs may be enhanced. By the same token, if you choose to concentrate enforcement efforts on a particular type of criminal behaviour, like marijuana grow operations, you will undoubtedly generate statistics that will support an argument that this is an expanding problem in the community.

Statistics Canada is a federal government agency that gathers and publishes criminal justice statistics, much of it based on reports provided by police services across the country. I haven't figured out Statistics Canada's angle yet, if they have one, but I certainly find it informative to visit their website at <www.statcan.gc.ca>. Was the crime rate up or down last year? What has the trend been over the past 10 years, or 20? Which cities, provinces or territories are the safest? Where am I most likely to be victimized? Is firearm use in the commission of crime on the increase? Is youth crime up or down? How about drug charges?

All of this information can be accessed on the website. Full year statistics may lag a year or two behind the current year, but you can certainly follow trends over a number of years. I never cease to find surprises, with my most recent visit being no exception. Would you believe that Ontario and Quebec had the lowest per capita crime rate in the country, or that Nunavut had the highest?

Did you know that the risk of being murdered in Winnipeg or Regina is more than twice as high as the risk if you live in Toronto? Would it come as a shock to you to realize that the use of firearms in the commission of robberies has been declining steadily for years? In fact, violent crime in general has declined significantly over the past 20 years.

Seniors, who are often quite fearful of becoming victims of violent crime, have no statistical support for their fear whatsoever. Although Canadians over the age of 65 make up almost 13 per cent of the population, they represent less than two per cent of the victims of violent crime. In fact, statistics tend to show that young men between the ages of 15 to 19 are about eight times more likely to be violently victimized. Most of the members of this age group seem to strut around without a worry in the world. Maybe it is because, statistically, they are also the group most likely to be committing violent crimes. Even focusing on these statistics, it is important to keep in mind that well over half of the charges that make up the "violent" crime statistic are for common assault.

Would you be surprised to discover that the most common type of criminal charge against adults that our courts process is "administration of justice charges"? These are offences like failure to appear in court, failure to comply with a court order, or breach of probation and they make up approximately 20 per cent of all charges. The next most common adult charge is impaired driving, which represents about a tenth of all the adult court cases. Homicide (murder or manslaughter) charges, thank goodness, constitute less than a tenth of one per cent of all court cases.

In looking at corrections statistics, it is clear that the cost of incarcerating offenders continues to increase. Government policies to increase the number of minimum sentences and toughen up parole eligibility requirements could create significant cost increases with more inmates in custody for longer periods. Restricting the range of offences for which conditional sentences can be used is also problematic. If you are a taxpayer, you should be concerned, since supervision of convicts who serve their time in the community costs about a fifth as much as locking them up. You'd also have cause for dismay if the number of female inmates rises. It is significantly more expensive to incarcerate women, partially because of the small numbers, yet there's a need for specially designated correctional institutions in each region of the country. The overall cost of our prison system is up. Part of this may be accounted for due to the fact that there are higher percentages of prisoners over the age of 50 than there were 15 years ago, likely afflicted by all of the regular health problems associated with aging. Upward of 40 per cent of the prison population has been diagnosed as having mental health problems.

We continue to incarcerate more than twice as many people on a per capita basis than countries like Norway and Denmark, but rank pretty close to Australia and Britain. The U.S. is lock-up crazy, slamming the door on seven times as many inmates as we do in Canada. Do people in the U.S. feel safer as a result? Considering their relative crime rates, that would be foolish. You may well ask why Canadian governments would ever want to emulate failed American approaches to sentencing and corrections.

All statistics need to be viewed with some skepticism and in the broader context of related statistics and the social trends that may contribute to the numbers appearing as they do. For example, many experts have pointed to simple demographic analyses that show that Canada's population is aging. If you have a smaller percentage of your population in the younger age groups, where criminal behaviour is more common, you are likely to have lower crime rates. A new baby boom would bring the expectation of increased crime rates, 15 to 20 years into the future.

Changes to the law and enforcement policies can also affect the statistics that are generated. According to Statistics Canada data, drug charges seem to fluctuate significantly from year to year. What doesn't seem to change much is that over half of the reported incidents relate to the possession of marijuana. Does society's use of marijuana products fluctuate drastically from year to year, or do enforcement policies or allocation of enforcement resources shift? What would happen to drug statistics if marijuana possession were legalized? Over 4,000 licences have already been issued to Canadians for medical use of marijuana, primarily as a method of treating chronic pain.

People who are planning to work in the justice system need to be able to critically evaluate the statistics that are generated in order to use them wisely.

ABORIGINAL OVER-REPRESENTATION IN CANADIAN PRISONS

One disturbing element of our criminal justice system presents an interesting intersection of the issues discussed in the previous two sections of this chapter. It has been over 14 years since the Supreme Court of Canada's ruling in a case called, *R. v. Gladue* drew attention to a provision in section 718.2(*e*) of the *Criminal Code* which says, "all available sanctions other than imprisonment should be considered for all offenders, with particular attention to the circumstances of aboriginal offenders". The Supreme Court encouraged sentencing judges to use the impetus of this section as a justification for the increased use of restorative justice approaches to sentencing, particularly as a method of looking for systemic alternatives to the serious problem of the over-representation of aboriginal Canadians in prisons.

If this was a systemic problem back in 1999, it appears that despite the Supreme Court's nudge, little has been done to bring about enduring change. Statistics generated to the end of 2007 show that while aboriginal Canadians make up less than four per cent of our population, they account for 24 per cent of the people being sentenced to custody in federal and provincial prisons. Further statistics demonstrate that Ontario, has been jailing twice as many aboriginal youth as non-aboriginal youth for the same offences. Sadly, in the 2012 decision of the Supreme Court of Canada, *R. v. Ipeelee*, Justice LeBel noted, "... statistics indicate that the overrepresentation and alienation of Aboriginal peoples in the criminal justice system has only worsened". Justice LeBel cited disturbing statistics indicating that while crime rates and incarceration rates among Canadians generally had been declining, they were actually increasing among Aboriginal Canadians.

Ontario Justice Patrick Sheppard, who was one of the judges responsible for the creation of the five special "Gladue" courts that exist in Ontario, has been quoted as saying, "… the justice system is moving far too lethargically … I am really disappointed in the numbers". (*The Globe and Mail*, Dec. 26, 2009) Experts such as Jonathan Rudin, a lawyer who teaches at York University and is program director of Aboriginal Legal Services of Toronto, have pointed to the lack of funding for programs that would provide alternatives to jail, "I think the reality is that people have not wanted to commit the resources to make *Gladue* real."

COUNTER-TERRORISM INITIATIVES

Canada is part of a global community where highly publicized incidents of terrorism have generated national and international responses in the form of *conventions* and *treaties*, signed by Canada and other members of the United Nations and in the form of new laws and amendments to old laws at the federal and provincial levels within Canada.

Recent media reports indicated that the federal government has been spending so much money on terrorism initiatives that they had actually lost track of where almost $3 billion dollars was directed. While the Royal Canadian Mounted Police (RCMP) and the Canadian Security Intelligence Service have taken on important investigative and policing functions, they are not alone. Federal Departments of Justice and National Defence, Environment Canada, Transport Canada, Health Canada and agencies like the Canadian Nuclear Safety Commission, the Canada Customs and Revenue Agency, and a wide range of provincial and territorial departments and agencies have all been involved in planning and emergency preparedness.

Unprecedented security measures have been instituted in relation to land, sea and air transportation with Customs agents, police services and private security companies working with and developing a host of new technological devices, from iris scanning to sophisticated x-ray and vapour detecting devices. The training and utilization of dogs in the detection of a broad range of contraband and explosive devices has also expanded rapidly with the new demands.

The *Security Offences Act* and the *Canadian Security Intelligence Service Act* are important federal statutes in terms of defining threats to the security of Canada and for assigning responsibility for investigations and prosecutions. The federal *Anti-Terrorism Act* brought about changes to the *Criminal Code* to add preventative enforcement measures and investigative tools to assist in fighting terrorist activities.

Part II.1 of the *Criminal Code* contains the anti-terrorism provisions. Section 83.01 provides an extensive definition of terrorist activities, referring to a long list of United Nations conventions on air travel, the taking of hostages, terrorist bombings and the financing of terrorism. It also includes actions done for "... a political, religious or ideological purpose, objective or cause ..." and intended to intimidate the public. Being involved in conspiracies, attempts, or acting as an accessory after the fact to any of the outlawed activities also constitute terrorist activities.

There is a definition of a "terrorist group" since many of the terrorist-specific crimes relate to financing, aiding, or dealing in property on behalf of such groups. For greater certainty, the Solicitor General can recommend to Cabinet that named groups become part of a "list of entities" that fit the definition. This list has been established as a *regulation* under the *Criminal Code*.

It is illegal to provide financial services to a terrorist group and banks and other financial institutions are required to "... determine on a continuing basis whether they are in possession or control of property owned or controlled on behalf of a listed entity". Assets can be frozen and property controlled by terrorist groups can be seized.

According to section 83.2 committing *any indictable offence* on behalf of a terrorist group will attract a potential life sentence. As if that weren't clear enough, section 83.27 adds to the overkill by specifying that any indictable offence that could also be categorized as a terrorist activity attracts a life sentence.

The Code's anti-terrorism provisions also attempt to distort normal criminal procedures. For example, for any other offence, an accused person would be tried in a court in the territorial jurisdiction where the offence is alleged to have occurred. Section 83.25 purports to allow representatives of the Attorney General of Canada to start the trial process against someone alleged to have committed a terrorist activity in any territorial division in Canada. The rationale is unclear.

In addition, section 83.26 requires that a judge who sentences an offender in relation to a terrorist offence must make the sentence *consecutive* to any other sentence imposed, even if the other offence arose out of the same incident. This is normally the type of situation in which a judge would be entitled to exercise his or her discretion to impose a *concurrent* sentence.

Special provisions are included in section 83.28 of the *Criminal Code* to allow a peace officer to apply to a judge for *an order for the gathering of information*. If the officer believes a terrorist offence has been, or may be committed, the officer can ask the judge for an order that would require a named individual to come forward and provide any information he or she has about the offence or the whereabouts of any individual. This is unprecedented in our criminal justice system as a crime control measure. The person who is called is entitled to a lawyer, but cannot refuse to testify because the evidence he or she gives may be incriminatory. A person who tries to avoid the process could be arrested and a refusal to testify could result in continued custody for contempt of court.

Section 83.3 of the *Criminal Code* allows a peace officer who suspects that a terrorist activity may be carried out to have the suspect brought before a judge. If the officer believes the situation to be "exigent" (an emergency), the officer could arrest the suspect without a warrant. The judge will then listen to any evidence the peace officer has to support his or her belief in the risk presented. If the officer is believed, the judge can require that the suspect enter a *recognizance*, which is basically a promise to keep the peace and to comply with a number of conditions that could be added by the judge, including a prohibition from possessing any firearms or explosives. If the suspect refuses to sign the recognizance, he or she can be locked up for up to 12 months.

When law-makers become zealous in drafting pro-active security measures, there is always a risk that the rights of citizens will be compromised. It was inevitable that legal challenges to some of this legislation would be mounted under the *Canadian Charter of Rights and Freedoms*. The investigative order provisions in section 83.28 were challenged in the case of *R. v. Bagri*. In that 2004 decision, the Supreme Court of Canada ruled that while the section did not violate sections 7 or 11(*d*) of the *Charter*, judges dealing with these applications would have to be vigilant in ensuring that they were based on truly relevant evidence.

It is interesting to note that from the time of the creation of this legislation, the government was concerned it was overreaching with the information gathering orders and the streamlined process to haul suspects before a judge. When these provisions were enacted, the government also required the publication of an annual report on their usage and a review of their utility within three years. The required annual reports indicate that the arrest powers in section 83.3 were never used by any police service. Section 83.32 was set up as a "sunset clause", requiring that if the federal government did not pass a resolution for sections 83.28 through 83.3 to continue in effect by early 2007, these sections would cease to have any effect. In February of 2007, the federal government killed the sections by voting not to extend their validity. Sections 83.28 through 83.3 ceased to have any effect in March of 2007, but their provisions were revived by the federal government in 2013.

The concept of security certificates has been around much longer, though their practical utility has been seriously challenged in recent court decisions. Since 1978, the *Immigration and Refugee Protection Act* and laws that preceded that statute have allowed federal Cabinet ministers to sign these certificates, authorizing the incarceration and removal from Canada of individuals on the basis of a "reasonable suspicion" that the person was a threat to national security. While the Act allows for a Federal Court judge's review of the validity of the certificates, the person who could be locked up and deported is not allowed to see the "intelligence" information that purportedly provides the justification for these drastic attacks on the person's freedom. Not surprisingly, the atmosphere of tightened security, triggered by 9/11 increased the use of these certificates. Increased use inevitably led to legal scrutiny from the courts because the process of using the certificates appears to violate several of the fundamental legal protections provided in the *Canadian Charter of Rights and Freedoms*.

In the 2007 Supreme Court of Canada case, called *Charkaoui v. Canada*, a permanent resident named Adil Charkaoui and two foreign nationals named Hassan Almrei and Mohamed Harkat challenged the security certificate issuance and court review procedures set up under the *Immigration and Refugee Protection Act*. The Supreme Court recognized that security concerns may necessitate extraordinary measures, but were not prepared to tolerate the fact that the court review process set up under the Act violated numerous fundamental principles of a fair hearing and sections 7, 9 and 10(*c*) of the *Canadian Charter of Rights and Freedoms*. They allowed the government a year to change the law to address their concerns and the process has since been revised, adopting a slightly less secretive approach.

Strict restrictions on the freedom of the three individuals who were involved in the 2007 case have been challenged in a series of subsequent cases at the Federal Court level. As a result, Charkaoui and Almrei gained complete freedom from the security certificate controls by the end of 2009. A major factor in judges easing the restrictions was because agents of the Canadian Security Intelligence Service refused to present any evidence at all to justify ongoing security concerns, claiming that to do so might jeopardize their "confidential" sources. It is logical that some of these sources are agents in the employ of foreign governments and a great deal of media speculation raises the possibility that some of the initial information may have come from sources tortured by foreign operatives. With the results of these court cases, the continued utility of the security certificate process has been seriously questioned.

EMPLOYMENT OPPORTUNITIES IN THE JUSTICE SYSTEM

There will always be a wide variety of career opportunities in the justice system for people who are prepared to accept and embrace change and are dedicated to continuing to educate themselves on the effect new court precedents and statutory revisions have on the way the law impacts on the lives of Canadians. Nothing about the law is static. People who choose to not keep up will soon be left behind.

Financial pressures on municipal governments have led to increased demands that police budgets be cut. It seems inevitable that police services will need to introduce differentiated roles, like those employed in the United Kingdom where community support officers handle a more limited range of duties and are paid about two-thirds as much as regular officers.

Some functions may have to be privatized and others eliminated from a police service's duties. Police can expect extra scrutiny over everything they do and the expenditures they make. For example, do police in Canada really need the massive, gas-guzzling vehicles they seem to prefer when officers in other parts of the world seem to operate effectively with much less ostentatious, environmentally friendly forms of transportation?

Correctional personnel who have the flexibility to work in community corrections, as well as secure institutions, are prepared to adapt to legislative changes and government policies that alter the emphasis on the way society deals with offenders.

Forensic investigators and analysts live in a world where technological change and scientific development is the norm. Changes to the law will just be another dynamic factor in their lives.

Law clerks, paralegals and lawyers in the traditional legal services fields quickly learn that their employment environment is very much affected by the economy. When the economic climate is buoyant, people are buying houses and starting new businesses. They need legal service providers who can facilitate real estate transactions and set up corporations. There is a great deal of work for law clerks or paralegals capable of assisting lawyers in these tasks. When the economy takes a downturn, expertise in bankruptcy and inventive ways of collecting from people who are finding it difficult to pay their bills can be valuable skills. Nevertheless, law firms themselves may have to reduce their staff complement as clients find it increasingly difficult to pay for expert legal help. Even if crime or the rate of family break-ups doesn't change significantly, the financial ability of people to hire lawyers or agents and their support staff to assist with these issues can be affected. An inability to adapt quickly to whatever service needs remain can be a real impediment to continued employment.

Private security, computer security and risk management expertise have never been in higher demand and the expectation for the range of legal knowledge for people in these fields continues to grow exponentially. Keeping up with technological advances is an additional career challenge which makes this work fascinating and challenging.

The same sorts of challenges and opportunities face people training to work in the customs and immigration sectors. Booming international trade, combined with drastically heightened concern around security issues and extremely complex legislation affecting the field, continue to keep the demand for qualified experts at a very high level among private businesses and the government agencies.

Hopefully, this book has provided a useful overview of the Canadian justice system regardless of your career path. With this context, you should be able to expand your knowledge in the direction that excites you the most. Good luck in pursuing a career in the justice system!

KEY TERMINOLOGY

alternative measures	community based remedies for criminal behaviour which allow an accused person to avoid having the matter dealt with in the court system
concurrent sentence	a sentence that is served at the same time as the sentence for another offence
consecutive sentence	a sentence that will be added on to another sentence and served after the initial sentence expires
conventions	international agreements to treat legal issues in a particular way — commonly used among United Nations membership
extrajudicial measures	remedies provided outside the court process
information	the document that starts the court process for most criminal charges
order for the gathering of information	special anti-terrorism measure that allows a judge to order a witness to attend for questioning in relation to a potential terrorist attack or the whereabouts of terrorism suspects
recognizance	a promise to keep the peace and comply with listed conditions
regulations	government-created legal details added to statutes
restorative approaches	community-based initiatives that emphasize healing rather than punishment when dealing with criminal offenders
treaties	legal agreements between countries

STATUTES MENTIONED

Anti-terrorism Act, S.C. 2001, c. 41

Canadian Charter of Rights and Freedoms, Part 1 of the *Constitution Act, 1982*, being Schedule B to the *Canada Act 1982* (U.K.), 1982, c. 11

Canadian Security Intelligence Service Act, R.S.C. 1985, c. C-23, as am.

Divorce Act, R.S.C. 1985, c. 3 (2nd. Supp.), as am.

Immigration and Refugee Protection Act, S.C. 2001, c. 27

Security Offences Act, R.S.C. 1985, c. S-7

Youth Criminal Justice Act, S.C. 2002, c. 1, as am.

CASES MENTIONED

Charkaoui v. Canada, [2007] S.C.J. No. 9, [2007] 1 S.C.R. 350 (S.C.C.)

Application under s. 83.28 of the *Criminal Code* (Re), [2004] S.C.J. No. 40, [2004] 2 S.C.R. 248 (S.C.C.) (*R. v. B.*)

R. v. Gladue, [1999] S.C.J. No. 19, [1999] 1 S.C.R. 688 (S.C.C.)

R. v. Ipeelee, [2012] S.C.J. No. 13, 2012 SCC 13 (S.C.C.)

R. v. Parker, [2013] O.J. No. 1755, 2013 ONCJ 195 (C.J.)

USEFUL WEBSITES

Online: Statistics Canada <www.statcan.gc.ca>

TEST YOURSELF

1. Consider the career path you have chosen in the Canadian justice system. Discuss how the trends addressed in this chapter will impact on your career choice. If you feel that the impact will be minimal, support this assessment.

2. Quickly review the range of legal issues covered in this text. Select three that you feel will be of particular importance for someone on the career path you are currently pursuing. Detail your plans for expanding your knowledge of those legal issues as you progress down the career path. List any resources you feel will assist in accomplishing the required knowledge acquisition.

Appendix 1

Glossary of Terms

absolute discharge — a sentence that enables the offender to claim he or she has not been convicted of a criminal offence, this type of discharge is effective as soon as the judge makes the order

absolute liability — proof of the *actus reus* component of this type of criminal or quasi-criminal charge is enough to get a conviction

acceptance — an unconditional positive response to a contract offer

acquitted — being judged "not guilty"

actus reus — an illegal action or omission

adjourn — postpone, or set over to a later date

administrative law — category of law that involves boards, tribunals and government officers who make legal decisions (not courts)

admissibility — the issue of whether or not evidence can be used during a trial — judge decides

adversarial system — our trial system — involving a contest between the parties, with a judge acting as an independent arbitrator

agent — someone authorized to enter into contracts on behalf of another

aggravating circumstances — factors related to the offence that could justify a judge imposing a more severe penalty

alternative measures — community-based remedies for criminal behaviour which allow an accused person to avoid having the matter dealt with in court

amend	to change a law
amending formula	the requirement that the federal government and two-thirds of the provinces have to agree to any change to Canada's constitution
amendments	changes made to existing laws
appeal courts	courts that deal with challenges to decisions made by other courts
appearance notice	document used by police to get an accused to court for a first appearance on a summary, hybrid or section 553 *Criminal Code* offence
appellant	the person who starts an appeal of a court decision
arbitrarily	without a legitimate legal reason
arraignment	first appearance in court to face a criminal charge
arrest	interfere with someone's freedom by preventing freedom of movement
arrest warrant	court order authorizing police to arrest a named individual
assault	an uninvited threat of force, with a reasonable fear it will be acted upon, or an uninvited application of force
automatism	acting while in an involuntary or unconscious state
bail	a process for releasing someone who has been arrested from custody pending his or her trial
balance of probabilities	the standard of proof in the civil justice system
battery	an uninvited application of force
beyond a reasonable doubt	standard of proof in the criminal justice system
bill	proposal for a government-created law
binding	a court decision that a judge has a legal obligation to follow in dealing with another case

breach of contract	not doing what was agreed to be done
breach of the peace	actions that could result in actual or threatened harm to someone, or to a person's property in the person's presence
by-law	a written law made by a municipal government
cabinet	the key members of the party in power in the federal or provincial government who act as special advisors to the Prime Minister or the premiers and guide government policy decisions
cabinet minister	a member of the party in power who has been given special responsibilities for overseeing a government department and attends cabinet meetings
capacity	having the maturity and mental capabilities to enter into a binding agreement
case report	the written judgment or decision of a court case that includes the judges' view of the facts of the case, the legal issues that must be resolved and the judges' decision on the correct resolution
case reporting service	a service that collects, organizes and publishes case reports
cause of action	legal justification for suing someone
caution	a warning not to get involved in future criminal behaviour, could include a warning against associating with certain individuals or being in certain locations
challenge for cause	one of the reasons listed in the *Criminal Code* for keeping someone off a jury
chattels	personal property with intrinsic value, also known as "goods"
child in need of protection	child who has been neglected or subjected to physical, mental or emotional abuse
choses in action	documents that have value due to financial commitments written on them

citation	reference information for locating a statute or case report
clause	a portion of a subsection of a statute, labeled with a small case letter in parentheses
closing statement	a last attempt to convince a judge or jury by an advocate acting on behalf of one of the parties at a trial
common law	a system of resolving common legal disputes in a common way by relying on precedents
community supervision	a sentence served in the community with conditions attached and a community correctional worker monitoring compliance
compulsion by threats	a potential defence for some criminal charges for someone who has been threatened with physical harm
concurrent sentence	a sentence that is served at the same time as a sentence for another offence
conditional discharge	a sentence that includes a period of probation, but if that is completed successfully it would allow the offender to claim that he or she has not been convicted of a criminal offence
confirmed	judge or justice of the peace will review and endorse an appearance notice, promise to appear or recognizance issued by a police officer
consecutive sentence	a sentence that will be added on to another sentence and served after the initial sentence expires
consideration	a promise that something of value will be exchanged
constitution	the fundamental legal basis on which the government of Canada is organized
consumer protection laws	laws that are intended to protect consumers from questionable business practices
contempt	a wilful failure to follow a court order

contracts	agreements that courts will help enforce
contributory liability	when the plaintiff's actions are a contributing factor in the harm done
contributory negligence	the plaintiff has contributed to his or her own injuries through lack of care
conventions	international agreements to treat legal issues in a consistent way — commonly used among United Nations membership
counsel	legal representative — lawyer or paralegal
counter-offer	an alternative proposal of an offer made during contract negotiations
CPIC	Canadian Police Information Centre — a central computer-based data bank containing criminal records of members of the public
credibility	whether or not a witness can be believed
criminal charge	the allegation that a person has violated a particular section of a criminal statute
criminal record	a record of convictions for federal criminal offences
cross-examine	challenge the testimony of an opposing witness with probing or leading questions
damages	financial compensation ordered for someone who has won a lawsuit
dangerous offender	a label attached at the time of sentencing to convicts who have committed particularly violent offences, showing a lack of regard for others — carries an indeterminate sentence
decision	a judge's answer to the legal issues that have to be resolved in a court case
defamation	published statements that damage someone's reputation

defence	a rationale for the defendant's actions that eliminates or reduces liability or in a criminal case may entitle the accused to be acquitted or convicted of a reduced charge
defence of mental disorder	suffering from a mental condition that renders a person incapable of knowing that what he or she is doing is wrong
defence of person	protecting yourself or another person
defence of property	protecting your property from harm
defendant	the accused person in a criminal trial or the person who is being sued in a civil trial
detain	prevent someone from going where he or she wants to go
direct taxation	a taxing power given to the provinces — the person being taxed has to be made aware of the tax
discharge	a special form of sentence that may include a period of probation but will enable the offender to claim he or she has not been convicted of a criminal charge
disclose	provide evidence to the other party in advance of a trial
discovery	exchange relevant documents, question key opposition witnesses prior to a civil trial
dismiss	court order eliminating a criminal or quasi-criminal charge against an accused person
drunkenness	intoxication, can be used as a partial defence to some criminal charges
dual procedure offence	also called "hybrid", prosecutor has the choice to use summary conviction or indictable process
due diligence	exercising care to avoid doing something illegal
duress	a defence based on being forced to act through threats of physical harm

duty of care	the duty to be careful toward others
elect	to make a choice
endorse	a local judge re-affirming the effect of a court order made in another jurisdiction
enumerated powers	listed law-making powers given to a particular level of government
evidence	information that can be considered by a judge, jury or administrative tribunal in making a decision
expert witness	a witness with special knowledge or training, whose opinion would be helpful to a judge, jury or administrative tribunal in making a decision
extrajudicial measures	remedies provided outside the court process
failure to appear	didn't show up at the time and place appointed for an appearance in court or for fingerprints and photos
false arrest	stopping someone from going where he or she wants to go without a legitimate legal reason
false imprisonment	confining someone without a legitimate legal reason
federal	the central government with power to create laws that apply across the country
fine option program	provincially or territorially initiated programs that allow offenders to work off their fines
first appearance	also called an "arraignment", initial time in court to face a criminal or quasi-criminal charge
fixtures	goods that are permanently attached to real estate, becoming part of the realty
force of law	having the same impact as a valid government-created law
goods	personal property having intrinsic value, also known as "chattels"

habeas corpus	the right to be brought before a judge to have the validity of incarceration assessed
hearsay evidence	out of court statements being presented by someone other than the person who initially made the statement
hierarchy of courts	ranking some courts as more influential than others; for example, appeal courts are more influential than trial courts and the Supreme Court of Canada is the most influential of all
hybrid offence	also called "dual procedure", prosecutor has the choice to use summary or indictable process
identity	identifying who committed an offence
indeterminate sentence	a sentence with no set expiry date, used for dangerous offenders who will only get out of jail when the Parole Board is convinced they are no longer a danger to society
indictable offence	serious criminal offence
indictment	document used in processing indictable offences
influential	convincing, likely to affect another judge's approach to dealing with a legal issue
information	the document that starts the court process for most criminal or quasi-criminal charges
injunction	court order preventing someone from doing something
intellectual property	a bundle of rights, including ownership in relation to business concepts, inventions and creative works
intention	the mental element of criminal behaviour; meaning to bring on a particular result, or being reckless as to consequences
intention to be legally bound	a desire to enter into a binding contract
intermittent sentence	a sentence that can be served on weekends — can't be longer than 90 days

interpretation section	a portion of a statute that provides definitions for terminology used in that law
intoxication	a partial defence to some criminal charges based on being so impaired that the person is unable to form a specific intent
intra vires	within the law-making power of a particular level of government
intrusion upon seclusion	a common law right to sue for an invasion of a person's private affairs
judicial interim release	the name used for "bail" in the *Criminal Code*
jurisdiction	legal responsibility based on geography or division of legislative powers
jury	a group chosen from the community to decide on the guilt or innocence of an accused person in a criminal case, or on liability of someone who is being sued
jury summons	a court order requiring a person to attend a jury selection process
justice of the peace	an administrative officer appointed by the province to perform a variety of functions in the criminal justice process
leading question	a form of question that suggests the answer
leave	seeking the permission of a court of appeal to proceed with an appeal
legal aid	a scheme to provide expert legal representation for people who fall below the limits of a financial means test and face serious legal consequences in court
legal dictionaries	special dictionaries dealing with legal terminology
legal issues	the questions that have to be answered by a judge or jury in resolving a legal dispute
legislation	statutes, or written laws

lesser and included offence	another, less serious charge that includes many of the same elements
liable	legally and/or financially responsible
lien	a legal claim to some of the value of a piece of property
long-term offender	special label given to violent offenders who will need a long period of community supervision (up to 10 years) after their jail sentences expire
malpractice	negligence by a doctor or other medical expert
maximum penalty	the largest penalty stipulated for breaking a law
mens rea	the mental element that may have to be proven to secure the conviction of someone accused of committing a crime
minors	people who are under the age of majority set by a province or territory
mitigate	keep the damages as low as possible
municipal clerk	local government administrator with special responsibility for organizing, filing and making municipal by-laws available to the public
negligence	a lack of care that entitles someone to sue
no force and effect	a law that is invalid, cannot be enforced
non-necessary	not a necessity for a particular person
not criminally responsible	a possible trial outcome for someone suffering from a mental disorder that renders the person incapable of knowing that what was done was wrong
nuisance	doing something on your own property that damages the value of someone else's property
object	ask a judge to rule that certain evidence should not be admissible or that conduct of opposing counsel is inappropriate

offer	a tentative promise of an exchange
officer in charge	the police officer in charge of the local lock-up, given extra release powers in the *Criminal Code*
onus	the responsibility for proving something
opening statement	an initial oral presentation by an advocate representing one of the parties, outlining key points in the case that will be presented on behalf of that party
opinion evidence	an expert's point of view on an evidentiary issue
order for the gathering of information	special anti-terrorism measure that allows a judge to order a witness to attend for questioning in relation to a potential terrorist action or the location of terrorism suspects
order-in-council	cabinet decision
ownership	the largest bundle of property rights
pardon	government permission to relieve the negative ramifications of a criminal record
parliamentary process	process followed by government to enact laws
parole eligibility dates	the dates at which offenders sentenced to jail will become eligible to apply for various types of supervised release into the community
partial defence	an explanation of an accused's conduct that may result in a conviction for a lesser and included offence rather than for the more serious charge
parties	individuals directly involved in a lawsuit, criminal trial or administrative hearing
passing off	an attempt to have people falsely believe that a product is affiliated with an established brand
patent agent	an expert who could assist a person applying for patent protection for an invention

peace officer	defined in the "interpretation" section of the *Criminal Code* — includes police officers, correctional officers, customs officers and others
penalty	punishment for breaking a law
penitentiaries	federally operated jails, house prisoners with sentences longer than two years
peremptory challenge	being able to keep a potential juror off the jury panel without having to provide a reason
personal property	goods or chattels and choses in action
plaintiff	the person who starts a lawsuit
possession	the control of property
preamble	an introductory portion of a statute, often outlines the purpose of the law
precedents	previous court decisions that may be influential or binding on a judge dealing with a similar legal issue
preliminary inquiry	a process during which the prosecutor is required to produce enough evidence to convince a provincial court judge that an indictable case is worth sending on to a superior court for trial
pre-sentence report	background information to assist the judge at the time of sentencing someone who has been convicted of an offence — usually prepared by a probation officer
presumed	a judge will assume a particular state of affairs unless he or she receives contrary evidence
presumed innocent	an assumption that an accused person is innocent until proven guilty in court
presumptive offences	list of serious offences that will require a youth to face an adult sentence unless the youth court is convinced that it would be inappropriate

prima facie case	this is what the prosecutor has to establish at a preliminary inquiry to convince a judge to send the case to superior court for trial — some evidence of each of the elements of the charge as described in the charging statute
primary ground	the necessity to keep an accused person locked up or otherwise restricted with bail conditions to ensure that he or she will show up in court to face a criminal charge
principles of fundamental justice	common law principles of justice preserved by section 7 of the *Canadian Charter of Rights and Freedoms*
privative clause	a provision in a statute that purports to prevent a court from reviewing the decisions of an administrative tribunal
privilege	a special legal right
privity	the requirement that there be a direct contractual relationship between people involved in a lawsuit for breach of contract
procedural fairness	a process that enables an affected party to make submissions to a decision-maker before a decision is made
promise to appear	a document used by an officer in charge of a lock-up to release someone facing a relatively minor charge who is prepared to sign a promise to attend court for a first appearance
property	a collection of rights that includes ownership in relation to land, goods, business concepts, inventions or artistic creations
protective custody	special security provided for a prisoner who may be targeted by others
provinces	10 distinct geographic portions of Canada that have designated law-making power

provincial trial courts	courts with provincially appointed judges; trials are held by judge alone without a jury — busiest criminal courts, handling all summary charges, first appearances on most other charges and indictable charges when the accused person chooses this venue
provocation	a wrongful act or insult that is enough to deprive an ordinary person of self-control
quasi-criminal	having many of the same characteristics as a criminal offence, an offence created by a province, territory or municipality
Queen's Printer	government agency responsible for making laws available to the public
readings	stages in the parliamentary process for creating laws, may involve a literal reading, referral to committees for further review or a vote
real property	land and fixtures permanently attached
reasonable and probable grounds	the standard of belief required of a police officer to apply for a warrant or to lay a criminal charge
reasonable limits	restrictions on rights protected by the *Canadian Charter of Rights and Freedoms*
reasonably foreseeable	predictable
recidivism risk	the likelihood of someone committing another criminal offence
recognizance	a document used by an officer in charge of a lock-up or a judge to release someone who is prepared to deposit money or commit to paying an amount to secure release and agrees to other release conditions
record suspension	having a criminal record separated from records that could harm a person's employment or travel options
reformatory prisons	provincial jails

regulations	government-created legal details added to statutes
related statutes	written laws from the same level of government that deal with some of the same issues, or use the same terminology
relevant	having probative value with respect to an issue of importance in a trial or other hearing
remedies	solutions that a court can order following a civil trial
reprimand	verbal denunciation of a youth's criminal action
restorative approaches	community based initiatives that emphasize healing rather than punishment when dealing with criminal offenders
right to an impartial decision-maker	a right to have decisions made by someone who is unbiased
right to be heard	includes a right to a reasonable notice that a decision will be made and a right to make submissions to the decision-maker prior to that decision
right to exclude others	a right to deny access to your property
Sable Island	island off the east coast of Nova Scotia
secondary ground	the necessity to keep a person locked up or otherwise restricted with bail conditions to ensure he or she won't commit another offence or interfere with the administration of justice prior to first appearance in court
section	the primary division of a statute
self defence	acting to protect oneself from serious bodily harm
sentencing	the process of determining the appropriate punishment for someone who has been convicted of a criminal or quasi-criminal offence
sessional volume	a book containing the statutes created by the federal government or a provincial or territorial government during a particular year or sitting of the legislators

show cause hearing	another name for a "bail" hearing — prosecutor must convince a judge or justice of the peace that the accused person should be kept in custody or that restrictions be placed on release
small claims court	a civil court, using simplified procedures to deal with claims involving dollar amounts under a limit set by statute
solitary confinement	prison punishment involving isolation from others
special handling unit	a specially designed prison unit with extra security for the inmates that pose the greatest risk of escape or danger to others
specific intent	a particular mental element to a crime required by the wording of the charging statute
standard of care	the degree of care that must be exercised
standard of proof	the degree to which something must be proven
stare decisis	the common law system of relying on precedents that considers court decisions from a higher level of court binding and decisions from the same level, or from another jurisdiction, influential
statement of claim	the document used to start a lawsuit
statement of defence	the document used to respond to a statement of claim in a lawsuit
statutes	government-created written laws
strict liability	being civilly liable without the ability to use being careful or any other excuse as a defence; OR criminal or quasi-criminal charges that don't require proof of *mens rea*, but may enable an accused to use a due diligence defence
subsection	a portion of a section of a statute, grammatically it will be a sentence and will be labelled by a number in parentheses

summary offence	all provincial, territorial and municipal charges and less serious federal charges
summons	a judge's order that an accused person attend court to face a criminal or a quasi-criminal charge
superior trial courts	trial courts with federally appointed judges; jury trials are an option
Supreme Court of Canada	highest level of appeal court in the country; its decisions are binding on all other judges
surety	a family member or friend who is prepared to pledge money or property to secure an accused person's release from custody and to guarantee that the accused will attend court to face a charge
suspicion	an inkling that someone may be responsible without much proof to support the belief
thin skull rule	being responsible for all damage caused even if the victim was particularly sensitive
threat	causing someone to fear harm
torts	non-contractual justifications for suing someone
transcript	a written record of the questions asked, answers given and statements made when someone is speaking in court or during another type of legal proceeding
treaties	legal agreements between countries
trespass	encroaching on someone else's property without permission or any other legal reason
trial courts	courts where evidence is provided by witnesses to assist a judge or jury in arriving at a decision involving a criminal charge or civil lawsuit
trier of fact	the judge or jury required to make a decision about what happened and whether or not it fits the elements of a crime; guilty or not guilty

ultra vires	beyond the law-making power of a level of government
undertaking	a signed promise that an accused person will attend court to face charges, could include conditions that must be followed during the period of release from custody
unfit to stand trial	suffering from a mental disorder to such an extent that the person would not be able to understand what is happening during a trial or to instruct a lawyer providing representation
uninvited	without any prompting or invitation
vicarious liability	holding employers legally and financially responsible for the actions of their employees
victim impact statement	a written submission to a court by a victim, describing the way in which an offence has impacted on the victim and his or her family
warrant	a court order authorizing a search, seizure or arrest
warrant expiry date	the date on which a prison sentence imposed by a judge expires and correctional supervision of a convict ends
youth court	the court designated in each province to deal with charges under the *Youth Criminal Justice Act*

Appendix 2

Excerpts from the
Constitution Act, 1867

VI. DISTRIBUTION OF LEGISLATIVE POWERS

POWERS OF THE PARLIAMENT

Legislative Authority of Parliament of Canada
91. It shall be lawful for the Queen, by and with the Advice and Consent of the Senate and House of Commons, to make Laws for the Peace, Order, and good Government of Canada, in relation to all Matters not coming within the Classes of Subjects by this Act assigned exclusively to the Legislatures of the Provinces; and for greater Certainty, but not so as to restrict the Generality of the foregoing Terms of this Section, it is hereby declared that (notwithstanding anything in this Act) the exclusive Legislative Authority of the Parliament of Canada extends to all Matters coming within the Classes of Subjects next hereinafter enumerated; that is to say,

1.   Repealed. (44)
1A. The Public Debt and Property. (45)
2.   The Regulation of Trade and Commerce.
2A. Unemployment insurance. (46)
3.   The raising of Money by any Mode or System of Taxation.
4.   The borrowing of Money on the Public Credit.
5.   Postal Service.
6.   The Census and Statistics.
7.   Militia, Military and Naval Service, and Defence.
8.   The fixing of and providing for the Salaries and Allowances of Civil and other Officers of the Government of Canada.
9.   Beacons, Buoys, Lighthouses, and Sable Island.
10. Navigation and Shipping.
11. Quarantine and the Establishment and Maintenance of Marine Hospitals.
12. Sea Coast and Inland Fisheries.
13. Ferries between a Province and any British or Foreign Country or between Two Provinces.
14. Currency and Coinage.
15. Banking, Incorporation of Banks, and the Issue of Paper Money.
16. Savings Banks.
17. Weights and Measures.

18. Bills of Exchange and Promissory Notes.
19. Interest.
20. Legal Tender.
21. Bankruptcy and Insolvency.
22. Patents of Invention and Discovery.
23. Copyrights.
24. Indians, and Lands reserved for the Indians.
25. Naturalization and Aliens.
26. Marriage and Divorce.
27. The Criminal Law, except the Constitution of Courts of Criminal Jurisdiction, but including the Procedure in Criminal Matters.
28. The Establishment, Maintenance, and Management of Penitentiaries.
29. Such Classes of Subjects as are expressly excepted in the Enumeration of the Classes of Subjects by this Act assigned exclusively to the Legislatures of the Provinces.

And any Matter coming within any of the Classes of Subjects enumerated in this Section shall not be deemed to come within the Class of Matters of a local or private Nature comprised in the Enumeration of the Classes of Subjects by this Act assigned exclusively to the Legislatures of the Provinces. (47)

EXCLUSIVE POWERS OF PROVINCIAL LEGISLATURES

Subjects of exclusive Provincial Legislation
92. In each Province the Legislature may exclusively make Laws in relation to Matters coming within the Classes of Subjects next hereinafter enumerated; that is to say,

1. Repealed. (48)
2. Direct Taxation within the Province in order to the raising of a Revenue for Provincial Purposes.
3. The borrowing of Money on the sole Credit of the Province
4. The Establishment and Tenure of Provincial Offices and the Appointment and Payment of Provincial Officers.
5. The Management and Sale of the Public Lands belonging to the Province and of the Timber and Wood thereon.
6. The Establishment, Maintenance, and Management of Public and Reformatory Prisons in and for the Province.
7. The Establishment, Maintenance, and Management of Hospitals, Asylums, Charities, and Eleemosynary Institutions in and for the Province, other than Marine Hospitals.
8. Municipal Institutions in the Province.
9. Shop, Saloon, Tavern, Auctioneer, and other Licences in order to the raising of a Revenue for Provincial, Local, or Municipal Purposes.
10. Local Works and Undertakings other than such as are of the following Classes:

(*a*) Lines of Steam or other Ships, Railways, Canals, Telegraphs, and other Works and Undertakings connecting the Province with any other or others of the Provinces, or extending beyond the Limits of the Province:

(*b*) Lines of Steam Ships between the Province and any British or Foreign Country:

(*c*) Such Works as, although wholly situate within the Province, are before or after their Execution declared by the Parliament of Canada to be for the general Advantage of Canada or for the Advantage of Two or more of the Provinces.

11. The Incorporation of Companies with Provincial Objects.
12. The Solemnization of Marriage in the Province.
13. Property and Civil Rights in the Province.
14. The Administration of Justice in the Province, including the Constitution, Maintenance, and Organization of Provincial Courts, both of Civil and of Criminal Jurisdiction, and including Procedure in Civil Matters in those Courts.
15. The Imposition of Punishment by Fine, Penalty, or Imprisonment for enforcing any Law of the Province made in relation to any Matter coming within any of the Classes of Subjects enumerated in this Section.
16. Generally all Matters of a merely local or private Nature in the Province.

NON-RENEWABLE NATURAL RESOURCES, FORESTRY RESOURCES AND ELECTRICAL ENERGY

Laws respecting non-renewable natural resources, forestry resources and electrical energy
92A. (1) In each province, the legislature may exclusively make laws in relation to

(*a*) exploration for non-renewable natural resources in the province;

(*b*) development, conservation and management of non-renewable natural resources and forestry resources in the province, including laws in relation to the rate of primary production therefrom; and

(*c*) development, conservation and management of sites and facilities in the province for the generation and production of electrical energy.

Export from provinces of resources
(2) In each province, the legislature may make laws in relation to the export from the province to another part of Canada of the primary production from non-renewable natural resources and forestry resources in the province and the production from facilities in the province for the generation of electrical energy, but such laws may not authorize or provide for discrimination in prices or in supplies exported to another part of Canada.

Authority of Parliament
(3) Nothing in subsection (2) derogates from the authority of Parliament to enact laws in relation to the matters referred to in that subsection and, where such a law of Parliament and a law of a province conflict, the law of Parliament prevails to the extent of the conflict.

Taxation of resources
(4) In each province, the legislature may make laws in relation to the raising of money by any mode or system of taxation in respect of

    (a)   non-renewable natural resources and forestry resources in the province and the primary production therefrom, and

    (b)   sites and facilities in the province for the generation of electrical energy and the production therefrom,

whether or not such production is exported in whole or in part from the province, but such laws may not authorize or provide for taxation that differentiates between production exported to another part of Canada and production not exported from the province.

"Primary production"
(5) The expression "primary production" has the meaning assigned by the Sixth Schedule.

Existing powers or rights
(6) Nothing in subsections (1) to (5) derogates from any powers or rights that a legislature or government of a province had immediately before the coming into force of this section.

EDUCATION

Legislation respecting Education
93. In and for each Province the Legislature may exclusively make Laws in relation to Education, subject and according to the following Provisions:

(1) Nothing in any such Law shall prejudicially affect any Right or Privilege with respect to Denominational Schools which any Class of Persons have by Law in the Province at the Union:
(2) All the Powers, Privileges, and Duties at the Union by Law conferred and imposed in Upper Canada on the Separate Schools and School Trustees of the Queen's Roman Catholic Subjects shall be and the same are hereby extended to the Dissentient Schools of the Queen's Protestant and Roman Catholic Subjects in Quebec:
(3) Where in any Province a System of Separate or Dissentient Schools exists by Law at the Union or is thereafter established by the Legislature of the Province,

an Appeal shall lie to the Governor General in Council from any Act or Decision of any Provincial Authority affecting any Right or Privilege of the Protestant or Roman Catholic Minority of the Queen's Subjects in relation to Education:

(4) In case any such Provincial Law as from Time to Time seems to the Governor General in Council requisite for the due Execution of the Provisions of this Section is not made, or in case any Decision of the Governor General in Council on any Appeal under this Section is not duly executed by the proper Provincial Authority in that Behalf, then and in every such Case, and as far only as the Circumstances of each Case require, the Parliament of Canada may make remedial Laws for the due Execution of the Provisions of this Section and of any Decision of the Governor General in Council under this Section. (50)

Quebec
93A. Paragraphs (1) to (4) of section 93 do not apply to Quebec.

Appendix 3

Constitution Act, 1982

Enacted as Schedule B to the *Canada Act 1982* (U.K.) 1982, c. 11, which came into force on April 17, 1982

PART I
Canadian charter of rights and freedoms

Whereas Canada is founded upon principles that recognize the supremacy of God and the rule of law:

Guarantee of Rights and Freedoms

Rights and freedoms in Canada

1. The *Canadian Charter of Rights and Freedoms* guarantees the rights and freedoms set out in it subject only to such reasonable limits prescribed by law as can be demonstrably justified in a free and democratic society.

Fundamental Freedoms

Fundamental freedoms

2. Everyone has the following fundamental freedoms:
   (*a*) freedom of conscience and religion;
   (*b*) freedom of thought, belief, opinion and expression, including freedom of the press and other media of communication;
   (*c*) freedom of peaceful assembly; and
   (*d*) freedom of association.

Democratic Rights

Democratic rights of citizens

3. Every citizen of Canada has the right to vote in an election of members of the House of Commons or of a legislative assembly and to be qualified for membership therein.

Maximum duration of legislative bodies

4. (1) No House of Commons and no legislative assembly shall continue for longer than five years from the date fixed for the return of the writs of a general election of its members.

Continuation
in special
circumstances

    (2) In time of real or apprehended war, invasion or insurrec-
tion, a House of Commons may be continued by Parliament and a
legislative assembly may be continued by the legislature beyond
five years if such continuation is not opposed by the votes of
more than one-third of the members of the House of Commons or
the legislative assembly, as the case may be.

Annual sitting
of legislative
bodies

    5. There shall be a sitting of Parliament and of each legislature
at least once every twelve months

Mobility Rights

Mobility of
citizens

    6. (1) Every citizen of Canada has the right to enter, remain in
and leave Canada.

Rights to
move and
gain liveli-
hood

    (2) Every citizen of Canada and every person who has the
status of a permanent resident of Canada has the right
        (*a*) to move to and take up residence in any province;
        and
        (*b*) to pursue the gaining of a livelihood in any province.

Limitation

    (3) The rights specified in subsection (2) are subject to
        (*a*) any laws or practices of general application in force
        in a province other than those that discriminate among
        persons primarily on the basis of province of present or
        previous residence; and
        (*b*) any laws providing for reasonable residency require-
        ments as a qualification for the receipt of publicly pro-
        vided social services.

Affirmative
action pro-
grams

    (4) Subsections (2) and (3) do not preclude any law, program
or activity that has as its object the amelioration in a province of
conditions of individuals in that province who are socially or eco-
nomically disadvantaged if the rate of employment in that province is below the rate of employment in Canada.

Legal Rights

Life, liberty
and security
of person

    7. Everyone has the right to life, liberty and security of the
person and the right not to be deprived thereof except in accordance with the principles of fundamental justice.

Search or
seizure

    8. Everyone has the right to be secure against unreasonable
search or seizure.

Detention or
imprisonment

9. Everyone has the right not to be arbitrarily detained or imprisoned.

Arrest or
detention

10. Everyone has the right on arrest or detention

(*a*) to be informed promptly of the reasons therefor;

(*b*) to retain and instruct counsel without delay and to be informed of that right; and

(*c*) to have the validity of the detention determined by way of *habeas corpus* and to be released if the detention is not lawful.

Proceedings
in criminal
and penal
matters

11. Any person charged with an offence has the right

(*a*) to be informed without unreasonable delay of the specific offence;

(*b*) to be tried within a reasonable time;

(*c*) not to be compelled to be a witness in proceedings against that person in respect of the offence;

(*d*) to be presumed innocent until proven guilty according to law in a fair and public hearing by an independent and impartial tribunal;

(*e*) not to be denied reasonable bail without just cause;

(*f*) except in the case of an offence under military law tried before a military tribunal, to the benefit of trial by jury where the maximum punishment for the offence is imprisonment for five years or a more severe punishment;

(*g*) not to be found guilty on account of any act or omission unless, at the time of the act or omission, it constituted an offence under Canadian or international law or was criminal according to the general principles of law recognized by the community of nations;

(*h*) if finally acquitted of the offence, not to be tried for it again and, if finally found guilty and punished for the offence, not to be tried or punished for it again; and

(*i*) if found guilty of the offence and if the punishment for the offence has been varied between the time of commission and the time of sentencing, to the benefit of the lesser punishment.

Treatment or
punishment

12. Everyone has the right not to be subjected to any cruel and unusual treatment or punishment.

Self-
crimination

13. A witness who testifies in any proceedings has the right not to have any incriminating evidence so given used to incriminate that witness in any other proceedings, except in a prosecution for perjury or for the giving of contradictory evidence.

Interpreter

14. A party or witness in any proceedings who does not understand or speak the language in which the proceedings are conducted or who is deaf has the right to the assistance of an interpreter.

Equality Rights

Equality before and under law and equal protection and benefit of law

15. (1) Every individual is equal before and under the law and has the right to the equal protection and equal benefit of the law without discrimination and, in particular, without discrimination based on race, national or ethnic origin, colour, religion, sex, age or mental or physical disability.

Affirmative action programs

(2) Subsection (1) does not preclude any law, program or activity that has as its object the amelioration of conditions of disadvantaged individuals or groups including those that are disadvantaged because of race, national or ethnic origin, colour, religion, sex, age or mental or physical disability.

. . . . .

Enforcement

Enforcement of guaranteed rights and freedoms

24. (1) Anyone whose rights or freedoms, as guaranteed by this Charter, have been infringed or denied may apply to a court of competent jurisdiction to obtain such remedy as the court considers appropriate and just in the circumstances.

Exclusion of evidence bringing administration of justice into disrepute

(2) Where, in proceedings under subsection (1), a court concludes that evidence was obtained in a manner that infringed or denied any rights or freedoms guaranteed by this Charter, the evidence shall be excluded if it is established that, having regard to all the circumstances, the admission of it in the proceedings would bring the administration of justice into disrepute.

General

Aboriginal rights and freedoms not affected by Charter

25. The guarantee in this Charter of certain rights and freedoms shall not be construed so as to abrogate or derogate from any aboriginal, treaty or other rights or freedoms that pertain to the aboriginal peoples of Canada including

(*a*) any rights or freedoms that have been recognized by the Royal Proclamation of October 7, 1763; and (*b*) any rights or freedoms that now exist by way of land claims agreements or may be so acquired.

. . . . .

Application to territories and territorial authorities

30. A reference in this Charter to a Province or to the legislative assembly or legislature of a province shall be deemed to include a reference to the Yukon Territory and the Northwest Territories, or to the appropriate legislative authority thereof, as the case may be.

Legislative powers not extended

31. Nothing in this Charter extends the legislative powers of any body or authority.

Application of Charter

Application of Charter

32. (1)This Charter applies
(*a*) to the Parliament and government of Canada in respect of all matters within the authority of Parliament including all matters relating to the Yukon Territory and Northwest Territories; and
(*b*) to the legislature and government of each province in respect of all matters within the authority of the legislature of each province.

Exception

(2) Notwithstanding subsection (1), section 15 shall not have effect until three years after this section comes into force.

Exception where express declaration

33. (1) Parliament or the legislature of a province may expressly declare in an Act of Parliament or of the legislature, as the case may be, that the Act or a provision thereof shall operate notwithstanding a provision included in section 2 or sections 7 to 15 of this Charter.

Operation of exception

(2) An Act or a provision of an Act in respect of which a declaration made under this section is in effect shall have such operation as it would have but for the provision of this Charter referred to in the declaration.

Five year limitation

(3) A declaration made under subsection (1) shall cease to have effect five years after it comes into force or on such earlier date as may be specified in the declaration.

Re-enactment   (4) Parliament or the legislature of a province may re-enact a declaration made under subsection (1).

Five year
limitation   (5) Subsection (3) applies in respect of a re-enactment made under subsection (4).

Citation

Citation   **34.** This Part may be cited as the *Canadian Charter of Rights and Freedoms.*

Appendix 4
Sample Statutes

Identification of Criminals Act
R.S.C. 1985, c. I-1

CHAPTER I-1

An Act respecting the identification of criminals

SHORT TITLE

Short title

1. This Act may be cited as the *Identification of Criminals Act.*
R.S., c. I-1, s. 1.

HER MAJESTY

Binding on
Her Majesty

1.1 This Act is binding on Her Majesty in right of Canada or a province.
1992, c. 47, s. 73.

IDENTIFICATION OF CRIMINALS

Fingerprints
and photographs

2. (1) The following persons may be fingerprinted or photographed or subjected to such other measurements, processes and operations having the object of identifying persons as are approved by order of the Governor in Council:

(*a*) any person who is in lawful custody charged with or convicted of

(i) an indictable offence, other than an offence that is designated as a contravention under the *Contraventions Act* in respect of which the Attorney General, within the meaning of that Act, has made an election under section 50 of that Act, or

(ii) an offence under the *Security of Information Act*;

(*b*) any person who has been apprehended under the *Extradition Act*;

(*c*) any person alleged to have committed an indictable offence, other than an offence that is designated as a contravention under the *Contraventions Act* in respect of which the Attorney General, within the meaning of that Act, has made an election under section 50 of that Act, who is required pursuant to subsection 501(3) or 509(5) of the *Criminal Code* to appear for the purposes of this Act by an appearance notice, promise to appear, recognizance or summons; or

(*d*) any person who is in lawful custody pursuant to section 83.3 of the *Criminal Code*.

Use of force   (2) Such force may be used as is necessary to the effectual carrying out and application of the measurements, processes and operations described under subsection (1).

Publication   (3) The results of the measurements, processes and operations to which a person has been subjected pursuant to subsection (1) may be published for the purpose of affording information to officers and others engaged in the execution or administration of the law.

R.S., 1985, c. I-1, s. 2; 1992, c. 47, s. 74; 1996, c. 7, s. 39; 1999, c. 18, s. 88; 2001, c. 41, ss. 23.1, 35.

No liability for acting under Act   **3.** No liability, civil or criminal, for anything lawfully done under this Act shall be incurred by any person

(*a*) having custody of a person described in subsection 2(1);

(*b*) acting in the aid or under the direction of a person having such custody; or

(*c*) concerned in the publication of results under subsection 2(3).

R.S., 1985, c. I-1, s. 3; 1992, c. 47, s. 75.

DESTRUCTION OF FINGERPRINTS AND PHOTOGRAPHS

Destruction of fingerprints and photographs   **4.** Where a person charged with an offence that is designated as a contravention under the *Contraventions Act* is fingerprinted or photographed and the Attorney General, within the meaning of that Act, makes an election under section 50 of that Act, the fingerprints or photographs shall be destroyed.

1992, c. 47, s. 76; 1996, c. 7, s. 40.

Trespass to Property Act
R.S.O. 1990, c. T.21

Amended by: 2000, c. 30, s. 11.

Definitions
1. (1) In this Act,

"occupier" includes,
  (a) a person who is in physical possession of premises, or
  (b) a person who has responsibility for and control over the condition of premises or the activities there carried on, or control over persons allowed to enter the premises,
even if there is more than one occupier of the same premises; ("occupant")

"premises" means lands and structures, or either of them, and includes,
  (a) water,
  (b) ships and vessels,
  (c) trailers and portable structures designed or used for residence, business or shelter,
  (d) trains, railway cars, vehicles and aircraft, except while in operation. ("lieux") R.S.O. 1990, c. T.21, s. 1 (1).

School boards
  (2) A school board has all the rights and duties of an occupier in respect of its school sites as defined in the *Education Act*. R.S.O. 1990, c. T.21, s. 1 (2).

Trespass an offence
  2. (1) Every person who is not acting under a right or authority conferred by law and who,
  (a) without the express permission of the occupier, the proof of which rests on the defendant,
      (i) enters on premises when entry is prohibited under this Act, or
      (ii) engages in an activity on premises when the activity is prohibited under this Act; or
  (b) does not leave the premises immediately after he or she is directed to do so by the occupier of the premises or a person authorized by the occupier,
is guilty of an offence and on conviction is liable to a fine of not more than $2,000. R.S.O. 1990, c. T.21, s. 2 (1).

Colour of right as a defence

(2) It is a defence to a charge under subsection (1) in respect of premises that is land that the person charged reasonably believed that he or she had title to or an interest in the land that entitled him or her to do the act complained of. R.S.O. 1990, c. T.21, s. 2 (2).

Prohibition of entry

3. (1) Entry on premises may be prohibited by notice to that effect and entry is prohibited without any notice on premises,

(a) that is a garden, field or other land that is under cultivation, including a lawn, orchard, vineyard and premises on which trees have been planted and have not attained an average height of more than two metres and woodlots on land used primarily for agricultural purposes; or

(b) that is enclosed in a manner that indicates the occupier's intention to keep persons off the premises or to keep animals on the premises. R.S.O. 1990, c. T.21, s. 3 (1).

Implied permission to use approach to door

(2) There is a presumption that access for lawful purposes to the door of a building on premises by a means apparently provided and used for the purpose of access is not prohibited. R.S.O. 1990, c. T.21, s. 3 (2).

Limited permission

4. (1) Where notice is given that one or more particular activities are permitted, all other activities and entry for the purpose are prohibited and any additional notice that entry is prohibited or a particular activity is prohibited on the same premises shall be construed to be for greater certainty only. R.S.O. 1990, c. T.21, s. 4 (1).

Limited prohibition

(2) Where entry on premises is not prohibited under section 3 or by notice that one or more particular activities are permitted under subsection (1), and notice is given that a particular activity is prohibited, that activity and entry for the purpose is prohibited and all other activities and entry for the purpose are not prohibited. R.S.O. 1990, c. T.21, s. 4 (2).

Method of giving notice

5. (1) A notice under this Act may be given,

(a) orally or in writing;

(b) by means of signs posted so that a sign is clearly visible in daylight under normal conditions from the approach to each ordinary point of access to the premises to which it applies; or

(c) by means of the marking system set out in section 7. R.S.O. 1990, c. T.21, s. 5 (1).

Substantial compliance

(2) Substantial compliance with clause (1) (b) or (c) is sufficient notice. R.S.O. 1990, c. T.21, s. 5 (2).

Form of sign

6. (1) A sign naming an activity or showing a graphic representation of an activity is sufficient for the purpose of giving notice that the activity is permitted. R.S.O. 1990, c. T.21, s. 6 (1).

Idem

(2) A sign naming an activity with an oblique line drawn through the name or showing a graphic representation of an activity with an oblique line drawn through the representation is sufficient for the purpose of giving notice that the activity is prohibited. R.S.O. 1990, c. T.21, s. 6 (2).

Red markings

7. (1) Red markings made and posted in accordance with subsections (3) and (4) are sufficient for the purpose of giving notice that entry on the premises is prohibited. R.S.O. 1990, c. T.21, s. 7 (1).

Yellow markings

(2) Yellow markings made and posted in accordance with subsections (3) and (4) are sufficient for the purpose of giving notice that entry is prohibited except for the purpose of certain activities and shall be deemed to be notice of the activities permitted. R.S.O. 1990, c. T.21, s. 7 (2).

Size

(3) A marking under this section shall be of such a size that a circle ten centimetres in diameter can be contained wholly within it. R.S.O. 1990, c. T.21, s. 7 (3).

Posting

(4) Markings under this section shall be so placed that a marking is clearly visible in daylight under normal conditions from the approach to each ordinary point of access to the premises to which it applies. R.S.O. 1990, c. T.21, s. 7 (4).

Notice applicable to part of premises

8. A notice or permission under this Act may be given in respect of any part of the premises of an occupier. R.S.O. 1990, c. T.21, s. 8.

Arrest without warrant on premises

9. (1) A police officer, or the occupier of premises, or a person authorized by the occupier may arrest without warrant any person he or she believes on reasonable and probable grounds to be on the premises in contravention of section 2. R.S.O. 1990, c. T.21, s. 9 (1).

Delivery to police officer

(2) Where the person who makes an arrest under subsection (1) is not a police officer, he or she shall promptly call for the assistance of a police officer and give the person arrested into the custody of the police officer. R.S.O. 1990, c. T.21, s. 9 (2).

Deemed arrest

(3) A police officer to whom the custody of a person is given under subsection (2) shall be deemed to have arrested the person for the purposes of the provisions of the *Provincial Offences Act* applying to his or her release or continued detention and bail. R.S.O. 1990, c. T.21, s. 9 (3).

Arrest without warrant off premises

10. Where a police officer believes on reasonable and probable grounds that a person has been in contravention of section 2 and has made fresh departure from the premises, and the person refuses to give his or her name and address, or there are reasonable and probable grounds to believe that the name or address given is false, the police officer may arrest the person without warrant. R.S.O. 1990, c. T.21, s. 10.

Motor vehicles and motorized snow vehicles

11. Where an offence under this Act is committed by means of a motor vehicle, as defined in the *Highway Traffic Act*, or by means of a motorized snow vehicle, as defined in the *Motorized Snow Vehicles Act*, the driver of the motor vehicle or motorized snow vehicle is liable to the fine provided under this Act and, where the driver is not the owner, the owner of the motor vehicle or motorized snow vehicle is liable to the fine provided under this Act unless the driver is convicted of the offence or, at the time the offence was committed, the motor vehicle or motorized snow vehicle was in the possession of a person other than the owner without the owner's consent. 2000, c. 30, s. 11.

Damage award

12. (1) Where a person is convicted of an offence under section 2, and a person has suffered damage caused by the person convicted during the commission of the offence, the court shall, on the request of the prosecutor and with the consent of the person who suffered the damage, determine the damages and shall make a judgment for damages against the person convicted in favour of the person who suffered the damage, but no judgment shall be for an amount in excess of $1,000. R.S.O. 1990, c. T.21, s. 12 (1).

Costs of prosecution

(2) Where a prosecution under section 2 is conducted by a private prosecutor, and the defendant is convicted, unless the court is of the opinion that the prosecution was not necessary for the protection of the occupier or the occupier's interests, the court shall determine the actual costs reasonably

incurred in conducting the prosecution and, despite section 60 of the *Provincial Offences Act*, shall order those costs to be paid by the defendant to the prosecutor. R.S.O. 1990, c. T.21, s. 12 (2).

Damages and costs in addition to fine

(3) A judgment for damages under subsection (1), or an award of costs under subsection (2), shall be in addition to any fine that is imposed under this Act. R.S.O. 1990, c. T.21, s. 12 (3).

Civil action

(4) A judgment for damages under subsection (1) extinguishes the right of the person in whose favour the judgment is made to bring a civil action for damages against the person convicted arising out of the same facts. R.S.O. 1990, c. T.21, s. 12 (4).

Idem

(5) The failure to request or refusal to grant a judgment for damages under subsection (1) does not affect a right to bring a civil action for damages arising out of the same facts. R.S.O. 1990, c. T.21, s. 12 (5).

Enforcement

(6) The judgment for damages under subsection (1), and the award for costs under subsection (2), may be filed in the Small Claims Court and shall be deemed to be a judgment or order of that court for the purposes of enforcement. R.S.O. 1990, c. T.21, s. 12 (6).

Sample Cases

Court of Appeal of Ontario

Between:

Joey Boudreau

Plaintiff
(Appellant)

– and –

Bank of Montreal, Rogers Communications Inc., Nike Inc., Umbro Inc., TDL Group Corporation, State Farm Insurance, Bick Financial Ltd., Dan Lawrie Insurance Brokers Ltd., Michael Lamont, AON Inc., and Hamilton Tiger Cats Football Club Inc.

Defendants
(Respondents)

Indexed as: *Boudreau v. Bank of Montreal*

Neutral citation: 2013 ONCA 211

Docket: C55980

Heard: March 27, 2013
Judgment: April 5, 2013

Present: J.L. MacFarland, D. Watt and S.E. Pepall JJ.A.

Counsel: Jane Poproski, for the appellant.

Irving Marks and Dominique Michaud, for the respondent, Bank of Montreal.

Peter J. Pliszka and Andrew M. Baerg, for the respondents, Rogers Communications Inc. and Umbro Inc.

On appeal from the judgment of Justice Thomas R. Lofchik of the Superior Court of Justice, dated July 31, 2012.

Civil litigation — Civil procedure — Disposition without trial — Dismissal of action — Action unfounded in law — Appeal by plaintiff from order dismissing action against three defendants dismissed — Plaintiff brought action for damages following incident in which he was rendered paraplegic while playing soccer at indoor field — Plaintiff alleged that sporting association had inadequate insurance and that responding defendants, each of whom sponsored association, had duty to inquire whether association and stadium operator had sufficient insurance — No facts pleaded which supported existence of duty of care between plaintiff and responding defendants — Plaintiff had cause of action against those with direct involvement in incident.

Tort law — Negligence — Duty and standard of care — Duty of care — Appeal by plaintiff from order dismissing action against three defendants dismissed — Plaintiff brought action for damages following incident in which he was rendered paraplegic while playing soccer at indoor field — Plaintiff alleged that sporting association had inadequate insurance and that responding defendants, each of whom sponsored association, had duty to inquire whether association and stadium operator had sufficient insurance — No facts pleaded which supported existence of duty of care between plaintiff and responding defendants — Plaintiff had cause of action against those with direct involvement in incident.

ENDORSEMENT

The following judgment was delivered by

THE COURT: —

[1]   The appellant was injured during a soccer game and rendered a paraplegic. The soccer game was organized by the Ontario Soccer Association ("OSA"), and took place at the Soccerworld facility in Hamilton. The OSA had obtained insurance for its members, however its coverage for the appellant's injuries was limited to $40,000.

[2]   The appellant commenced numerous lawsuits against many defendants, including the OSA, Soccerworld, players and referees.

[3]   The appellant also commenced an action against the corporate sponsors of the OSA, namely, the respondents Bank of Montreal, Umbro Inc., and Rogers Communications Inc. The OSA is not a party to that action. The statement of claim alleged that the OSA carried inadequate accident insurance for the soccer players; that it was foreseeable to the corporate sponsors that a player would get hurt; and that the corporate sponsors had a legal duty to the appellant to inquire into the adequacy of insurance coverage for the players

or, if they did inquire, to ensure that adequate insurance coverage was available. The appellant pleaded that the respondents extensively and publicly identify themselves as corporate partners of OSA and are major financial OSA sponsors.

[4]   The respondents moved to strike the statement of claim on the basis that it did not disclose a reasonable cause of action. The motion judge agreed that the claim as against the corporate sponsors should be struck out. He found that the facts pleaded did not establish a relationship of sufficient proximity between the appellant and the respondents to ground a duty of care or to support the appellant's claim in negligence.

[5]   The appellant appeals that order. Counsel argues that the OSA had a close partnership relationship with the respondents capable of grounding a legal duty to OSA's members and, as such, the pleading should not have been struck out.

[6]   The motion judge analyzed the statement of claim, applied the correct test, and considered the relevant case law. He was alive to the partnership issue as pleaded. He correctly concluded that a duty of care as alleged had not been recognized before in Canadian law. Nor had an analogous duty been recognized. Furthermore, the motion judge found that the appellant had not pleaded the facts necessary to establish a relationship of sufficient proximity between the appellant and the respondents to ground a new duty of care.

[7]   We see no error in the motion judge's decision. The pleading is bald. It discloses no relationship between the appellant and the corporate sponsor respondents, apart from the one that normally exists between a commercial corporation and its target market. Although the statement of claim refers to the respondents' presence on the Soccerworld field and related OSA and Soccerworld websites, the only example provided is the respondents' posting of advertisements in the "physical or cyber space under the authority and occupation of the OSA and Soccerworld."

[8]   Indeed, the pleading discloses no organizational role played by the respondents in operating the league or the specific game in which the appellant was injured, apart from their status as sponsors; no possession, control or responsibility by the respondents for the Soccerworld facility; and no role played by the respondents in overseeing or selecting insurance coverage for the appellant. Further, there are no facts pleaded in support of any reliance by the appellant on any of the respondents, and no assertion that it was in the reasonable contemplation of the respondents that the appellant was relying on them to ensure that his accident insurance was adequate.

[9]   Apart from other policy reasons that might be available to negate any finding of proximity, we would note that the appellant has a cause of action against those with direct involvement in the incident.

[10]   The appeal is dismissed.

[11]   The appellant shall pay the respondents' costs fixed in the amount of $12,500 inclusive of disbursements and applicable taxes.

J.L. MacFARLAND J.A
D. WATT J.A.
S.E. PEPALL J.A.

Yukon Territory Small Claims Court

Between:

Glanzmann Tours Ltd.

Plaintiff

– and –

Yukon Wide Adventures

Defendant

Indexed as: *Glanzmann Tours Ltd. v. Yukon Wide Adventures*

Neutral citation: 2012 YKSM 3

Docket: 11-S0062

Judgment: May 10, 2012

Present: J. Faulkner Terr. Ct. J.

Counsel: Peter Sandiford: Counsel for Plaintiff.

Thomas de Jager: Appearing on own behalf for the Defendant.

REASONS FOR JUDGMENT

[1]   J. FAULKNER TERR. CT. J.: — This is the tale of a very nice photograph of the aurora borealis or northern lights and of two tourism operators, Glanzmann Tours Ltd. and Yukon Wide Adventures.

[2]   The plaintiff, Glanzmann Tours Ltd., is a Yukon corporation owned and operated by Beat Glanzmann. The defendant, Yukon Wide Adventures, is a sole proprietorship owned and operated by Thomas de Jager. Both businesses are closely-held "one man" operations and in the reasons that follow I use the terms "plaintiff" and "defendant" interchangeably to refer to either the corporation, the proprietorship or their principals.

[3]   The plaintiff, Glanzmann Tours Ltd., offers guided adventure and sight-seeing tours in the Yukon, primarily to a German-speaking clientele. To promote its tours, Glanzmann Tours maintains a website.

[4]   In addition to operating tours, Mr. Glanzmann is also a professional photographer and derives a significant portion of his income through the licencing of photographs he has taken. To market his photographs, Mr. Glanzmann utilizes the services of Corbis Corporation, a large international photo marketing business.

[5]   In 1996, Mr. Glanzmann took a stunning photograph of the aurora borealis. The photograph was not sent to Corbis, but was retained by the plaintiff. Around 2007, Mr. Glanzmann uploaded a digital copy of the photo to his own website. According to Mr. Glanzmann, Corbis permits such personal use, so there was still the potential to licence the aurora photo to Corbis. The copy of the photo displayed on the plaintiff's website had no copyright or watermark on it, however, the website itself had a notice that all its contents were copyright protected.

[6]   Around December of 2011, a copy of the aurora photo appeared on a website maintained by the defendant, Yukon Wide Adventures. Yukon Wide offers tour services similar to those marketed by Glanzmann Tours. Both cater almost exclusively to the German market. In short, Mr. Glanzmann and Mr. de Jager are direct competitors. Indeed, the aurora photo was being used by Yukon Wide to promote a Northern Lights Tour: Mr. Glanzmann offers a similar tour and was using the photo on his website to the same purpose.

[7]   After Mr. Glanzmann became aware that his photo was being used, he contacted Mr. de Jager who immediately removed the photo from Yukon Wide's website.

[8]   As indicated, both businesses cater almost exclusively to the German-speaking market. However, the plaintiff's aurora photo only appeared on the English language portion of the defendant's website. The defendant never, in fact, sold or ran any of the Northern Lights Tours and so made no profit from the use of the photo.

[9]   It is clear, and the defendant does not seriously dispute, that it infringed the plaintiff's copyright in the aurora photo. Mr. de Jager claims that the infringement was inadvertent. He testified that he found the photo among computer files he inherited when he bought the business in 2003. There was no indication of copyright and he assumed that it was permissible to use the photo.

[10]   The plaintiff, however, says that he did not put the photo on his own website until 2007 and since the photo had never been published anywhere else, the photo could only have been obtained from the Glanzmann Tours website. By 2007, Mr. de Jager was in sole control of Yukon Wide Adventures.

Consequently, the plaintiff says that if the photo was on the defendant's computer, it was Mr. de Jager who downloaded it.

[11] However, it is difficult to believe that Mr. de Jager would be so rash as to deliberately copy the photo from the website of another local tourism operation marketing an identical product. This is especially so given that similar aurora photos are readily available for nominal fees from internet-based stock photo agencies. I note that the history of the aurora photo from the time it was digitized, including the copies of it that made their way into the Glanzmann Tours and Yukon Wide Adventures websites, might have been discoverable by reference to the metadata that accompanies digital photo files. Metadata can include when an image was created and when a computer copy of it was made or manipulated. However, neither party offered such evidence.

[12] At the end of the day, it remains unclear how the plaintiff's aurora photo found its way onto the defendant's computer and website. However, it is not a defence to the present action that the copyright infringement was inadvertent. The plaintiff is still entitled to damages equal to the loss he suffered from the infringement.

[13] This is where the real issue in the case arises.

[14] Mr. Glanzmann's position regarding his alleged losses was fraught with problems. Originally, the plaintiff claimed damages of $5,000.00. On the day of the trial he sought to amend his claim to seek $7,500.00. I refused to allow the amendment as it came far too late in the day.

[15] To support the claim for damages, Mr. Glanzmann swore an affidavit claiming revenues from sales of certain of his photos of as much as $20,000.00. However, during his testimony at trial, it became clear that the figures in the affidavit were wildly inaccurate, as the revenues that he calculated in dollars were often paid in other currencies such as German marks. Moreover, it also became apparent that the figures were gross revenues, whereas the plaintiff actually receives 37.5% of the licencing fees.

[16] Nevertheless, it was eventually established that some of the plaintiff's photographs have earned considerable revenue – netting him $5,000 or more in licencing fees. Typically, a licencee would pay much less for a one-time use, but some photos are licenced multiple times. Other photos have generated four figure fees from a single licencing.

[17] Mr. Glanzmann produced at trial a number of his photographs as well as agency records showing the fees he received following sales by Corbis. The difficulty with this evidence is that there is no way to determine in advance what sort of revenue a particular photograph will produce. Some will sell well, others less so, and some not at all.

[18]   The aurora photo is, to my eye, a very nice photo, but as I have indicated, similar photos are readily available for nominal fees. Interestingly, some of the plaintiff's photographs that did generate considerable income were, again to my eye, rather ordinary looking, something the average tourist might have taken while on vacation. So, the potential value of a particular photograph is difficult to predict.

[19]   As indicated, Mr. Glanzmann produced evidence concerning the sales of some, but by no means all, of his photographs. How he selected them is unclear. He gave no evidence regarding the average market value of all his photos. He did testify that his annual earnings from photography have varied between five and twenty-five thousand dollars.

[20]   None the less, given Mr. Glanzmann's undoubted success as a photographer and some of the sales he has enjoyed, it is reasonable to assume that the aurora photo has considerable value: potentially several thousand dollars in all and a single-use value of as high as $1,000.00.

[21]   However, the plaintiff does not, as one might expect, claim damages on the basis of a single use – i.e. what Yukon Wide would have to pay to properly licence and use the photograph. Rather, the plaintiff claimed that the defendant's use had destroyed any and all commercial value the photograph had and he claimed damages on that basis.

[22]   Mr. Glanzmann claimed that his understanding of his contract with his agent, Corbis, was that Corbis would not accept photos that had been used elsewhere.

[23]   When the court expressed some skepticism about the value of Mr. Glanzmann's interpretation of a legal document he had not produced in evidence, he sought, and was granted an adjournment in order to obtain the contract and it was later provided to the court.

[24]   Unfortunately for the plaintiff, the contract does not contain what he says it does. In the first place, it is apparent that Corbis will accept photos that have been used before since, on the plaintiff's own evidence, it has accepted photos which the photographer has published himself – on his own website, for example. Moreover, the contract clearly contemplates the non-exclusive licencing of photos. Even where the licencing argument is exclusive, the contract simply provides that the photographer must make Corbis the exclusive agent for the photo and must warrant that he has not previously licenced the photo to anyone else. None of this would in any way prevent Mr. Glanzmann from licencing the aurora photo to Corbis.

[25]   Mr. Glanzmann also testified that he had a telephone conversation with a representative of Corbis and was told that they would no longer be interested in the aurora photo if it had been used elsewhere. There are at least three problems

with this evidence. First, the evidence is hearsay. Second, it contradicts the wording of the agency contract itself. Third, it is far from clear that the scenario the plaintiff presented to the Corbis representative concerning the provenance of the aurora photo was an accurate representation of what actually occurred in this case. The aurora photo has not been previously licenced and it appeared but briefly on the defendant's English language website – a site which, given the defendant's clientele, is probably little viewed.

[26]   I have already noted that, thus far, the plaintiff has made no attempt to market the photo in question. It may be reasonable to assume that the value of the photo has been diminished somewhat, but there is no evidence capable of showing that the value of the aurora photograph, whatever it was, has been completely and utterly destroyed by the actions of the defendant.

[27]   In my view, the only reasonable estimation of damages in this case must be based on a *reduction* in the market value of the photo. One measure of that reduction in value would be the cost of a single use licence – which would be unlikely to have netted the plaintiff more than $400.00 to $500.00, especially considering that the plaintiff receives 37.5% of the gross revenue.

[28]   Even assuming that the aurora photograph's history of misuse by the defendant might complicate its marketing and further reduce its value, the plaintiff's losses have not been proven to exceed $1000.00 and I give judgment for the plaintiff in this amount.

[29]   With respect to costs, I find that success has in a sense been divided. Moreover both parties, but the plaintiff in particular, caused the proceeding to become needlessly protracted. In the result, each party will bear their own costs.

J. FAULKNER TERR. CT. J.

Supreme Court of Canada

Between:

Her Majesty the Queen

Appellant

– and –

Abede Burke

Respondent

Indexed as: *R. v. Burke*

Neutral citation: 2009 SCC 57

File No.: 33031

Heard: November 19, 2009
Judgment: December 4, 2009

Present: LeBel, Deschamps, Fish, Abella, Charron, Rothstein and Cromwell JJ.

Counsel: Sonia Lebel and Benoît Lauzon, for the appellant.

Louis Belleau, as amicus curiae.

ON APPEAL FROM THE COURT OF APPEAL FOR QUEBEC

Criminal law — Arrest without warrant — Reasonable grounds — Accused acquitted at trial of narcotic offence — Trial judge finding police officer did not have reasonable grounds to arrest accused without warrant — Whether trial judge imposed burden more onerous than "reasonable grounds" standard for arrest without warrant — Criminal Code, R.S.C. 1985, c. C-46, s. 495(1)(c).

A police officer arrested the accused without a warrant and, following a search incidental to arrest, found a bag of crack in the accused's pocket. The arresting officer did not investigate the accused's claim that he was the brother of the person sought by the arrest warrant at the time of the arrest. At the police station, however, the accused was confirmed not to be the person sought by the warrant. The trial judge acquitted the accused on a charge of possession of cocaine for the purpose of trafficking, finding that, despite the resemblance between the accused and his brother, the officer did not have objective grounds for the arrest because he had not investigated the accused's claim of mistaken identity at the time of the arrest. She concluded that the arrest was illegal, the subsequent search was unreasonable and excluded the evidence. The Court of Appeal, in a majority decision, upheld the acquittal. The issue in this appeal as of right was whether the trial judge erred in law by substituting a more onerous standard for the requirement of reasonable grounds that a peace officer must have in order to make an arrest without warrant pursuant to s. 495 of the *Criminal Code*.

Held (Deschamps and Cromwell JJ. dissenting): The appeal should be dismissed.

Per LeBel, **Fish**, Abella, Charron and Rothstein JJ.: The trial judge's conclusion that the reasonable grounds required under s. 495 had not been made out in the particular circumstances of this case rested essentially on an appreciation of the evidence before her. Her reasons explained why the arresting officer's evidence was inconsistent, contradictory and wanting as to the circumstances of the arrest.

Per Deschamps and **Cromwell** JJ. (dissenting): The trial judge's reasoning imposed a heavier onus than that required by s. 495(1)(*c*). It required the officer to be certain, or at least persuaded, that the person about to be arrested is the one against whom a warrant of arrest is in force, rather than simply to have reasonable grounds to believe so.

Statutes and Regulations Cited

Criminal Code, R.S.C. 1985, c. C-46, s. 495.

APPEAL from a judgment of the Quebec Court of Appeal (Chamberland, Vézina and Côté JJ.A.), 2009 QCCA 85, 63 C.R. (6th) 277, [2009] J.Q. n° 222 (QL), 2009 CarswellQue 11110, upholding the accused's acquittal. Appeal dismissed, Deschamps and Cromwell JJ. dissenting.

The judgment of LeBel, Fish, Abella, Charron and Rothstein JJ. was delivered by

FISH J.: —

[1]   This is an appeal by the Crown, as of right, from a decision of the Québec Court of Appeal affirming the respondent's acquittal at trial on a charge

of possession of cocaine for the purpose of trafficking (2009 QCCA 85, 248 C.C.C. (3d) 450).

[2]   The decisive issue on the appeal is whether the trial judge erred in law, as the Crown contends, by substituting a more onerous standard for the requirement of reasonable grounds that a peace officer must have in order to make an arrest without warrant pursuant to s. 495 of the *Criminal Code*, R.S.C. 1985, c. C-46.

[3]   We are not persuaded that she did. Rather, the trial judge concluded that the reasonable grounds required under s. 495 had not been made out *in the particular circumstances of this case*. And her conclusion in this regard rests essentially on an appreciation of the evidence before her: The trial judge's reasons, delivered orally, explain in detail why she found the evidence of the arresting officer inconsistent, contradictory and wanting as to the circumstances surrounding the respondent's arrest.

[4]   Accordingly, with respect for those who are of a different view, I would dismiss the appeal.

English version of the reasons of Deschamps and Cromwell JJ. delivered by

CROMWELL J. (dissenting):—

[5]   I have read the reasons of my colleague Fish J. and, with respect, I am unable to agree with him.

[6]   The question of law in this appeal is whether the trial judge imposed a burden more onerous than the one provided for in s. 495(1)(*c*) of the *Criminal Code*, R.S.C. 1985, c. C-46. I agree with Chamberland J.A., the dissenting judge in the Quebec Court of Appeal, that the answer is yes, for the following reasons:

[TRANSLATION] The trial judge stated that she was unable to "conclude that the officer had objective grounds for the arrest". Why? Because "he did not investigate when the identification of the accused was contested, even though he was told that the person being sought after by the warrant was the brother". Similarly, she "considers that the officer was obliged, on the face of the protest and information given by the accused to proceed to a verification" and adds that "the attitude of arresting a person without further verification ... appears capricious".
In my view, and with the greatest respect for the trial judge, this reasoning is erroneous in that it imposes on the officer a different and heavier burden than what is required in s. 495(1)(*c*) *Cr. C*. It would require the officer to be certain, or at least persuaded, that the person

about to be arrested is the one against whom a warrant of arrest is in force, rather than simply to have reasonable grounds to believe so.

(2009 QCCA 85, 248 C.C.C. (3d) 450, at paras. 23-24)

[7] Despite the able submission of Mr. Belleau, the *amicus curiae* in this case, I would allow the appeal and order a new trial.

Appeal dismissed, DESCHAMPS *and* CROMWELL JJ. *dissenting.*

Solicitor for the appellant: Director of Criminal and Penal Prosecutions of Quebec, Montréal.

Solicitors for the amicus curiae: Filteau & Belleau, Montréal.

INDEX